Advance Praise for
Nothing Ventured | An American Life
In Alphabetical Order

More than anything else I was struck by how frequently Steve Pease breaks away from his narrative in order to emphasize that he's stayed in touch with people he's worked with or otherwise crossed paths with in earlier years. Although he also makes the point in the text that he chose specific business ventures because he valued opportunities to make decisions independently, his independence in decision making has coexisted throughout with long term personal investments in relationships. An excellent balance, I believe.

—Kevin Calhoun
Senior Engineer, Apple

Good job, great read! What are the odds that a Spokane boy and a Spokane girl, former husband and wife, both end up moving to a small town in Northern California, to live a few blocks from each other, participate in the same community organizations, and to share friends? After your description of my days as a Goldwater Girl and Republican operative, I may have missed your mention of the fact that I have fully recovered, and am now a registered Independent.

—Karen Collins
Sonoma's 2019 Alcadessa
(honorary mayor)

How does a Protestant boy from a traditional upbringing in mid-century America discover a rich cultural heritage in his own country so fascinating that he gives up a highly rewarding career to venture into a scholarly study of two centuries of Jewish achievement and then tell the story to the world? Read this endearing memoir to learn how and why.

—Marilyn Hewitt
Journalist, Author,
This Is a Soul: The Mission of Rick Hodes

Steve Pease's memoir is a tale of growing up in what arguably were the years of America's maturation—revealing the powerful combination of opportunity, education, and initiative that enabled tens of millions to enjoy productive lives. Steve has written a journal of the quintessential American story. From modest middle class beginnings to the fulfillment of the American dream, with experiences and unique insights that are particularly needed now, in the last quarter of the game, Steve Pease's sage reflections are particularly valuable and meaningful for all.

—David M. Hirsch
Chairman, Warren Alpert Foundation,
Trustee, Rensselaer Polytechnic Institute

An engrossing and personable look at real-life business decisions and the man behind them.

Between his personal life and business dealings, Pease traveled to Russia some 50 times. Drawing on this experience, he provides insights into the present-day situation in the country as well as some more general political and personal views. He also discusses (and later delineates the points of) his published works on the success of Jewish people.

On the whole, readers get not just textbook management cases, but a well-rounded picture of the business world. An engrossing and personable look at real-life business decisions and the man behind them.

—Kirkus Reviews
"36 Indies Worth Discovering" 2023

You will get to know Steve Pease in *Nothing Ventured | An American Life*, and you will understand how his life is a testament to the daring concept that titles his memoir.

Steve has enjoyed a fascinating personal life, and it is a delight to read his fusion of memories. He skillfully integrates cultural history with political and business events, and his intelligent musings about life, people and the times are entertaining, engrossing, and riveting.

—Katy (Hungerford) McGovern
Former wife of Mark Hungerford

Steve Pease is a marvel. He deftly presents an extraordinary life as a series of learnings—not as a literary device, but because it sheds light on who he is as a person, ready for any new insight that crosses his path. A generous author in every sense, and well worth reading.

—Lucy Merello Peterson
Author and entrepreneur

Steve Pease's book is a very well-written tale of an exciting and meaningful life.

—Harold (Hal) Phillips
Educational entrepreneur

The content of Steve Pease's book is informative about the nature of his character and of business in general. His work does a good job in distilling the essence of the times in the more particular details of the life of an individual. I was taken by the unique structure and dynamism of the early era of American venture capitalism as well as the unprecedented global interconnectedness and optimism ushered in by the end of the Cold War. A good read!

—Julien Stefanki Segre
Student of Russian language and literature, Stanford University

I arrived at work with ambitious plans for the day. Your biography derailed them. I never should have opened the book because I have not been able to put it down. As a minor "Russia Hand" who is honorary president of the Russian cardiology congress and who (with Maxime Osipov) has written a Russian medical textbook (*Echocardiology*), I found your extensive adventures there insightful and riveting.

Self-revealing, interesting anecdotes told with candor, and the sense that, as readers, we are both welcome and eavesdropping, your memoir is a very well written and thought-provoking read. My only advice for you is to keep writing because you have so much to say and say it so well.

—*Dr. Nelson Schiller,*
UCSF Professor of Medicine and Anesthesia,
Founder, Echocardiology Lab
and Adult Congenital Disease Service,
Director of Research, Cardiac Physiology Lab
Cardiovascular Research Institute

This well-written tale of how Steve Pease, a native of Spokane, Washington, found his calling as a company turnaround specialist, venture capitalist, Russian business investor, philanthropist, and as an unexpected admirer of Jewish culture and achievements, rewards us with an unforgettable, informative personal history.

—*Jeff Splitgerber*
San Francisco real estate investor, retired

What a great biography! Well written and thoroughly researched, Steve Pease's story shows the fruit of his hard work, ambition, creativity and entrepreneurial skills. His life demonstrates the importance of both culture and serendipity, and provides a wonderful example of the many people who created the vital and vibrant country that is America.

—*Dr. John Stace*
Rural medical practitioner, Australia

My sense is that Steve Pease epitomizes genuine entrepreneurship – in spirit and natural faculties. He seems blessed with everything one needs to become a successful businessman and venture capitalist, namely a sense of adventure, the ability to take risks, face challenges, and take the untrodden path. These qualities also shine through in other important aspects of his life such as philanthropy, community service, and scholarly research.

Learning what the United States, its Enterprise Fund (TUSRIF) and Foundation (USRF) did to advance the development of Russia's market economy—and help transform Russian society after the collapse of the Soviet Union—was of great interest to me. The author served as a leader of TUSRIF AND USRF and was central to those progressive efforts. It saddens me to see how Russia has reversed course and is now destroying those positive and transformative reforms.

—*Yegor*

Yegor's story is told in this memoir on pages 172-73, 180-82, 199 and 338.

Nothing Ventured

An American Life

by
Steven L. Pease

Azalea Art Press
Sonoma | California

© Steven L. Pease, 2022.
All Rights Reserved.

Hardcover:
978-1-943471-65-2

Trade Paperback:
978-1-943471-74-4

Ebook:
978-1-943471-62-1

Library of Congress Control Number: 2022918040

Cover Photo:
*The cover photo was taken by my dad
at Fish Lake in 1947 or 1948,
using a Brownie camera.
On the back, my mother wrote:
"My favorite shot of Steve, fishing."*

Dedicated to:

My mother, Ruth Pease.
Her unconditional love and support
mattered most in shaping who I became.

Steve Pease | Age 4

CONTENTS

Preface   *i*

Chapter One
Growing Up in Spokane and Seattle   1

Chapter Two
Business School,
Management Consulting,
and Corporate Staff   18

Chapter Three
Real Estate Data Inc.   45

Chapter Four
Wallbangers
and Liquid Crystal Technologies   65

Chapter Five
Joyce and Me   79

Chapter Six
PLM, PLM Railcar Maintenance,
PLM International, Transcisco
(and SFAT)   90

Chapter Seven
Deucalion Venture Partners,
Venture Capital and Its Present Scale   114

**Introduction
to the Russia Chapters**   136

Chapter Eight
The U.S. Russia Investment Fund	138

Chapter Nine
The Center for Entrepreneurship	154

Chapter Ten
The U.S. Russia Foundation for Economic
Development and the Rule of Law	161

Chapter Eleven
Working with USAID	184

Chapter Twelve
Russian Updates and Remembrances	191

Photos	201

Chapter Thirteen
Writing About Jews	214

Chapter Fourteen
Threads, Inspirations, and Politics	237

Chapter Fifteen
Giving Back	255

Chapter Sixteen
Taking Stock	272

Appendices

Appendix I
A Summing Up—
Achievements of Jews   282

Appendix II
More Thoughts on Jewish Culture   284

Appendix III
Statistics and Stories
of Jewish Accomplishments   295

Appendix IV
Historical Events that Influenced the
Jewish Culture of High Achievement   303

Appendix V
Theories of Jewish Achievement   306

Index   312

Acknowledgments   336

About the Author   341

Contact   342

Book Orders   342

ஓ ஓ ஓ

Preface

Not long ago, I met my friend, Jeff Splitgerber, for lunch. As we swapped stories about our lives, he was intrigued with my business experiences in Russia and with the two books I'd written about the astonishing achievements of Jews. "Have you ever thought about writing your *own* story?" he asked me.

I thanked Jeff for the compliment but said that although my life has been wonderful and interesting for me, my story is small potatoes compared with the many remarkable people who have achieved much, become famous, and occasionally become very wealthy in the process. I also felt that my family would have little interest in a memoir since they already know much of my story.

Yet, as I reflected on his suggestion, several new ideas ran through my mind. Writing is the best single discipline I know for thinking through and clearly expressing one's thoughts. As Søren Kierkegaard once observed, "Life can only be understood backwards; but it must be lived forwards." In essence, life often seems like chaos as you live through it, but as you look back, it takes on the character of a finely crafted novel.

From my first years at Harvard Business School, my three years as a management consultant, and throughout my fifty years of running companies, venture investing, and entrepreneurial endeavors, writing has proven to be invaluable for me.

It occurred to me that writing my memoir might help Joyce and me sort through some of the questions I had about the future of my family and my country.

Equally important, my wife and I had been considering the best way to distribute our estate. We knew that half would go to our family and the other half would be devoted to philanthropic causes. Although we had some good ideas, those ideas needed to be clarified in more specific terms. Writing my memoir would help us make sure those causes reflected our core beliefs and values.

America is a unique and exceptional country that provided remarkable opportunities for me and my generation. That is one reason I chose *An American Life* for the subtitle of this memoir. In our recent, ever more tumultuous times, the days of entrepreneurial meritocracy, free enterprise, and individualism are losing out. Writing my memoir would allow me to tell the story of one person who prospered greatly (as have many) in an era whose values now seem to be coming under attack.

In that sense, my story may prove emblematic of the end of an era. And maybe, just maybe, I can tell that story in an interesting way.

—Steven L. Pease
November 1, 2022

Nothing Ventured

An American Life

৩ ৩ ৩

Chapter One

Growing Up in Spokane and Seattle

Skies are blue and friendships true . . .
—First line in Spokane's 1950s theme song

Growing up in Spokane, Washington, was as close to ideal as a kid might hope for. I have often said it is the farthest west midwestern city in the United States. It was, and still is, a relatively small town with midwestern values, agricultural and mining roots, ski mountains just a few hours drive in one direction and numerous lakes for water skiing less than an hour away in other directions. There was the annual Lilac Parade and a schmaltzy song we learned when I was young: "Skies are blue and friendships true in sunny old Spokane. Stay a while you'll learn to smile in sunny old Spokane . . ." Spokane had great schools and a politically conservative friendly atmosphere.

My first memories, from when I was probably 3 or 4, are of our move into an old house in a lower middle-class neighborhood. I still have a couple of pictures from that time. One shows me in cowboy garb sitting on the back of a pony in front of our house. It was probably taken by a photographer who took pictures of many kids on that horse to make a living. The other image is a black-and-white photo of me with a fishing pole in hand, probably taken at Fish Lake (about fifteen miles from Spokane) where my grandparents (on my mother's side) lived.

Born in 1943, I'm shown in baby pictures as a smiley healthy eight-pound kid with light brown hair, blue eyes, and his thumb in his mouth.

My grandparents from my father's side and my mother's side were quite different from one another. My dad's father, Glendon "Glen" Pease was quite gentle, but he was badly injured in a flour mill explosion and died in 1948 when I was 5. His wife, Lillian, was one of three sisters. They all went to a "normal school" where they were taught to become schoolteachers. In her later years she worked for the local newspaper in Spokane, and she hosted many of our family holiday events.

My mom's parents, Raymond and Happy Shepard, were "born-again" Christians. Raymond's father was alcoholic, so he and Happy had a strong aversion to alcohol. My folks drank in moderation, but out of concern for my grandparents, we all had to hide the liquor whenever they came to visit. Years later after Happy had succumbed to breast cancer and I was helping my grandfather mow, rake, and bring in the hay on his farm, we would watch television in the evening. At the time, liquor could be advertised on TV. My grandfather would become very agitated and speak loudly to the television set complaining it was a damn shame they could do that. I had never seen him so angry.

My father, LeRoy Pease, born in 1915, and my mother, Ruth Shepard Pease, born in 1919, were part of the "Greatest Generation." Both lived through all of the Great Depression followed shortly after by World War II. They faced roughly fifteen years of very hard times and lived with limited means and all the stress and fears that lasted until the war was over and Dad had a decent secure job making good money.

There were four of us. My dad was a dispatcher at a moving and storage company in Spokane. My mom was a housewife, but she aspired to become a beauty operator. This meant going to beauty school, getting her license, and then being able to earn some money and gain some independence.

My parents graduated from high school but neither went on to college. It was the same for most of my friends' parents. My sister, Glenna Rae, was six years older than I was. She lived with us, but the age difference meant we were never in the same school at the same time. We liked each other, but our friends and activities were totally different.

I had some medical issues, including losing an eardrum to infection when I was six months old. I fell down a flight of steps to the basement, landing on my head, and had other ailments as well. But my sister went through much more. She was born three months premature in 1937 and weighed less than three pounds at birth.

Her first three months of life were spent isolated in an incubator. She had almost no contact with our mother in that important time for breast-feeding, holding, caressing, talking, and bonding. She often seemed estranged, unhappy with both our mom and dad. She married the first time shortly after high school. I thus became something of an "only child" from age 10 or 11 on. For all of her life she tended to be sickly, and ultimately developed cirrhosis despite not drinking. She had three husbands and I liked them all. Of the three, the last was the best. Ed Keller was wonderful to her. She also had three great kids (Tami, Diane, and Steve) and I became an uncle at age 12 or 13.

I was fine with being an only child. The most important person in my life was my mother, and I believe she felt the same toward me. She was unconditionally loving. My father, like most men of that time, was not particularly affectionate. He had a job to get to. In the 1930s he began driving trucks moving household goods and during the war he was promoted to being a dispatcher. Later, he became the manager, and after that he bought and ran his own small moving and storage company. It was a challenge for him. There was a lot of stress and for a time he took Valium to manage it as best he could. Both he and my mom would have a drink now and then but neither abused alcohol, and I never saw either one of them drunk. They tended to be hardworking salt-of-the-earth folks.

So, I got all the attention and loving affection from my mother who was never doting or demanding but always warm and supportive. She trusted me and my decisions.

After World War II when the men came home, most families seemed to have a single male breadwinner. Not having been drafted because of tendon injuries on his right hand, the draft board said Dad would have problems shooting a rifle and thus could not serve. Nonetheless, he was considered essential since many troops and others were being moved all over the country. I think he always felt a bit embarrassed for not having served, but he also thought he should be the sole breadwinner. My mom's wish to become a beauty operator was threatening to him. I do not believe my father ever hit or cursed at her, but I do remember them down on the carpet with him holding her down as they fought verbally about her plans.

Meanwhile, my father also suffered from undiagnosed high blood pressure. He could become very frustrated, and it showed. I remember him losing a fish one day when we were trolling on a local lake. He literally pulled the rod back, broke it into small pieces and tossed them into the lake. His anger could be shocking and embarrassing, but he was never brutal. Like all kids in that era, I might get a spanking, but those were rare. Meanwhile, as much as I hated to be told I had to spend the day helping him out on a project at home, he trained me well in basic electricity, plumbing, general repairs, and carpentry. I learned decent mechanical skills from him, and they still come in handy.

Mom was not about to be dissuaded, so she enrolled and spent a year in beauty school. After that, she was required to work in someone else's beauty shop for a year before she could open her own "Crown Beauty Salon" in what had been my bedroom. It meant she would always be there when I got home from school. Years later she was very well thought of by her peers and her clients. She was recruited to join the State Board of Cosmetology that administered and oversaw all of the licensing of beauty operators and beauty shops in Washington State.

But the tensions at home remained for as long as I lived with my parents. At one point I really wanted them to divorce. I thought it would have been better for all of us, but they never did, and they stayed together until Dad died of heart disease in 1978 at the age of 63.

The Cold War also added to the tensions of the times. In kindergarten and the early grades, we held civil defense drills in the school basement with our heads tucked between our knees as the sirens sounded all over town. Because Fairchild Air Force Base—with its bombers and nukes—was just a few miles west of downtown Spokane, nuclear war with the Soviet Union was always thought possible. Fairchild was a likely target, and a Soviet nuclear weapon would have destroyed the city. In those same postwar years, an ever-increasing number of books were published that described the brutal history of World War II. Documentaries, such as *War at Sea* and *The World at War* appeared on television chronicling the terror and the massive death tolls (an estimated 75 million soldiers and civilians including six million Jewish victims of the Holocaust).

At the same time, we all began to learn more about the horrors of the Soviet Union. In nearly every respect, Stalin was as evil and as diabolical as Hitler. Most estimates put the numbers of Russians killed by Stalin's regime at 20 million. Mao was much the same, and his regime is thought to have killed 60 million Chinese during his lifetime. The twentieth century was brutal.

Stories of Stalin and Hitler conscripting young Germans and Russians to report on their parents horrified me. Similarly, mostly following the Israeli victory in establishing the country of Israel, I began to read about the kibbutzim with its sabra class of youth, many of whom were supposedly raised by the entire kibbutz rather than living with their own mothers and fathers. I simply could not imagine growing up that way. I wanted to have my dedicated mom and a two-parent family.

Later, in October, 1957, the Soviets launched the rocket carrying the Sputnik satellite. They had not only copied our nuclear bomb technology, they had also beaten us to space. Many Americans felt we were falling behind the Communists, and through those same years, concerned scientists kept the "Doomsday Nuclear Time Clock" that usually showed the clock was only minutes from midnight when a nuclear war would kill us all.

I think most who grew up in those years went through much the same insecurities and fears as I did, but I made mine even worse by discovering Hostess cupcakes, Twinkies, and Coca-Cola. I got fat. Over the middle years of grade school, I grew to 180 pounds when I was only 5' 3" tall. I became ever more shy but was still a good student and got decent grades. The teachers were great, and as I neared the time I would head for high school, my work mowing lawns and bagging groceries at a local grocery store helped me slim down a bit as I also grew taller. But even after all these years, I still think of myself as overweight.

Never a great athlete, I learned one important life lesson from a baseball coach while playing right field. He told all of us to "Anticipate!" By that, he meant we should never just daydream while we were in the outfield. We should always simply anticipate what we would do if a ball was hit in our direction. Were there runners on base? Where were first, second, and third basemen? Should I catch the fly and try to create another out by throwing to the base if the runner lacked time to get back to it safely? Or should I throw to first base to get the hitter, or to home plate to block the runner coming from third base? The message stuck and still does. In 2015, when the Russian government was cracking down on NGOs (nonprofit non-governmental organizations) such as one I co-chaired, the issue was to think through specifically what the U.S. Russia Foundation (USRF) would do if the organization was named "undesirable." We were. It gave us a great head start. We knew exactly what we would do.

In 1957, I entered Lewis & Clark High School. It was a completely different world. I had been one of 60 members of my grade school class. At high school, I was one of 520.

After a couple of years, I turned 16 and could drive. It was marvelous. It also meant I could spend my summers working on my dad's trucks moving household goods and also doing the packing and unpacking for most moves. I worked with all the men employed by my father. I took the view that because my dad owned the business, I would have to work harder than the others and never be thought of as being a slacker ("the boss's son"). I also never wanted any of the men to think I might say anything negative about them to my dad. As it turned out, I developed friendships with them all. The nature of the work also made me stronger and slimmer. A grade school friend had told me years before that I might become a good-looking kid if I took off a few pounds. Moving household goods did that. At 5' 10" tall, my weight dropped to 165 pounds.

My grades were always pretty good. I was never the best student or a candidate for valedictorian, but I got nearly all A's and B's. I developed some close friendships. Ken Garceau, one of the students at Gonzaga, the parochial high school he attended, was always part of my life in those years. He was the best man at my first wedding, and we still stay in touch. Just a couple of months ago he gave me a call. Another went on to join me at the University of Washington, and we joined the Sigma Alpha Epsilon fraternity together. Two high school classmates, Nancy Tefft and Lee Hatch, became good friends. I never dated either one—they were like my sisters.

Certainly, one of the most important things that happened during my high school years was to meet my first serious girlfriend, Glenda Stallcop. She was cute, fun to be with, and an accomplished artist who wanted to become an art teacher. She had a great family and her father, Dave, became a mentor to me. He lived in Spokane but had gone to college, become a pharmacist, and with a partner, purchased a drugstore in Cut Bank, Montana, where he worked about half the year and managed it even when he was home in Spokane. I liked him a lot and even years later, after Glenda and I split up and I was in Boston, he let me know he would be traveling there and would love to have dinner together. Even when I was in high school, he had encouraged my early interest in going to Harvard Business School after college. Glenda's sister, Linda, was two years ahead of us and became a good friend.

One of the nicest aspects of Spokane was the relative absence of racism. At Lewis & Clark High School, the Gaskins twins were Black, a year behind me, and stars of the football team. One of them was elected student body vice president. One of my mom's friends, Fumi, was a Japanese American whose family had a truck farm on the outskirts of town. Though Spokane was notably Republican, nearly all of us disdained the neo-Nazi types who lived in Northern Idaho, whose hero was George Lincoln Rockwell.

One of the more questionable aspects of my high school years, with my access to my own car, was taking a liking to beer and wine. My friends introduced me to the idea that if we found an old guy leaving a bar, we could offer him a generous tip if he bought us a bottle of wine or a six-pack of beer. So, in addition to smoking, which I did for roughly thirty years before I stopped, I also partied with my friends. I never got into trouble because of drinking except for two times, the first when I got sick in my closet at home. The next morning, my dad smiled as he said,

"Don't you ever do that again." But while I never again got sick at home, I did continue to party.

After graduating from Lewis & Clark, I was accepted at the University of Washington (U of W) in Seattle. During that summer, U of W fraternities held rush parties in Spokane. One with several Spokane members was Sigma Alpha Epsilon (SAE), and they invited me to an August rush party at Coeur D'Alene Lake located thirty miles east of Spokane in Idaho. There, the legal drinking age was 18—which I would not be for another month. The guys were all older and asked me to join them at a local bar for a beer which I did, sitting on a stool in the middle of the bar. Coeur D'Alene was the site of a major hydroplane race slated for the next day, and the town was crawling with people planning to attend. As I was sitting there in the bar, we noticed that the cops were coming through the front and back doors. All I could do was sit there as they worked their way to the center asking to see IDs. When they got to me, it was curtains. I found myself sitting with fifty or sixty others on the concrete floor of a jail cell until the next

---

HBS
Harvard Business School

MBA
Master of Business Administration

NGO
Nonprofit non-governmental organization

SAE
Sigma Alpha Epsilon fraternity

SBA
Small Business Administration

U of W
University of Washington

morning when I was released to my parents who came to get me.

Fortunately, Glenda's older sister, Linda, was then dating an SAE, David Whitney, whose father was wealthy and influential. Ultimately all of the charges for me and the others were dropped, and the records were purged. In a month, I would be asked to join the fraternity, which I did.

When I arrived at the university, I would be one of more than 18,000 students. The campus was beautiful, extending over nearly a square mile (634 acres). It was immense. As soon as Rush Week was over, and I found myself living in the fraternity house, I immediately discovered the fraternal camaraderie disappeared for us "pledges." From mid-September, 1961, through mid-spring, 1962, we were hazed and harassed. We were awakened at two or three in the morning to clean the house, with the sophomores yelling at us, forcing us to eat raw onions and raw eggs; we occasionally got paddled too. It was awful.

In addition, most of us were studying night and day with little time for anything else. To make it even worse for a Spokane kid, it rained. Spokane is 300 miles east of Seattle, generally sunny, hot in the summer and cold during the winter. It snows, and summer rains can pour down, but most days are sunny and nice. In Seattle, it rained every day for more than thirty days from the day I entered the university. I was miserable. But thank God, I still had Glenda and friends who provided a respite from the wet weather and the hassles and worries about grades.

It all came to a rather glorious ending in spring after "Hell Week." First, we were then full members of SAE. We were no longer hassled. We had completed two quarters of study, gotten good grades, and all of a sudden, with little rain, on a clear day Seattle and the U of W campus became one the most beautiful places to be. Situated in North Seattle, with beautiful gothic architecture; from the red brick plaza in front of the Suzzallo Library you could see Mt. Ranier in the distance. It was spectacular. Moreover, if you were high enough up, you could see the snow-capped Cascade Mountains to the east across Lake Washington as well as the peaks of the Olympic Mountains west across Puget Sound. I loved the school and enjoyed the city and campus for the remaining three years before I graduated.

I think it was sometime during my junior year at U of W that Glenda and I agreed to end our courtship. She had a new boyfriend who planned to become a doctor. I wanted to play the field and date others.

During summers, I returned to Spokane and would work on the trucks in my dad's business and make good money.

One Christmas holiday when I returned to Spokane, my father asked me to help with a major problem: An Air Force officer was being transferred from Fairchild Air Force Base to Minnesota. Dad was the contractor, and the military business was important for him. His Spokane company was an affiliate of Global Van Lines, one of perhaps five to ten major U.S. moving and storage companies at the time.

Dad's crew had loaded the furniture into a trailer and Global Van Lines assigned a driver to drive his tractor to Spokane where he would hook up to the trailer and drive it to Minneapolis. It was cold and snowing. The driver had no experience driving on snow. He got as far as Great Falls, Montana, and refused to drive farther. Dad asked if I and a long time employee, Kenny Osso, would drive a tractor to Great Falls, hook it up to the trailer, pull it to Minneapolis and then return to Spokane. We said we would give it a go. The weather was so bad and the tractor so unstable we slid off the highway twice en route to Great Falls. The first time it happened we figured out how to get the tractor back on the highway ourselves. A tow truck helped us the second time. Finally, we got to Great Falls.

We hooked up to the trailer and immediately began the trek across Montana. It was very treacherous. Montana, that far east, is flat, and we had about 300 miles of two-lane roads covered with fresh snow making it difficult to figure out where the shoulder of the road was. I was terrified that Kenny or I would lose control and run into a car coming in the opposite direction. But we kept going, mile by mile. Finally, we got to Miles City and U.S. 94, a four-lane freeway that was plowed and generally clear. We drove the remaining 600 miles and dropped the trailer with the company that would do the local delivery.

We turned around and headed back to Spokane, the two of us alternating driving and resting. We never turned the engine off during the whole trip. Ironically, we had made it that far, but as Kenny was driving on the freeway toward the exit for his own house, I noticed he had missed the exit. When I spoke up to tell him, I found he had fallen asleep at the wheel. Fortunately, he was not startled when I woke him, and we got him home, and I then drove the tractor back to the office and headed home myself. It was a "character building" few days and a trip I'll never forget.

I helped my dad with another problem during those years. He was turned down for a SBA (Small Business Administration) loan, which he badly needed and thought he qualified for. I took it upon myself to write a letter to the office of Senator Warren G. Magnuson, then chair of the Senate Commerce Committee and one of Washington State's two senators. I made the pitch in the letter and asked if he might be helpful. He was, and my dad got the loan.

Meanwhile my wish to go on for an MBA from Harvard Business School (HBS) became an important priority. Even then, the admission rate was very low and good grades were not enough. Fortunately, my fraternity supported me, knowing that if I ran for student body office I would likely win, and they could benefit from my academic record as well as my political reputation. I ran for sophomore class vice president. In the process, I came to know and work with Larry Levy, who was elected president. I'd had Jewish friends since kindergarten when Steve Brilling lived less than a block away. In high school, Clark Gemmell became a friend as did Ellen Wolff with whom I still share emails or exchange messages. Larry was something special. Always smiling and outgoing, he was a delight to be with. His plan was to become a lawyer, and he did.

That introduction to campus politics led me to run for student body vice president. No one filed to run against me, so as a senior I served. Those and other activities complemented my academic record. Once I had a feel for how to study and participate in class, I also found I was a good student. I was named the university's "Outstanding Marketing Student" in my senior year. I graduated magna cum laude, and to my surprise, I was selected by the university to become a member of Phi Beta Kappa. I had no idea a business student could be elected, but it was a very nice honor to be nominated and accepted.

Meanwhile, after "playing the field" in dating other girls, I met Karen Saldin while double-dating with Gary Webster, a fraternity brother and friend who brought her. He thought of her as more of a friend than a serious romantic interest, and when I asked if I could call her for a date, he encouraged me to do it. She was special. She would graduate from Whitworth College. She liked politics and was working for the King County Republican Central Committee under the leadership of Ken Rogstad, who would come back into my life again a few years later.

She was very unusual and very smart. A "Goldwater Girl" and more conservative than I was, she was very articulate and could meet others easily. Without fail, they liked her. Those talents would serve her well over the coming years.

So, as I graduated from U of W, I found myself destined to move to Boston and Cambridge for business school that coming fall. At the same time, Karen would be headed to Washington, D.C., to get her master's degree.

Chapter Two

Business School, Management Consulting, and Corporate Staff

Never make a decision until you have to.
—HBS professor

In the fall of 1965, after a summer spent earning money for graduate school by moving household goods, I loaded my small car with my belongings and those of Mike Stansbury, the U of W student body president when I was vice president. He was headed for Harvard Law School, and I was headed to Harvard Business School (HBS). I had never been east of Chicago.

We had our first dose of major changes in scenery and culture as we drove up the New Jersey Turnpike en route to Manhattan. It was early evening, and we passed mile after mile of ugly black refinery towers on both sides of the highway all belching their smoke. After we crossed under the Hudson River, we emerged into Manhattan in the midst of a huge garbage strike. The sidewalks were full of cans and bags of garbage, with some of the bags broken and spilling over onto the sidewalks and streets.

We headed to dinner on the Upper West Side with two of Mike's friends. We parked my car in the street, found their apartment, and had a nice meal and conversation. Afterward, as we emerged from the building and walked to my car, we saw two cops leaning against an adjacent building. As I unlocked the car doors they came over and asked who we were (with our Washington State license plates). We explained we were on our way to Boston and school. The cops were not threatening but they told us we should never leave any contents in our car when we parked on a Manhattan street. They had been standing there to make sure no one broke into the car. We greatly appreciated what they had done, but we knew at the time that things were really different here—such risks were very rare in Spokane or Seattle.

Harvard was beautiful and intimidating. There were about 650 members of our class. HBS divided us into seven sections ("A" through "G") with roughly ninety students in each section. We all sat in large rooms with five or six horseshoe-shaped tiers of seats and countertops. That first year men and women wore business attire to classes which were held Monday through Saturday morning. During our first year, all of the classes were with our section mates. Only in the second year could we select from a wide variety of classes and in that way be exposed to other classmates.

Most students, male or female, lived on campus. They were housed in suites of four bedrooms (each sleeping two of us) and sharing common toilets, sinks and shower facilities. Married students lived in separate dorms and a few students lived in apartments or homes off campus. In the evening we studied written cases for each class the next day. The cases were generally five to thirty pages describing a business problem or circumstances where decisions were required. At first, classes began with the professor calling on one student to respond by telling the professor and the classmates what the protagonist in the case should do. Fellow classmates then either volunteered or were designated by the professor to comment on that initial analysis. Those discussions went on for approximately ninety minutes. It could be terrifying and as one of the youngest in my section, I was more terrified than most.

Add the fact that the large number of cases each day made reading and mastering all of them impossible. Thus, the first lesson for entering students was the impossibility of doing all the work presented. Over time, most of us learned to raise our hand and volunteer for a case we studied closely the night before and for which we were prepared to venture our thoughts. You might do well, and likely you would not be called on by the professor for some time as long as you periodically volunteered to begin the discussion or respond to someone else's comment. Most students spoke several times a week in each class. Part of your grade was based on your classroom participation. There was always the risk that if you hadn't studied a particular case (having focused instead on a different class), you would get nailed. But if you mastered prioritizing which cases to study and picked your openings in class, you could do well. I tried that but I was generally more quiet than most. HBS also encouraged students to form small study groups to share their thinking about assigned cases the night before.

Our classmates were impressive. They came from a wide variety of backgrounds including military service, foreign nationals, wealthy scions, and middle-class kids like myself. One student I particularly came to like was Finn Jacobsen who was part of my study group along with Bill Douglas, a fellow U of W alum and football player, and Rick Kroon, a very smart Yale graduate. Finn was Norwegian. He arrived speaking almost no English. He taught me how quickly necessity could promote rapid learning. Within a month or two he became sufficiently proficient to express his thoughts in English about the cases we were assigned. He had a wonderful sense of humor including putting down the Swedes, and he later headed the Arthur Anderson practice for all of Scandinavia. Arthur Anderson was one of the major accounting firms in the world at the time. When I saw him in Norway a few years ago, he kiddingly smiled as he told me that when a Swedish employee misbehaved, he would shut down that office!

About once a month a single case would be assigned to everyone in all seven sections. The task was to prepare a written (typed) report on his or her analysis of the case and what the protagonist must do. That report had to be dropped into the receptacle chute by Saturday evening at 6 P.M. This was the first of two formative experiences in writing my own analyses and recommendations for problem cases. That experience has served me well ever since.

Generally, everyone in the class was ambitious and experienced, but I never sensed any cutthroat competition. Perhaps the fact that we were all faced with the same pressures and circumstances built a sense of camaraderie. There was also a broad sense of modesty about attending HBS, as symbolized in a way by the language in many of the cases that said that the protagonist had attended a "well-known Eastern business School." The word Harvard never appeared. I may be wrong. Perhaps Harvard was more mindful of selling the cases they produced to other business schools and that was the driving force, but I always felt the approach played down any sense of elitism or prestige in the minds of students.

One part of that first year I will never forget were the classes focused on human behavior and culture. Some of those got more than a little "touchy-feely" when the professor and students were playing armchair psychologists or psychiatrists. Many students found those discussions annoying, and some were not reluctant to let the professor know it. Those students were older, more experienced and pragmatic, and they disliked the cloying human behavioral analysis. More than one professor was known to feel a bit uncomfortable and put upon by the class discussions.

There were other highly respected professors that were tough as nails. General Georges Doriot, a French immigrant who served in the American military during World War II, was one of them. He taught production and is considered one of the fathers of America's venture capital industry. He was a legend and he demanded much.

Many relationships built during those two years continued after graduation. Some members of my section still get together every couple of years and we stay in touch now and then.

Between years at Harvard, Mike Stansbury and I decided to try to get a job in Washington, D.C. I am not sure if he initiated the contact or if I did, but we contacted Warren G. Magnuson's senate staff and asked if they might be able to help us find summer jobs. Soon, we were in touch with Gerald Grinstein, one of Magnuson's aides who came up with an opening for Mike, if I recall correctly, at the Federal Trade Commission and for me at the Federal Aviation Agency. My job consisted of forecasting future flight traffic at airports around the United States. I quickly found it was not particularly demanding. My boss was a very nice guy, but my job was to develop data and graphs based on traffic over preceding years, merely extrapolating past numbers into the future. The experience made me skeptical that much of what passed as expert forecasts by Washington bureaucrats had a solid grounding based on a thorough analysis.

Nonetheless, the job gave me real insight into D.C., and the way the bureaucracy operated, and it introduced me to some of the young staff members serving the senators and representatives in Congress.

All of that came in handy when my mother told me she would like to come to Washington, D.C., to see me, tour the city, and perhaps ride up to Boston with me on my way to my second year at HBS. So, I called a girl I had met who was part of the staff of Congressman Tom Foley, whose district encompassed Spokane. I told her my mother had never been to Washington, D.C., and I would like to give her a tour of the Capitol and asked if we might poke our heads into the offices of the congressman. Without missing a beat, she said, "Yes!" and encouraged us to show up around 11:30 A.M. in a few days. We did, thinking she would show us the offices and tell us about her job. Instead, shortly after we arrived, Tom Foley (who later became speaker of the House) came out, introduced himself, and asked if we would join him for lunch in the Congressional Dining Room. My folks never made a political donation in their lives and, while my mom was nominally a Democrat, she was never active. Beyond a simple act of kindness toward a constituent, there was no reason for the congressman to be so thoughtful. We both enjoyed talking with him for almost an hour and, of course my mom was thrilled.

In the years since, I have thought many times about that lunch and Congressman Foley's behavior. I do not think it could ever happen today. So much of today's focus is on fundraising, dealing with fellow politicians, lobbyists, and major supporters—a gesture like his is highly unlikely. It is a shame.

In the end, I am glad I went to Harvard Business School. I learned from the experience and formed some lasting friendships. I learned the importance of living with pressure and knowing you cannot possibly do everything you think you should do—you have to prioritize the tasks and you have to live with risk. Another great maxim from one of my professors was, "Never make a decision until you have to." It seemed almost like sacrilege when he said it, but we soon learned from his wisdom. To perform in the business world (and other domains as well) is to operate in an ever-evolving, rapidly changing arena. You never have all the facts and new facts may well emerge. If you are too eager to reach a decision, you may deprive yourself of late-breaking facts or information that will improve your decision. So, with that in mind, "Never make a decision until you have to!"

In the spring of my second year at HBS, the place was packed with recruiters on campus looking for candidates to hire. I thought about industries and companies that might interest me and probably interviewed with at least ten companies or

> **ACI**
> Arcata Communication Information
>
> **AOL**
> America Online
>
> **CMP**
> Cresap, McCormick & Paget
>
> **GEG**
> Airport code for Spokane International Airport, derived from its original name, 'Geiger Field'
>
> **HBS**
> Harvard Business School
>
> **NASDAQ**
> National Association of Securities Dealers Automated Quotations—global electronic marketplace for buying and selling securities
>
> **REDI**
> Real Estate Data Inc.
>
> **TWA**
> Trans World Airlines
>
> **VC**
> Venture capitalist
>
> **YVCAA**
> Yakima Valley Community Action Agency

partnerships. Trans World Airlines (TWA) interviewed me and immediately asked me for the airport code of Spokane International Airport. When I responded "GEG" (and not SIA) I passed the test. They flew me to New York a few days later for a second round of interviews. Levi Strauss flew me to San Francisco where I was interviewed by senior officers including Peter Haas, the then president. I interviewed in Seattle with Simpson Timber and was impressed with their young (age 39) CEO.

But at some level, I was lured by the idea of management consulting. It was the favored choice of many graduating students in those years before going to Wall Street became more attractive in the 1980s.

To some extent, consulting was an extension of business school with problems to analyze and recommendations to make for which you would be well compensated. It was a staff job rather than a line job where I could run a business, but it was a good place to start. Two firms were very interested in hiring me.

One was McKinsey, the legendary firm then led by Marvin Bower. These were "the best and brightest" working in offices in major cities all over the United States and abroad.[1] They not only set up multiple interviews with

---

[1] One amusing story highlighting the clever chutzpah of McKinsey associates about that time involved the fact that McKinsey required their consultants to wear suitable businessmen's hats. A new associate bought one and put it on his travel expense form. He got the form back with a note saying, "McKinsey does not pay for hats." The next time he submitted his expenses, there was a footnote on the bottom of the form. It said, "Find the hat!"

junior and senior staff, and partners, they also hired a psychologist who spent hours checking out each candidate, testing him and writing up an overall assessment. Apparently I passed, and they made me an offer to work for them in their Los Angeles office. They were impressive and I gave it serious thought. One drawback was their "up or out in two years" policy which struck me as risky. Who wanted to ever go back into the job market as a former McKinsey consultant who ended in two years being "Out" rather than "Up"?

The other offer came from Cresap, McCormick & Paget (CMP), a smaller boutique firm with offices around the United States and in some foreign cities. They were very different. Their staff was more varied and in most offices you could work on a much wider variety of assignments. I liked the partners and they offered me a job in San Francisco. Another difference from McKinsey was the requirement for written reports for clients. They had professional editors to help in producing those reports and after my experience at Harvard Business School, I liked the approach. I also much preferred San Francisco and soon accepted the offer. I would join them in June 1967.

Meanwhile, after almost breaking up with Karen Saldin when she moved back to Seattle the summer I was in D.C. (she was dating an old flame in Seattle), we patched things up and, for a time we considered marrying before I returned to HBS for my second year. Fortunately, my mother sent us a thoughtful and beautiful letter recommending we both hold off until we had graduated with our respective master's degrees. We did that and agreed to marry in Seattle in September of 1967.

It was a very nice ceremony at a church adjacent to the University of Washington campus. That was convenient for Karen's family and friends in Seattle, and Spokane was only a five-hour drive away for those coming from my hometown. Our parents had known each other for many years before Karen and I met, so it was a friendly relationship between the two families. I will also never forget that one of her father's friends, Jim DiJulio, gave us a huge pepperoni as a wedding present!

Because I had joined CMP just a few months before, we did not take a long honeymoon. Instead, we first spent a weekend in Victoria, British Columbia (a charming place), and a few months later, we flew to Acapulco and stayed at Las Brisas Resort in a lovely casita with its own small swimming pool. Because we had to fly home from Mexico City, a few days later we had to drive there from Acapulco. It was a 235-mile drive. About halfway there, the rental car began to sputter. I could just see us missing our flight back to San Francisco because we could not get the car fixed in a backwater Mexican village where the mechanic might view us as easy picking. As it turned out, the guy at the garage was very knowledgeable, friendly, and fair. The price was right, he moved quickly, and we made our flight, so I showed up at the CMP office on time the next Monday. Whew!

I spent three years at CMP and loved it. The senior San Francisco partner was in his 60s and an HBS alumni.

He was a genuine rainmaker, bringing in business of all kinds. We also worked closely with the Los Angeles office and one partner there had a fascinating mix of clients. The consultants were also very interesting.

One of them, Kenny Uston, was Japanese American, a Yale grad who went to Harvard Business School where he was chosen to be a Baker Scholar, a wonderful honor. He was very bright, knew a lot about computing, was a good jazz pianist, loved to party, and had a wife, two daughters and a son. We never worked together but we became good friends. He was very interested in blackjack and had read the original Edward Thorpe book *Beat the Dealer* about card counting as the way to win at the table. We first practiced in Kenny's Tiburon home using matches as chips. I enjoyed playing in casinos and did fine in counting. But after I left CMP, he also left to become a senior vice president at the Pacific Coast Stock Exchange. Later, he was recruited to head strategic planning for American Cement. But he was bored. He began playing serious blackjack, worked with and put together groups of players who would cooperate to make large sums of money. He played in casinos all over the world and was barred from many casinos (including one at Lake Tahoe when my wife and I were with him). He was also a *60 Minutes* feature in which Harry Reasoner played blackjack with him, and then tested his counting by turning a full deck over, card after card, and without revealing it, asked Kenny, "What is the last card?" As you might expect, Kenny got it right.

Unfortunately, he died in a Paris hotel room at age 52. It was "Life in the Fast Lane" for Kenny.

Another colleague who became a close friend was Frank Caufield. He, too, was an HBS guy. He was the son of a two-star Army general who had preceded Frank's attendance at West Point. After graduating from West Point, Frank served four years in the Army before he arrived at HBS. We both worked on the Atlantic Richfield consulting job, and he moved to the San Francisco office after I left and had gone to work at Arcata National. We stayed in touch. After his CMP years, he helped Paul Cook, founder and CEO of Raychem, who had made some questionable venture investments in Mexico. He hired Frank to help him bail out of some of them, and they structured it as a partnership akin to a venture capital partnership.

Frank was successful, earned good money, and shortly after was asked to become a founding partner of Kleiner, Perkins, Caufield & Byers. It became legendary. Among Frank's more notable deals, he worked with Jim Kimsey, also a West Point grad, to fund and build what later became America Online (AOL). One time when another venture capitalist (VC) was touting his own success, Frank allowed as how he hadn't done that bad with AOL. He had invested $250,000 in the original company and, if I recall correctly, he said, when its successor AOL was merged with Time Warner, that stake was worth $500 million. At the time, the carried interest share earned by Kleiner Perkins from the deal was 30 percent of the gains—

approximately $150 million. Frank would have gotten the largest check for his lead role in the deal.

There were others, also very interesting, but Ken and Frank illustrate the unique talents uncovered by CMP that made the three years interesting.

After I joined CMP, one of my first assignments involved a family-held oil company (the Berry Holding Company) in Taft, California. The founder, Clarence Berry, raised in Fresno, had made a fortune in the late 1890s and early 1900s prospecting for and mining gold in three Alaska locations. In the early 1900s he and his wife moved to Taft, where previously he had been involved in startup oil companies. With his gold mining wealth, he bought up tracts of land near Taft where he successfully drilled for oil. This was adjacent to the infamous Teapot Dome oil fields.

Clarence Berry had a large number of siblings, plus two subsequent generations of family members. His will encompassed all three generations of beneficiaries who, after he died, would receive dividends from the shares owned by Berry. All family members of the first (oldest) generation would receive an equal share of the 37.5 percent of dividends allotted to that generation. If a member of that group passed away, his or her share was reallocated equally among the surviving peers. Thus, each surviving member benefited when his peers died. When the last member of that first generation succumbed, its 37.5 percent share of the dividends all went to the second generation—which was already receiving its own 37.5 percent from the original bequest. The same rules continued. If a member of the second generation died, the remaining members of that generation benefited by getting an equal share of what had been earned by the deceased. Then, later, when all members of the first and second generations died, the 75 percent that was originally set aside for them all went to augment the 25 percent of dividends originally allocated to the third generation. And of course, if you were the last surviving member of the third generation, it was a bizarre, almost Russian roulette arrangement in which each surviving member benefited from the demise of the others. We often wondered if those at family events spent a good deal of time asking about the health of others.

The family's question for us was whether or not they should diversify away from drilling and pumping more oil. They thought, for example about buying franchises of restaurant chains. I/we recommended they not do that. The math was pretty clear. The probabilities of success in drilling more "development" wells on property they already owned were very high while the risks of entering a different industry in which they had no experience were far from a sure thing. They took our advice. We also chose never to comment on the unique arrangement for passing wealth among surviving family members.

I suspect by now that most or all of the family members have died. Meanwhile, the company still exists. It is a NASDAQ-listed company with 2019 annual revenues of $559 million.

Another assignment was to prepare an outdoor recreation plan for the state of Alaska. This arose from a new federal program to subsidize such planning all over the United States. I worked directly with key state employees over roughly a year surveying existing recreation resources, documenting usage rates, projecting them forward and laying out a plan for further investment needed to develop the infrastructure to support the future growth. It was a delightful assignment involving many flights to Juneau, Anchorage, and elsewhere.

Western International Hotels CEO Edward Carlson (who began his career as a bellboy), asked us to prepare a compensation plan for the hotel chain's senior executive positions. The CMP partner taught me how to do a compensation plan for which the principal task was to chart the existing compensation levels for the senior executives, benchmark them against peers at similar levels in other hotel companies and from those comparisons, plus projections of future inflation, make recommendations to the CEO. It was easy, and the CEO always had the benefit of explaining to his board and his direct reports that all of that work had been done by "independent expert compensation consultants."

World Airways was a large charter airline built by Ed Daly, who was said to have used proceeds from his poker winnings to buy the airline. The company actually had two businesses. The first was charters to fly tour company clients on their overseas vacation tours. Daly wanted our thoughts on how to improve the operations and efficiency of that business. The other business at the time was mainly flying American troops to and from the United States to foreign postings, most of which were in Vietnam.

In August, 1968, I was asked to fly to Europe on a World Airways charter flight to begin interviewing key overseas executives. The assignment was made more interesting by a mix-up in the plans to get me on a flight from New York to London. It turned out they did not have an empty seat. Instead, they flew me to Toronto, where they had an empty Boeing 707 that needed to be repositioned. As a result, I was the sole passenger on the airplane with a full crew, including five or six flight attendants. We flew to Lakenheath Air Force base about eighty miles northeast of London. It was my first trip to Europe, and made more interesting by the delightful bus trip across the wonderful English countryside en route to London.

Ed Daly was a strong leader and a good client. My lasting memory of him, however, comes not from the work we did but from the image of him in newspapers and magazines with his pistol in hand standing on the back stairway of a Boeing 727 as he escorted the remaining troops aboard the airplane—this in the final days as the United States evacuated all of its troops from Vietnam. Ed Daly was going to defend them and the aircraft so they could all get out safely.

I also was asked to do a job for the Yakima Valley Community Action Agency (YVCAA). This was one of perhaps hundreds of local operations created by Lyndon Johnson's Community Action Agency poverty programs.

Our job was to look at what YVCAA was doing well and not so well and make recommendations for how to be more effective. We did that over an assignment lasting about six months. Whether it made a difference I will never know. It was a very political and bureaucratic structure. Whenever I think of the project, I am reminded of Tom Wolf's book *Radical Chic and Mau Mauing the Flack Catchers*, in which the poorer population being served quickly learned they could improve the chance of getting something they wanted by intimidating (or Mau Mauing) the client facing individuals of the U.S. government poverty agencies.

Greatermans Stores was another interesting assignment. In March of 1969, Norm Clement, the Los Angeles senior partner, and I flew to Johannesburg, South Africa, to consult with Norman Herber, the Jewish chairman and CEO of South Africa's largest department store chain (Greatermans) and Checkers, its chain of grocery stores. Ostensibly, we were reviewing the structure of this large retailing combination. I interviewed senior management in Johannesburg, flew to Durban and did much the same. Norm Clement flew to Capetown, and we shared our notes and our thoughts. Mostly, the structure seemed appropriate and strong.

Then, Norman Herber asked us (Norm Clement, his wife, Lisa, and me) to join him and his wife, Toni, a Roman Catholic from New Jersey, to fly in a small plane to Kreuger National Park where we would stay in Mala Mala, one of South Africa's foremost safari resorts, for a three-day camera safari. We did and had to buzz the airport to get the giraffes off the landing strip. Over the next three days, the five of us plus our Swiss driver, Romeo, drove all over the park taking pictures including some with the resort's popular cheetah that was very handsome and quite tame.

After we flew back to Johannesburg and were back at our hotel, Norm and I discussed the engagement since I did not feel we delivered much in the way of substantive comments and certainly not a written report. Norm Clement then told me he was not sure either, but he thought the real purpose of the engagement was the opportunity to exchange thoughts about what Norman Herber should do. He was Jewish in country that was predominantly Black. It was an apartheid country ruled by the Afrikaner descendants of the seventeenth and eighteenth-century Dutch colonizers who were about 9 percent of the total population. There were also people from India, Britain, Ireland, and other countries, as well as Jewish people—but the dominant population was Black, roughly 75 percent of the total.

The Black population was growing restive, major countries around the world were increasingly critical of the government, and for Norman Herber, most of his past and nearly all of his money was in South Africa, mostly in Greatermans stock. What should he do? In that circumstance, our comments about the organizational structure were interesting, but the real task was Norman Herber picking Norm Clement's brain (and to a much less extent, mine as well.) It was a plum assignment for me.

A codicil: when I was in Johannesburg in 1968, the city was nice, reminiscent of a smaller Chicago or St. Louis, reasonably clean with some beautiful residential neighborhoods. I walked the streets when I could and felt completely safe. I was interested in Soweto, but it was not considered safe for tourists, so I did not go. In June, 2014, we and two couples of friends joined a Southern Africa tour that began in Johannesburg. The city was stark, and the tour operator told us not to go out on our own. The downtown that we saw through bus windows was dingy and dirty. Some major high-rise buildings had been taken over by homeless people. With no electricity, wood fires had been started for heat and those fires engulfed the upper floors. This was five years since the magical era of Nelson Mandela had ended. As it turned out, on that trip we went to and toured Soweto. It was marvelous, friendly, and colorful.

In the end, I never did find out what conclusion Norman and Toni Herber came to regarding their fortune and future.

There were other engagements such as Atlantic Richfield, a huge project managed out of CMP's New York office. Many consultants doing interviews for this ever-changing company required a great deal of travel, particularly to New York for me, and like, Greatermans, I am not sure of the benefits for Atlantic Richfield. I also consulted for Slakey Brothers Inc., a family-owned plumbing contractor. The variety of engagements always made it interesting.

With my three-year anniversary approaching, I concluded I had been very fortunate, but this was not a career I wished to continue for two reasons. First, the more successful you were, the more your job was simply signing up new clients. With success you would spend ever less time in any particular place or home and more of your time traveling between the various prospects and clients you had signed up. Second, my career goal was to operate a small- to medium-sized business where I would be in charge and make the key decisions. To do that, I had to begin to move to an operating business and migrate from staff to line jobs that would point me in that direction.

The opportunity that came was with Arcata National, a Fortune 500 publicly traded company based in Menlo Park, California. I would be assistant to Group Vice President Gardiner Hempel, who was responsible for four acquired companies of which one was sold or dissolved before I arrived. A second was a small microfilm and microfiche service company that microfilmed historical corporate and hospital records as a way of preserving access to the historical information while substantially reducing space required to store all the documents.

ACI
Arcata Communication Information

REDI
Real Estate Data Inc.

PLM
Professional Lease Management

The third company was Brand Rating Research, a marketing survey research firm based in New York that produced large surveys involving thousands of interviews exploring consumer preferences for products and companies. The data were used to help the companies refine their own product or service strategies and determine their marketing and advertising plans. The fourth company was Real Estate Data Inc. (REDI), a Miami-based entrepreneurial company that was America's foremost provider of information about real property. REDI produced books county by county of all the tax maps and the tax rolls showing ownership, assessed value, and taxes paid for each parcel. REDI also produced aerial atlases created to assist developers and governments in their planning.

The microfilm business was interesting but had only limited opportunities for growth given the technologies of the time and the options to gravitate to digital records that were more useful and flexible than microfilmed records. The Brand Rating Research business was exciting, but it later developed that the entrepreneur who founded it had fraudulently claimed the contracts for services were more numerous and of greater value than they really were. It was a fiasco that was never resolved while I was there. REDI was the star. As a result, I spent most of my time working in Miami with Dick First, the entrepreneur who founded the company. He was probably 40. I was 29 and we enjoyed working with each other.

At the end of my first year, Don Thompson, another Arcata group vice president, approached me asking me to move to Washington, D.C., and consider taking over as CEO of Arcata Communications Information (ACI). This company collected information about radio frequencies and the companies that owned them. It was a very small business producing publications of interest to a very limited audience run by a very nice guy who had no idea how to build it. As it turned out, neither did Don or I. It was another of the "back of the envelope deals" cooked up over a dinner and a few drinks by the young Turks running Arcata. I suggested they shut it down or sell it and they did.

Over the three months Karen and I were in Washington, D.C., Karen had worked in the Nixon administration finding candidates to fill openings for various federal boards and commissions. The job was relatively senior. Her boss reported to Fred Malek who led recruitment at all levels in the administration. A West Point standout, he was later to become executive vice president of Marriott Corporation, president of Northwest Airlines, and serve four presidents in senior roles. Karen also got to know John Clarke, a professional executive recruiter, who approached me about becoming a pro bono part-time White House advance man, which I did after my return to San Francisco and Arcata's corporate headquarters in Menlo Park.

Arcata had asked me to return and head up strategic planning for the corporation. I did that, reporting to Bob Dehlendorf, the CEO, and Bill Walsh, chief administrative officer. Walsh was a Harvard-trained lawyer who prosecuted Mafia mobster Vito Genovese, then joined McKinsey and was recruited to join Arcata where he handled most of Arcata's legal affairs. It was an interesting nine-month gig and, for me, it was my last "staff" job. It was about that time that I met Charlie McWhorter.

A Most Remarkable Man

There was simply no one like him.

One evening in the late 1960s or early 1970s, a colleague of Karen Collins working in Ronald Reagan's California political office invited me to join him at Basin Street West in San Francisco to hear some jazz. There I first met the political and arts patron Charlie McWhorter[2] and thus began our thirty-year friendship.

Charlie was a wonderful guy who would bend over backwards to help anyone who was part of his life. When I was working for Sanborn and did not want to take the train and rent a room in Pelham, I would sleep on the couch at his Greenwich Village apartment. He was always available at the other end of the phone.

He often took in young people in need of help. Charlie once told me about the "White Ghost"—who was really Charlie—who loaned a great deal of money to young

---

[2] Born in 1922 in Lewisburg West Virginia, he served as a lieutenant in Patton's 3rd Army during World War II. He was awarded a Bronze Star with two citations and a Purple Heart.

From 1957 to 1961, he was Vice President Richard Nixon's administrative assistant. In 1961, he turned down an offer to work in the White House and returned to New York to work for AT&T. Officially, he was in the legal counsel's office but in fact, for twenty-six years he was their chief political advisor.

people down on their luck or needing a loan. He told me he never lost a dime. The loans were always repaid.

I discovered early on that he seemed to know everybody. Charlie had an encyclopedic memory of nearly every Republican office holder not only at the national level but also in many states and counties. Because of his amiability, he also knew many of their counterpart democrats and, he introduced them to each other.

Charlie's passion for the arts was legendary.[3] He was willing to take me, a hick from Spokane, under his wing to teach me a good bit about music and dance. One night in Manhattan, he introduced me to Duke Ellington. Another night we went to Lincoln Center to see the opera *Boris Gudonov* featuring a superb Edward Vallela ballet.

For years, he had been a director of the Monterey Jazz festival and he had rights to about 18 superb seats. Every year, Charlie assembled a group of friends (akin to the movie "Same Time Next Year") to share a large house in Carmel and sit together at the festival.[4]

Charlie always sent his calendar out early each year listing when and where he would be over the coming twelve months. Washington Post columnist David Broder once wrote that the Republican Party was a loose amalgamation

---

[3] In 1961, Charlie became a member of the National Council of the Arts. He also served as president, vice chairman, and a director of the American Ballet Theater as well as a director of the Alvin Ailey Dance Company and many other arts organizations.

[4] For many of those years, the group included Mark and Katy Hungerford, Frank Caufield and his then girlfriend, Peter and Debbie Ehrlichman, Stan and Melba Sanders, and Karen or Joyce and me plus others. Charlie served as host and chef.

of people held together by Charlie McWhorter's Christmas card list. His was always the first card we received right after Thanksgiving. It went to 3,000 people with a printed tribute to Christmas plus a hand-written personal note.

When he was ailing in the mid-1990s and found it hard to walk, I asked if I could help. He was stoic and did not want any sympathy. His comment to me was, "Steve, the parts wear out!"

After he retired, Charlie became ever more prone to dressing very colorfully. There was no doubt that he had his own flamboyant sense of style. In restaurants, all eyes would follow him as he walked to and from his table. Frank Caufield had a smile on his face after lunch when he leaned over to ask me, "What the heck was that?"

It was a huge loss for us all when Charlie died in 1999. He was a true mensch.

On to REDI

Dick First and I had stayed in touch. He had told Arcata that he wanted REDI to be spun out of Arcata and become a publicly traded company for the second time in its existence. Dick wanted me to help complete the public offering, make acquisitions for REDI, be responsible for those acquisitions, and by the end of the first year to be named the chief operating officer of the company. Further, he said, in five or six years he planned to retire and would like me to become his successor.

I always thought we struck a great bargain. We liked each other. I greatly respected his entrepreneurial success and thought I could learn a lot from him. He respected my Harvard Business School sheepskin—he wanted me to do most of the work for the public offering, do acquisitions for REDI as well, and prove I could run the company.

So, in mid-1972, Karen and I packed up and drove from San Francisco to Florida, where I started at REDI, whose offices and book production plant were in North Miami. We bought a house in Coral Gables; it was a totally new environment for Karen and me.

Chapter Three

Real Estate Data Inc. (REDI)

Hit them over the head with your crutch.
—*Dick First*

When I accepted the offer to join Real Estate Data Inc. (REDI) in 1972, I already had a head start.

I had known the company founder and CEO, Dick First, as well as the senior management team for two years. At Arcata, I reported to Group Vice President Gardiner Hempel, and REDI was one of the subsidiaries in his group. I knew a good bit about the industry, the history, the personalities, and the issues, and I wanted to work with Dick.

Karen and I drove across the country and when we arrived, Dick provided temporary housing for us in the guest quarters adjacent to his house. He was a genial host, and his waterfront house, pool, tennis court, and grounds were impressive.

REDI was by far the largest provider of tax maps, tax rolls, and aerial photography in the United States. Dick founded the company in 1958, built it, took it public, and later sold it to Arcata, making serious money in the process. But he was tiring of dealing with and reporting to a large Fortune 500 company, impatient with some of the personalities, and ever more unimpressed with some of the young Arcata senior management that had made serious mistakes. Arcata had a long history as a Redwood logging company before the bright young "whiz kids" took control and diversified Arcata into printing and a variety of other industries. When they purchased three new and very expensive state-of-the-art printing presses and could not get them to work properly, *Forbes* magazine wrote a scathing article about the trouble. Their story ended with a jibe: "Let's hope Arcata is out of the woods before they are out of the Redwoods."

Dick arranged for a gentlemen's solution. REDI would be taken public again, with Arcata still its largest shareholder, but REDI would have a great deal of autonomy. From my standpoint it was a perfect fit. I would be with a small- to medium-sized company, help take it public, lead its acquisitions, become executive vice president within a year or so, and work with a proven street-smart entrepreneur who would teach me.

The job came with a nice office, about a third the size of Dick's, which was next to mine. Much like anything else involving Dick, there was a story behind it. When Dick owned the company and expanded its printing facilities, he added a regulation half basketball court on the roof of the plant. He was only 5' 7" or 5' 8", but he was athletic and he loved basketball. He knew Ronnie Watts, a young Boston Celtics team member who, when in Miami, would come over to practice and play with Dick and other friends. Among Ronnie's closest friends was Bill Russell, the legendary Celtic, who also used the court to practice when he was in Miami.

At one point Dick approached his bosses at Arcata for approval of a plan to further enlarge the printing plant. One of them suggested Dick could find space elsewhere in the existing plant to meet the need. When Dick said they could also use his office, the conversation ended. He had won. After that, Dick decided to convert the half basketball court into his office and mine with a regulation racquetball court behind mine, which I could use at any time I wanted.

One of the first things Dick asked me to do was review all of the written suggestions that came from his survey of employees' views. Roughly once each year, he would print more than 350 sheets of paper headed "REDI Employee Survey." Each had a signature line and even though signing was not mandatory, most employees signed it.

Dick would assemble all the employees in each department. As he was handing out surveys, he told them he would like for them to please write down their gripes as well as their suggestions for fixing the problems. In addition, if there were things they liked, they could add those as well. My job was to read all of the survey responses and provide Dick with a written report of what I found and what I would suggest. It was a very useful exercise and it provided good information while also supporting morale.

Dick told me at the time that a few years before he had learned there would be an effort to unionize all of REDI's employees. Fortunately, one of Dick's closest friends was Dick Cami, who owned one of the area's most popular restaurants, Top of the Home, in Hollywood,

Florida, just north of Miami. (While double-checking my recollection for this book, I discovered Dick Cami also wrote a memoir, titled, *A Look Back: My Fifty Years Hosting Entertainers, Celebrities, and the Mob.*) As it turned out, Dick first met Gil Davis at the Top of the Home and they became friends.

Gil was an officer of a Canadian Teamsters union. Dick called him for advice about what to do. Gil flew down and counseled Dick, telling him that he (Dick) was at a big disadvantage because the union organizers were well trained, they did this work full-time year-round at many companies, and knew exactly how to do their jobs.

Dick First had never faced such a challenge, but Gil gave him very good advice. He followed it and the unionization attempt failed. Dick was very discrete about how he had learned what to do. He did not want word to filter back to the Teamsters. He also gave Gil a very nice Rolex watch as a thank-you gift. This story represents one of many lessons I learned from Dick and one I used later in my career when a union attempted to organize workers at Professional Lease Management (PLM) Railcar Maintenance Company when I was its president. The unionization effort there failed as well.

Dick had learned the benefit of doing employee surveys, and he also began an employee suggestion program in which employees would be rewarded for suggestions they made based on the economic value to the company. That program, too, was very popular.

In taking REDI public, I would come to know James Freund, one of the top attorneys at Skadden, Arps, Slate, Meagher & Flom. One of Jim's bright young colleagues was Ted Kozloff, a partner and, if I recall correctly, the firm's seventeenth hire, who did much of the work. He would later become one of my closest friends for more than fifty years.

As it turned out, Jim Freund, Ted Kozloff, Dick First, Marty Zuckerman, the VP of sales, most of REDI's sales force, and David Nitka, a REDI competitor Dick had acquired, were all Jewish, as were many entrepreneurs in the real estate information industry at the time. This added immeasurably to my knowledge and admiration for the Jewish people, their history, their culture, and their accomplishments. It would later lead to my writing two books about Jewish achievements.[5]

During that first year or so at REDI, I led and learned much about the process and consequences of being

---

[5] Many who read this memoir will have been unaware of how important the Jewish people have become to me over the course of my lifetime. Most will likely have perceived by this point in the book that I had a few Jewish friends and acquaintances long before I joined REDI and that I already respected much of their difficult history and successful creation of Israel. But it was at REDI where I began to work closely with so many of them. There I also began to develop close personal friendships and an intuition that, as a group, they are disproportionately high achievers as compared to their numbers in the population as a whole. Later, I would prove that my intuition was correct and would write the books about it. So, please know that if in this book I identify some of these people as "Jews" or "Jewish" I do not mean those words in any pejorative sense, but instead, as a positive compliment.

a publicly traded company. It was invaluable in the coming years of my career and with that came relationships that were equally important, Ted Kozloff being one of them.

I also had the task of acquiring David Nitka's second real estate information startup. Before I joined Arcata, Dick had acquired David's first company, but they did not get along. For a time while serving as assistant to Gardiner Hemple, the Arcata group vice president to whom Dick First reported, one assignment was for me to serve as an intermediary between the two of them. David stayed for the time called for in the original purchase agreement and then left to start Damar, a new Los Angeles–based real estate information company. When I joined REDI, David was again making inroads into REDI's market with new products that drew on his superior knowledge of how computers could be used to add value to the information. David and I negotiated a new purchase agreement for REDI to acquire Damar and in it, David would report to me. Both he and Dick were satisfied with that arrangement.

I bought another direct competitor during that first year. It was owned by Jack Vinik, another Jewish entrepreneur. These were slick acquisitions because REDI already had the production, sales, and administrative staff. An acquisition was a better way to add revenues and profits than competing market by market.

We also acquired a very different kind of company. Charles Silberstein had bought Sanborn Map Company in 1968, and it had been losing money ever since, with losses of $300,000 in 1971. He wanted out and we saw an opportunity to integrate some of the Sanborn data into our real estate atlases.

Founded in 1867, Sanborn was a vital resource for the fire insurance industry. It mapped every U.S. city with a population of 5,000 or more.[6] The maps were very detailed showing size, layout, construction materials, names of businesses, and much more. The maps allowed underwriters to analyze the fire insurance risk they would be taking on in insuring the property, and they could also see any other properties in the immediate area they already insured. In addition, Sanborn would send their surveyors back into each town every few years. The surveyor would diagram every significant new or changed property since the prior atlas. This would result in "glue-on" modifications to the "base" map pages. The glue-ons were produced, printed, and colored at Sanborn's offices in Pelham, New York. Glue would be applied to the back of each one, they would be bagged in plastic bags, and an employee would go to every customer's office to glue the additions onto the appropriate map pages.

Ultimately, by the 1960s, the insurance industry found cheaper ways to get the information they needed, and customers stopped the service. Siberstein bought

---

[6] Once while I was in Washington, D.C., I visited the Library of Congress to ask about the Sanborn maps in their collection. They told me they were the largest of all their collections. The maps were seen as an immense repository of the history and evolution of America's cities from the 1860s to the 1960s. Later, to my chagrin, the maps were found to have another use. That concerns a story and one of the bigger mistakes I ever made—one I will describe in the next footnote.

control, tried to migrate to making aerial maps, and failed. I understood his problems reasonably well, and when I tried to reduce the price, he refused and walked away from the deal. When I explained what happened, Dick did not get angry, but he did pick up the phone, called Charles, and apologized if his new young employee had blown the deal. Charles was polite and agreed to resurrect it.

Within the following year, we were able to turn Sanborn around. We made $100,000 that first year and profits grew in every following year. I say "we" because the real secret was a longtime Sanborn employee, Joe Cirillo, who reported to me. For many months, I had to fly to New York Sunday nights, go to Pelham, stay in a hotel, and fly home Friday night. Joe had never been listened to, and he knew where all the bones were buried. He made suggestions for what to do. I agreed with almost everything he suggested and his ideas worked. He deserved the bulk of the credit for the turnaround and we stayed solid friends even after I left REDI.[7]

So, roughly a year or so after joining REDI, I was made executive vice president and chief operating officer. Everything reported to me. I was 30 years old. I had also developed a friendship with Richard Simonet, the Ernst & Young partner who served as our auditor. His wife Pat was

---

[7] "The one that got away:" In the 1980s I had a chance to buy Sanborn and offered $600,000. REDI accepted and we moved forward. At the last minute, they raised the price by $100,000. I bolted. Within a few years, those maps became invaluable for identifying underground gas storage tanks and other environmental risks. It was worth millions, and I had blown it. Damn!

office manager for a successful legal practice and later became the president of a firm of consultants that counseled legal firms all over the United States in how they should manage their offices for efficiency and to ensure everything they did was proper. At one point Dick came to San Francisco to mentor a young man, Greg Saunders, I had promoted to chief financial officer of a different public company. To this day, Dick and I talk often.

Meanwhile, Karen and I had purchased, fixed up, and added a back patio and pool to the home we bought in Coral Gables, Florida. We began to make friends. The Gables tended to be something of an insular community. If you did not graduate from Gables High, you were often seen as an outsider. Karen had been doing some writing for REDI, including help on its annual report (she was a very good writer) and did not have a lot of free time, but as she met more and more people in Coral Gables, her warmth and personality opened many doors. She made many friends and was invited into a club of women who each year sponsored and produced a charity fundraiser (the Beaux Arts Ball), for an art museum. Heading up the fundraiser terrified most of the members. Karen was asked to do it and carried it off easily and well. Our circle of friends expanded thanks to her.

As we were about to put this chapter to bed, Karen Collins wrote to remind me of a newspaper picture and story that were published shortly after we arrived in Miami and a memorable mid-1970s Coral Gables dinner party involving her dad and many of our friends.

The newspaper feature, that appeared about five months after we arrived, was our invitation to a black-tie event. I didn't own a tux so I rented one. About two weeks later my picture was one of five or six on a full-page story about the event and the men's formal clothing. Under my picture was the caption, "Steve Pease, the rental guy" and thus was I introduced to "polite society" in Miami and Coral Gables.

I really liked Karen's second idea and realized it would be a nice way to profile her dad, Jim Saldin, who was another important person in my life. He and Karen's mom, Montana, had known my parents for a very long time (both fathers spent many years working in the moving and storage industry.) Moreover, I aways thought my mom might just have had something of a crush on him. But I never met Karen's folks until she and I began to date in the late 1960s.

When we married, I had the issue of what I should call him. "Dad" did not seem to fit. I already had a dad. "Jim" seemed presumptuous to me. Finally, and I do not recall why, I took to calling him "Chief." It caught on and soon everyone who knew him used it as well.

He was soft spoken, warm, a great salesperson, and a terrific father to Karen, her sister, and two brothers. He also loved a great story and he told many of them. One involved him helping a very old Alaskan Indian woman cross a busy street in Anchorage. She was so grateful she gave him her secret tribal recipe for grilled salmon. We all got a kick out of his story and then we tasted the salmon. It was incredible and we smiled again, thinking about the story. When he came to Coral Gables, he usually grilled the salmon, word spread, and everyone wanted to be invited.

For one of our dinner parties, the Chief flew down from Seattle with fresh salmon filets on ice.

In the mid-1970s Miami was still living in the glory of the 1972 Dolphins who won the Super Bowl at the end of a 17-0 perfect season. Jack Clancy was a former Dolphin, an All-American wide receiver from the University of Michigan, and a great party guy. He was invited and like the Chief, he put on his chef's hat, called himself a sous-chef, and poured the Jack Daniels and water for everyone. He also helped the Chief keep the recipe hidden from the prying eyes.

We held the party at some friends' house because ours was being renovated. The hostess, never having tasted the salmon, brought out a new jar of tartar sauce. In a feigned act of anger, the Chief picked up the jar, tossed it against a rock wall and said his salmon did not do tartar! Everyone laughed, loved the salmon, and had a great time.

Whenever we were together for a family event, he was always the first person up every morning around 5 A.M. I copied him in that habit and still do, more than fifty years later. It is great for the quiet time, but it has also been practical when dealing with people on the East Coast, and even more so when the calls were to and from Moscow.

Oh, and by the way, having watched the salmon being prepared so many times, I was able to create my own variation of his secret recipe!

Over time, I learned many lessons from Dick First. He was constantly walking into my office with ideas for new products and other changes we should consider—and toward which I was often cool. But he was never angry about "the brake" sitting in the office next door. We got along very well. He always believed we learn much more from our failures than our successes—they hurt more than the pleasure we get from success, which we tend to take for granted; but if we are realistic about failures and how they happened, we grow.

Dick was the first person I ever knew who, when discussing good salespeople, told me that most successful ministers (and probably rabbis too, though he did not include them in his story) are very good salespeople. His point was that a good minister could deliver inspirational sermons to his members and visitors. They would praise him or her and be loyal. He would counsel them one-on-one if they asked for help. He could gently nudge them in useful ways and they would reward him in the form of a growing congregation and more tithes and gifts. It was an interesting insight.

Dick had also pioneered the real estate information business, and one of the ways he became successful was leasing the books rather than selling them. In effect, he had a subscription business that gave him a built-in renewal business. When pressed to sell books, he would tell customers that the leasing arrangement would benefit them as well. Once they knew how to use the books, they would discover they were quite valuable. They also knew there is constant change in the owners, in property values, new properties being built, and much, much more. They would want their information to be as up-to-date as possible and the leasing arrangement gave REDI the assurance of future customers when they updated the books, which they usually did each year. That allowed REDI to know how many customers to print books for, and that made his production much more efficient, a savings he passed along in the lease pricing. Of course, without saying it, it meant that if the customer did not renew, the salesperson who was attempting to make the renewal would take the old books with him as he left the customer's office. It was a wise way to operate the business, and most competitors had not successfully copied it.

Ironically, Dick had an occasional stutter and he knew it. He had also learned how to turn it to his advantage. He found many prospective customers and others would have some sympathy for him since he was so friendly and outgoing. His advice, arising from his own experience, was to "hit them over the head with your crutch." In essence, he had learned how to turn his speech impediment into an advantage.

As REDI's founder and first salesperson, Dick also knew how hard it could be to convince customers that first time. He learned from personal experience what to do and how to do it. Ultimately, he knew he needed a highly talented sales force. They had to be able to walk into a real estate broker's, appraiser's, surveyor's, or title company's offices, get past the receptionist, get into the prospect's office, lay down the books, explain why the prospect needed them and how he could make more money using them. He also had to explain the leasing arrangement and then get a signed check, sometimes for more than $1,000, leave the books, get out the door and on to the next prospect.

REDI's salespeople were on the road constantly going from county to county and they were paid hefty commissions. In the early 1970s, a good REDI salesperson could earn $75,000 to $100,000 a year, which was big compensation at the time.[8] Dick knew how demanding the job was, and he knew good salespeople were expensive but worth it. I would occasionally spend a day traveling with one of them to get to know him and develop a better sense for how they worked. Because I was usually much younger, they sometimes took great pleasure in seeing if they could put me on the spot in closing a sale or visiting the local tax assessor to ask for more information we might incorporate into our books. I developed some skill at finessing their challenges.

At one point, I did come up with a way to get access to the tax roll and tax maps from King County, Washington (Seattle). Because these are all public data, the assessor nearly always cooperated and released the data to us without any charges, and we would provide them with a complimentary set of books. But occasionally assessors refused and we could not publish those counties. Karen's old boss, Ken Rogstad, was in Miami. He had been active in King County politics for years, and I asked if he might

---

[8] REDI had only salesmen. The work was grueling. Fifty weeks a year you were only home on weekends. There was great pressure to make sales. At the time, few women would have considered the job safe or attractive. Today, who knows?

be able to help. A month or so later, he told me he had secured permission but would need to pay the assessor $5,000. I told him we could not do that. I told him I could pay him (Ken) a fee for having secured the permission, but I would not pay the assessor. He agreed. I paid Ken and we published King County.

Dick had seen competitors come and go. When he heard rumors of a new competitor about to sell their books in a market already served by REDI, he did not immediately renew all the customers. Instead, he would wait until he knew the prospective competitor had printed his books. Dick would then get the bulk of the REDI salesforce into that market and quickly renew and deliver new books to customers. If the competitor had already printed books, he was out of pocket a good deal of money. That being the case, the prospective competitor was unlikely to make another run at that county or any other. Dick also learned from that experience that he needed to have very complete records on all customers so that REDI knew a lot about them, who sold to them, how long they had been customers, whether they had written or called to complain or ask questions. All of it was useful.

He told me he admired Miami's Cubans and hired many of them to work, particularly in our short run printing plant. They were smart, hardworking and we paid them good wages. It was another case of Dick seeing great value in a group of people some others in Miami looked down upon.

He could be a tough boss and if someone was not performing, Dick could cut the cord. It did not happen often, but when it did, the message would go out—without embarrassing the former employee—how the performance had failed. The only employee he did not follow that approach with was his own younger brother. That was left to me, and Dick was not happy when that day came.

During my six years at REDI, there were also unusual and sometimes amusing things that came with the job. One was an unknown employee who was obviously unhappy and showed it in a very strange way—he would smear the bathroom walls with his feces. An employee wag dubbed the unknown person "the mad shitter." When the next person came to use the facilities, he was greeted with an ugly mess and a horrible odor. This went on for a few weeks and we had not figured out who it was or why it happened. We considered some kind of video or other identification technique, but we dropped it for privacy reasons. Ultimately the word got around to everyone, and many people had thoughts about who it might be. So when their candidate or candidates used the facilities the employee with some suspicions would be the next person to enter the bathroom after the suspect exited. Ultimately the person was identified and terminated, but I do not recall that we ever got a clear answer as to why.

I also had the pleasure of exploring the possibility of overseas markets. A Washington, D.C., competitor, Rufus Lusk, owned that market and we never tried to enter and compete with him. It was an active market, but he had been there many years and produced good products. Instead, we stayed in touch, and when one of his British relatives, Paul Ostromoff, was going to be in Miami, we offered to show him our plant and talk with him about the business. He told us he lived on the Channel Islands' Isle of Guernsey, had developed real estate in the U.K. and was interested in sharing in an exploration of Europe for possible countries where products might be marketed.

I flew over to the U.K. and spent some time with Paul and his family on Guernsey. He chartered a small plane that we flew to Paris and some other cities, but the laws in each country were not as hospitable as those in the United States. We decided not to pursue it, but it was an interesting research project and a nice way to visit the U.K., Guernsey, Paris, and other prospects. We stayed in touch, and later he returned to Coral Gables with his mother, and they stayed with us.

Because he reported to me, I spent quite a bit of time in Los Angeles with David Nitka at his offices. These were a smaller version of the offices we had in Miami. His brother, Martin, handled production and a former REDI salesperson, Bob Lynn, was often in the office.

Like Dick and the REDI sales force, Bob was an excellent salesperson, but if you have made thousands of presentations, you occasionally might get bored, or want to humor yourself. One way Bob did that was to modulate the volume of his pitch. As he got into it, he would sometimes slowly lower his voice and gradually get down to a whisper. As the customer leaned closer and closer, Bob would then quickly raise his voice and startle the customer. Both he and the customer might start to laugh since most brokers were also good salespeople and knew what he had just done.

David's parents had immigrated to Israel from a small Polish shtetel in the early 1900s. He and his brother, Martin, were born and grew up there. In the late 1940s, they joined the Haganah (self-defense force) and fought in the war that ended in an Israeli victory. In 1948, after the civil war was over and Israel became a country, David wanted to go to engineering college, but he could not find a school in Israel accepting applications. Instead, he headed to New York and later graduated from college. While there he met a very pretty and young Jewish girl, Laurette, a talented artist. She had little interest in moving to Israel, so instead he stayed in New York and later moved to Los Angeles. His engineering training gave him skills in math and logic that would later come in handy when programming a computer.

David also taught me a great deal about the politics of the Middle East, Jewish history, Arabs, Palestinians, and the incredible network of relationships all over the world arising from the Diaspora experience. David had traveled widely and, at one point, he established a partnership in the Philippines with a Filipino friend. In that business, David shipped microfilm copies of all deed transfers (property sales) in a particular county in the United States. English-speaking Filipinos would read the deeds and enter all that information into digital computer files that were transmitted back to Los Angeles over undersea phone lines where David would compile them into monthly publications that some customers found were valuable market information.

In 1978, as we neared the end of six years working together, I asked Dick about his personal plans to retire. Perhaps I should not have been surprised, but he told me he could not afford to retire. He said, "Steve, it now costs me $150,000 a year just to get up every day and pay the families' bills." He had seven kids (he was a superb father), a second wife, plus he paid support to his first wife. He lived pretty high, and I had never pressed him about his finances. Clearly, he was not going anywhere. His second wife told him I would never quit, and I think he believed her. Although I was disappointed, I was not angry. I had been a bit naive not to anticipate his response, but I had gotten an invaluable experience working with him. It was time to consider moving on.

I put the word out and found that racquetball was a rapidly growing sport all over the United States. In San Francisco, Wallbangers, a chain of six racquetball clubs, had been started by two entrepreneurs and it was struggling. It had venture capital financing and the board members were looking for a new CEO. The fact that I had a racquetball court right behind my office and had done a successful turnaround (Sanborn) gave me a leg up.

Leaving Miami and Coral Gables was much tougher than I would have ever believed when Karen and I arrived six years earlier. We thought South Florida was flat, hot, and lacking in culture, but over the years it grew on us. We ended up with many friends. Karen had run a part-time catering business and was active in the Beaux Arts group.

I had learned that flat as South Florida was, there was great beauty and pleasure to be had. Sailing on Biscayne Bay at sunset with friends was one of them. Watching the summer afternoon cumulus clouds form in the west over the Everglades was another. Often, they would produce brief downpours but usually the sun created silver linings as it set behind the towering clouds. This was dramatic beauty as wonderful as mountains in the Cascades, the Sierras or even the Swiss Alps. Miami was becoming an international art capital with galleries and museums. It had also become a hub for many immigrants and businesses, particularly from Central and South America and later from Europe as well.

For me personally, I could hardly have found a more rewarding job at that stage in my life. I learned many lessons from Dick First and David Nitka, worked with some great people, ran a small publicly traded company, developed my management skills, and made friends that have lasted a lifetime.

Chapter Four

Wallbangers and Liquid Crystal Technologies (LCT)

We learn more from our failures than our successes. They hurt more than the pleasure we get from success.
—Dick First

Wallbangers

Karen and I returned to San Francisco in 1978 when I became CEO and a director of Wallbangers. It was a Bay Area chain of six racquetball clubs that was losing money. The board wanted me to get it into the black. Meanwhile, Karen began to work with a political campaign management firm (Spencer, Roberts, Woodward, and McDowell) in California.

I did not know it, but the next two and a half years would be my most difficult and challenging on many fronts. Had I anticipated what would unfold, I likely would have opted to stay at REDI, but I did not. In retrospect, I learned so much from the hardships, it turned out to be one of the most important parts of my career and life.

I knew racquetball very well since I had a racquetball court behind my office in Miami, and there were courts I could use at the University of Miami, less than a mile from our house.⁹

To get to know the business, I visited all the Wallbangers clubs, met most of the employees, and worked in several clubs to get a feel for the operations part of the business and its relationship with members. I was behind the counter/cash register in the Palo Alto club when venture capital icon Don Valentine walked in and became intrigued in part because, as the new CEO, I was behind the counter learning what I could. He was interested in considering an investment, but at the time, our board was not taking new money. Later, Don and I got to know each other, and a couple of times I moonlighted for him looking over and providing my thoughts on two or three of his portfolio companies. I respected him greatly.

At the time, racquetball courts and clubs around the country were packed. For most, this was a brand-new sport, easy to learn, fast and exciting, and it burned roughly 1,000 calories per hour—great for keeping trim as well as fit. Our clubs were roughly 90 percent occupied from early morning to early evening seven days a week.

It did not take long to decide we needed to raise prices, something the two founders had been reluctant to do. Rather quickly, Wallbangers began generating a profit. Not huge, mind you, but promising. The board was

---

⁹ One Saturday, in the early 1970s, a good friend, Bill Mooney, and I squared off against Lyn D'Alemberte and Janet Reno in a doubles racquetball match at Lyn and Sandy's backyard court. Much to our chagrin, the two women cleaned our clocks. So much for my racquetball skills!

pleased. One of the two founders that I replaced chided me by calling me "Superman" with his tongue in cheek.

I was asked to join the board of the National Court Clubs Association and, in the process, I got to know other major owners and operators around the United States in this rapidly growing industry.

Before I joined Wallbangers, its founders had begun conversations to open clubs in Southern California, and landlords there were happy to construct "build to suit" buildings to accommodate the courts.

A racquetball court is 20 feet wide, 20 feet high and 40 feet long, with a back wall at least 12 feet high. Those dimensions can fit nicely within the shell of a two-story office or commercial building. The Wallbangers' Palo Alto club was part of a large office complex, and the Daly City club was part of an office building located at the edge of a shopping center. Architects used concrete tilt-slab exterior walls, and that was a very good surface for a racquetball court wall. They also designed prospective cutouts in the exterior walls so the cut-outs could easily be removed, and office windows installed if needed. All of this gave developers a way to convert buildings if racquetball proved to be something of a fad, and it made it easier to develop new clubs, albeit with the club operators such as Wallbangers committing to long-term leases, leaving them on the hook for the term of the lease if the business began to slump.

Wallbangers' board was venture capital-oriented. Bill Edwards was a distinguished guy with a long history of successful private investing. We were also fortunate to have Frank Caufield as a board member. He had suggested I take the job. Lloyd Dulbecco was a very smart guy who represented Wayne Prim, a wealthy San Francisco attorney who invested in venture deals. I was a director, and the fifth director was Tom Ford who later became a good friend. I mentored one of his sons for a time at a later company.

Tom was the managing partner of Ford Land Company, which owned many major Silicon Valley research and office buildings. Among them was 3000 Sand Hill Road, home to many if not most of the top venture partnerships in the area. I did not know Tom when I worked for Arcata, but their headquarters office was another of his properties at 2750 Sand Hill Road. The son of an Ohio judge, Tom was legal counsel for Stanford's business office and the director of their land development activities for ten years.

As he watched Silicon Valley develop, Tom approached Stanford about their willingness to sell some land or enter into long-term ground leases. They said yes. He resigned from Stanford and, over the years, built, leased, and managed thirty-nine properties mostly to venture capital firms. He did this with only five employees. He wanted a lean organization and he subcontracted other tasks to vendors. He was immensely successful and a very nice person. When he passed away in 1998, an estimated 1,500 people attended the service at Stanford Memorial Church.

At one point we considered merging with clubs outside California and began negotiations with an operator in Washington, D.C. The more we looked, the more skeptical I became about the geographic dispersion of our money and time at this early stage of our business. The D.C. owners wanted to proceed. When I briefed the board and recommended we not do it, they agreed and complimented me for not trying to move forward too quickly at that point.

We closely tracked occupancy at all our facilities. We gathered the data by hour, day, month, season, weather, holidays, and other factors that gave us a clear picture of what we believed was driving occupancy. We had the best coverage of any operator in the Bay Area. We also developed promotions to encourage membership that was relatively inexpensive, and play (which generated most of the revenues). We also sold equipment and lessons.

What we were not doing was operating like health clubs, which at the time generally had lousy reputations for suckering people in to buy annual memberships when most health club operators knew that new members joined in the passion of the moment, signed the contract, used the health club heavily for a month or two, began to lose interest and then were stuck paying dues for the rest of the year.

We did proceed with the two or three clubs in Southern California that the Wallbangers founders had pursued and were under construction.

At one point I was introduced to Regis McKenna, the head of his own advertising agency that had Apple as a client. He was a very smart guy and made a pitch to me. The problem was we had no more capacity. Our ads would tend to help our competitors as much or more than it helped us, and it would be quite expensive.

Things went very well for about six months but over the fall months we saw significant declines in occupancy. We checked with other operators who reported similar experiences. We developed more aggressive promotional programs to drive traffic and they did work for a while, but then the slide continued. There were many theories. One was that when one of the playing partners lost interest, got sick, or was injured, that meant his partner also dropped out. They often did not come back. Another theory was that unlike tennis, getting started in racquetball was very easy. It did not require the many long hours tennis does in order to learn how to serve, make a backhand return, and master various other strokes to play competently. You were unlikely to give up your commitment to tennis while, in racquetball, it was easy come, easy go.

Another problem was that lease rates for "build-to-suit facilities" tended to be high. Those were the largest operating costs for facilities like Wallbangers. In a way, racquetball was a high fixed cost, low variable cost business. When operating above the break-even occupancy level, you could make a lot of money, but if you fell below that level, you could lose a bundle.

At one point as the pressures were building, I was scheduled to give a speech to a group interested in the industry. I was jammed and only made a few notes about what I would say. I began the talk and quickly lost confidence in what I was saying. I felt I was spouting generalizations and pablum. It was the worst talk I had ever given, and I was embarrassed. After that experience, stage fright took over and inhibited my public speaking for years.[10]

By late September, we were operating on fumes and by mid-October we were nearly out of cash. The board had no suggestions, and our ideas were ever less successful. We decided to file for bankruptcy over the four-day Thanksgiving weekend, thinking, in part, the story would get lost what with Thanksgiving travel, family events, and football. It turned out Wallbangers was so well known we got a lot of ink. Nonetheless, our members took us at our word about continuity and they generally kept playing, albeit not as much as they did in the early days.

One early lesson for me was that bankruptcy attorneys could be scathing. They knew little about the businesses but could rail on before the court suggesting fraud, lying, and stupidity. Moreover, one of our shareholders was outspoken in his criticism. My naive view when I joined Wallbangers had been that if the sport proved to be a fad but I had done a good job, the shareholders would be supportive. That was not to be the

---

[10] Stage fright stayed with me for many years. I spent time with a psychiatrist to no avail. Ultimately, I generally overcame most of it. That was a case of just "getting back on the horse," time after time. Giving book talks and heading nonprofit organizations required an ability to stand up and make a presentation. Today, we know that behavioral training usually works best and is not expensive.

case at least for this critic. It was a very trying time and came with a good deal of stress over a period of many months. I think those stresses also contributed to difficulties at home because I was working long hours and under pressure to deliver. Meanwhile one of the two founders who had referred to me in jest as "Superman," let me know that my cape was falling off.

We sought a buyer and Jerry Sweeney, my Number 2, began a conversation with a local health club chain. They loved our locations and could modify some of the courts into exercise areas and training rooms, areas for weightlifting, treadmills, classes, and the like. In the end, we sold the company to them. We were able to pay off all of our debts and return much of the investment made by our shareholders.

It was considered a very successful bankruptcy and the first following enactment of a new national bankruptcy law. I learned a lot about the law, the nature of those who practice bankruptcy law, the sharks who prey on bankruptcy estates, and the judges, who greatly impressed me. All of that was to be very helpful later in my career.

I received a $100,000 bonus from the board for what Jerry and I had done. I knew I still did not want to work for a large company, and I would instead continue to seek and run small- to medium-sized companies. I would never have a large pension, but if I incorporated my own business, I could contract for my turnaround and management services and over time create and fund my own pension plan.

In seeking a name for my company, I asked my assistant, Joyce Sorem, to look at Greek and Roman gods and suggest some names that might be appropriate. One name she suggested was Deucalion, which I amended to Deucalion Securities Inc.

The story was that when Zeus, the king of the gods, resolved to destroy all humanity by a flood, Deucalion constructed an ark in which, according to one version, he rode out the flood and landed on Mount Parnassus. Deucalion and his wife, Pyrrha, then tossed stones over their shoulders. His stones became men and hers became women. Thus, Deucalion was a force driving the repopulation of humanity. It was a good "turnaround" fit and Deucalion continues to exist as of 2022, more than forty years since its creation.

Liquid Crystal Technologies (LCT)

With what was seen as a successful bankruptcy behind me and a little money in the bank, Frank Caufield asked if I would consider joining Liquid Crystal Technologies (LCT) as its CEO and a board member. This was more in the way of a consulting gig to be done by a person holding the CEO title and was done as a contract between LCT and Deucalion.

LCT began life as something of a novelty company started by Fred Davis, a chemist who knew how to blend temperature-sensitive crystals with the unique property of changing colors in response to changes in ambient temperature. The formulations were applied to surfaces and covered with Lucite or other plastics. Readers 50 years old or older may recall the mood rings (which reacted to finger temperatures) and digital thermometers (that reacted to the ambient temperatures in rooms where they were hung.)

Fred became one of the foremost developers of the technology, and later he developed a forehead thermometer that was helpful in surgeries to let the operating room staff, and particularly the surgeon, know if the patient's temperature was quickly rising or falling.

In addition, Eric Ephrati, a Jewish entrepreneur with family roots in the Egyptian cotton business (and whose family and business were forced to immigrate to Switzerland following the creation of Israel), somehow also found himself in the promotions business where Fred's technology was used to make stylish promotional novelties for companies that bought them and gave them to clients and prospects in France, Switzerland, and other European countries. Fred also developed similar items such as rulers and paperweights that showed a room's temperature. LCT sold them in the United States.

Somehow, out of the thermometer efforts, and with seed capital from investors, Fred began to develop an elastomeric material that could stretch and be wrapped around a woman's upper torso. Prospectively, this might be used in breast cancer screening. The premise was that breast tumor cancers grow more quickly than surrounding tissue. They require more blood flow to support the growth of the tumor which in turn elevates the surface temperature adjacent to the tumor. That surface temperature differential was displayed as different colors on the elastomeric liquid crystal halters. Thus, it might help in screening women for cancer risks.

Meanwhile in Westbury, New York, entrepreneur Howard Stern and his partner, Dr. Philip Meyers, a New Orleans radiologist, had come up with a product that solved the problem of contamination in barium enemas used in connection with X-ray exams of the lower intestinal tract. In 1962 each put up $1,000 to start E-Z-EM and develop and market the product.

Given Phil Meyers' radiology experience and E-Z-EM's medical industry credentials, in the 1970s they learned of LCT's prospective product and thought it worth exploring. They entered a joint venture to try to develop and market the product.

That effort attracted the interest of prospective investors, including proven venture investor Charles Crocker, and Kleiner, Perkins, Caufield & Byers in what would still be classed as a seed round investment. Later, Joel Murray, a Chicago attorney and friend of LCT's Sales Vice President Rocco Sappienza, invested and joined the board.

Dr. Phil Meyers believed he could see visible evidence of tumor activity when he looked at images made of women's upper torso wrapped in the elastomeric halter. He said he could see spots on the halters indicating warmer temperatures on the underlying skin. He also had other radiologists who thought they were on to something.

But the venture was not developing quickly. Frank Caufield encouraged hiring a new CEO to take a fresh look at LCT and the breast screening joint venture, as well as the overseas business. He and the other board members wanted to get a handle on the realistic prospects for creating a very profitable investment. That was my assignment as LCT's CEO.

Over a period of more than a year, I came to know Fred, Howard, Phil, Eric, Charlie, Rocco, and Joel. This was perhaps the most fascinating small mix of colleagues with whom I ever worked. It still makes me smile as I think of them. Rocco was a street-smart Chicago Italian kid with family roots in the Mafia; Joel had served as counsel to some mobsters. He traveled with large sums of cash and was incredibly smart. Always on the lookout for "some action," he was known to tape a $1,000 bill to his forehead as he walked around downtown San Francisco at night.

Charlie was perhaps a fourth- or fifth-generation scion of the Crocker family whose founder, Charles Crocker, was one of the "Big Four" who built the western half of the first transcontinental railroad. Charlie was a very smart and sophisticated guy. Howard was MIT-trained and a superb entrepreneur, and Phil was a big, gregarious radiologist who, early on, thought I was much too serious. He came up to me one day, put his arm over my shoulder, leaned down, and said, "Body contact, Steve, you need to develop a style with body contact!" Frank, as readers may recall, had been a friend since my management consulting days in the late 1960s. As recently as a couple of years ago, I had lunch with Eric Ephrati in Geneva to renew our acquaintance when I was there on other business.

During my roughly eighteen months at LCT, I spent time in Westbury talking with Howard and Phil about what they thought and why. In Chicago and San Francisco I got to know Rocco. Twice I went to Switzerland and toured other cities to meet customers. Once, over a weekend I had a day of clear skies and bright sunshine while skiing the Alps across from Mont Blanc. I had the mountain almost to myself. It was marvelous.

Ultimately, I concluded there would be no quick and inexpensive way to perform clinical studies of the breast cancer risk indicator in order to satisfy the FDA and others of the efficacy of the LCT halters. In many women, breast cancer develops very slowly. You could easily do testing of women with known tumors, but you would need to recruit a large number of other women and follow them for some time to see any visible evidence of new cancers and none at all for women who stayed cancer free.

I shared those views with the board. They decided to sell and asked me to first negotiate with Eric Ephrati to have him buy the European operation, which he did. The rest of the business was sold after I left to take a new job.

I had considered joining a venture capital firm, but it did not come together. Even more, in a world where a CEO would likely get stock options for 5 percent of a company's equity when he took over, I was offered 14 percent of Professional Lease Management (PLM), which was losing money hand over fist. The PLM name was later changed to PLM Railcar Maintenance Company, and still later, Transcisco.

Chapter Five

Joyce and Me

*But most of all
I love you 'cause you're you.*
—*Willie Nelson*

In late 1980 and early 1981 while I was wrapping up my work at LCT, Karen and I began to have serious differences. I think the pressures from my work made me difficult to live with, and certainly Karen had good reasons for being unhappy. She was engaged in political work and gravitated to government relations for two major companies, Container Corporation of America, and Del Monte. These were big jobs. She was very good at them, and it meant she spent a lot of time in Sacramento.

At one point we agreed to split up, though my recollection is that we were still living in our house in San Francisco. Later we had something of a dinner party at that house, and we both spent much of the evening separately talking with others. After that, we had a heart-to-heart. Karen wanted to give it another try and I agreed.

In August, 1981, we decided to take a vacation trip. We toured Switzerland staying in Basel with Swiss friends who had visited us in Coral Gables. We drove through France and Italy to Venice, and then down through Trieste to Split, Dubrovnik, and I believe we took a ferry to Corfu as well. It was fun, but after we got back to San Francisco our relationship again began to sour, and before long, we split for good.

I am pleased to say that after some chilly times between the two of us, we both ended up in Sonoma for different reasons and we restoked our friendship. We continue to communicate by email, phone, and in person. I remain tremendously impressed with her smarts and her friendly outgoing nature.

A few years ago, when concert pianist Lang Lang opened the new Weill Symphony Hall at Sonoma State University, Joyce and I bought a table for ten and invited Karen. A devilish computer must have done the seating. I arrived to find Karen's assigned seat on the left side of me and Joyce's seat on the right. Friends from Sonoma looked over, did a double-take, and then smiled.

A few years ago, Karen was chosen to be Sonoma's Alcaldessa—an honorary one-year mayorship of Sonoma—to acknowledge her many long and important contributions to our shared community.[11]

Shortly after our split, I moved to a rental apartment, and I made two decisions. The first was I would "play the field" for a few years. Karen and I had married shortly after our respective master's degree graduations. The other decision was that my first date would be with Joyce Sorem, who had worked with me at Wallbangers, but at the time

---

[11] Over time, Karen has migrated from conservative to liberal. Her view is a mirror image of Reagan's famous line ("I didn't leave the Democrat Party, the Democrat Party left me!") As she says, "The Republican Party left me." After some years as a Democrat, she is now a "No Party Preference."

we were both married to others and neither of us wanted to violate our vows.

Sometime in September, 1981, I took Joyce to dinner at a restaurant near her house on the Peninsula. I later learned one of her daughters asked "tongue-in-cheek" when I pulled up, "Is this our new daddy?"

Between late summer of 1981 and mid-1984, I often dated Joyce on Friday or Saturday night, and either stayed home or dated someone else on the other weekend night.

Joyce became the person I most loved being with. She was simply a gifted mother. She had three smart kids, (Bernadette, David, and Juliana), loved them deeply, and the same was true for animals. I often refer to her as the Mother Teresa of the animal kingdom. I will go to my grave remembering a night driving between St. Helena and Napa, California, when a cat ran under our car and was hit. Joyce was nearly inconsolable. I felt so very bad and was moved by her sorrow.

As the eighth of the nine siblings in the Ross family (Joyce's maiden name), she has been surrounded by loving siblings and relatives who genuinely care for each other. One measure of the closeness is that when Joyce was slated to enter UC Berkeley, her mirror image identical twin, Janice, backed out at the last moment. This meant Joyce would back out as well. She could not imagine going to university without Janice.

We took our first international trip together in 1982. We flew to London and the next day, boarded the Venice Simplon Orient Express train to Venice. After crossing the

English Channel, we dressed up for drinks and a superb dining car dinner as we traveled to Paris and then bed. We woke the next morning in the Alps and arrived a few hours later in Venice where we were met and taken by motorboat to the Cipriani Hotel for a few days.

We then flew to Athens and Piraeus where we met George, our captain for a five-day charter sail from Piraeus to Aegina, Hydra, Spetses, Poros, and Kea. Every morning we arose for a light early breakfast and bought picnic supplies before sailing till stopping in a harbor, taking a dive from the deck to swim, climbing back aboard for lunch and then sailing on to the next island. We had dinner at restaurants in each port and slept on board. What a beautiful way to spend five romantic days (and nights).

About that time, I bought a small condominium on the crooked part of Lombard Street in San Francisco with a great view of San Francisco Bay from Alcatraz to the Bay Bridge. It was perfect with an elevator that stopped at my entrance and as well as at the entrances of my neighbors in the condos immediately above and below me. We all became friends. It was great.

In Joyce and Joel's divorce, she got their Porsche 911. Having had two Porsches myself earlier in my life, we shared an interest in taking weekend trips in the 911.

She moved to an apartment in San Francisco, and with that, my dating of others slowed down, and we often took weekend drives to Tahoe, the Gold Country, Carmel, Mendocino, and other destinations only a few hours away. Sometimes, I pretended I could sing and would sing along with Merle Haggard or Willie Nelson while playing their songs on the CD player.

At some point after I had completed fixing up the condo, Joyce moved in with me. Earlier that year, I had purchased a 3.5-acre lot in a 1,000-acre subdivision on a hill just above the town of Sonoma. It was very rural with more than 500 acres of agricultural land devoted to farms and vineyards. There were wonderful views of the town and all of the North Bay. The plan was to build a new house on that lot for weekend use. Until then, we used the lot for occasional picnics and a late afternoon glass of wine.

She and I ripped pages out of architecture magazines and had a large stack of photos that we liked. At some point I began to consider architects and talked with Joyce about house plans. It didn't take long before Joyce let me know that she was not about to spend time planning for a new house that she would not share with me as husband and wife.

We decided to tie the knot, and at an early 1985 cocktail party at the condo, we used a series of messages on the various sides of the folded cocktail napkin to let people know we were getting married. One side said, "How long have they been dating?" Another, "Do you suppose they are serious?" etc., ending with the final note, "April 20, 1985."

When Joyce's boss refused to give his permission for more time off and told her she was Cooper Companies' only part-time/full-time employee, she asked if he would reconsider if it was her honeymoon? He relented.

So, we got married under a tree on a neighbor's meadow across the fence from where we would later build our house. Joyce's family stood on the hill as a local justice of the peace performed the ceremony. The next day we flew off on our honeymoon.

We called it our R & R—namely Russia and the Riviera. The first eight days were to be our initial visit to Russia, and the rest were to stay at great hotels in Paris, Côte D'Azur, and, along the way, driving north through Switzerland, Austria, and Germany to Amsterdam and our flight home.

Intourist Tour T51 began in Moscow, and later took us to Kiev (now Kyiv), and Leningrad (St. Petersburg). It was a remarkable introduction.

There must have been at least fifty people squeezed together trying get to the check-in desk at the Intourist hotel in Moscow. There was no queue. Earlier that day we had the same experience getting through customs at Moscow's Sheremetyevo Airport. We were very lucky that a kindly check-in woman realized we were newly married and gave us a honeymoon suite. We did not recognize any landmarks from our windows, but the next morning we found out we were only a couple of blocks from Red Square. In the years since that first visit, the Intourist hotel has been torn down and replaced with a very expensive Ritz Carlton.

The trip combined a bit of Transcisco business with lots of pleasure. We met with representatives of

AMTORG[12] to discuss my idea of a possible business partnership. The meeting ultimately led to the creation of Soviet-Finnish-America Transport (SFAT) a joint venture that converted and operated 5,000 Russian railroad tank cars that transported petroleum from Siberia to Tallin, Estonia, for export.

After a half-day guided tour of Moscow, we were free to go wherever we wished. We started with Red Square and watched the Soviet soldiers goose-stepping past Lenin's tomb while holding their rifles vertical in one hand. We walked all over, including to Gorky Park and residential neighborhoods. Many large apartment buildings were in what I came to call the Commie Modern style. The five- to ten-story buildings were filled with small apartments, some of which were nicely furnished by the residents, but

> **AMTORG**
> AMTORG Trading Company, short for *Amerikanskaya Torgovlya* in Russian
>
> **SFAT**
> Soviet-Finnish-America Transport —a joint venture Russian railway and river freight company specializing in the transportation of oil and other chemicals

---

[12] AMTORG was the acronym for an international trading company established in 1924 by merging a company controlled by Armand Hammer with several Russian entities. It was controlled by the People's Commissariat for Foreign Trade and consummated deals with the likes of Ford, General Electric, International Harvester, and other companies. Later, in the 1930s, it became involved with "subversive employees who were known spies and 'rezidents.' Nonetheless, it continued to be a way to "do deals" between Russians and Americans. As an arm of the Soviet state, it was a way to pursue a joint venture—which we did.

the building lobbies and elevators were dingy, and the landscaping was almost nonexistent.

After three days, a T51 car and driver dropped us off at a Moscow airport where we had to find our Aeroflot flight to Kiev (a daunting task for two tourists who did not speak the language or even know the alphabet). Our guided tour of Kiev was just for the two of us, and our guide, a woman who was certain that their lives in the Soviet Union were far better than ours in America. What impressed us most in Kiev was the immense Great Patriotic War Memorial Park and the 203-foot-tall titanium statue of a woman holding a sword skyward while facing the Dnieper River to the west (the direction from which the Nazi's invaded) with the implicit message "Never Again."[13]

There were only six of us on a 40-foot bus for the Tour T51 Leningrad visit, but we toured the Hermitage as well as the Summer Palace, which was still in the process of being repaired forty years after the massive damage inflicted by the Germans during their siege of the city.

We flew out of Leningrad to Finland and will never forget our fellow passengers (and us) clapping when we were "wheels up" on the flight taking us to Helsinki. We arrived on "May Day" and were struck by the prolific colors in Helsinki that so contrasted with the dark browns, blues, and grays of Moscow, Kiev, and Leningrad.

---

[13] It's ironic that as this is being written, the statue should be on the other side of the river pointing east, since that is the direction from which Ukraine is being invaded by Russia.

The next day's flight took us to Paris where we stayed at the Georges V Hotel. It was and still is among "la crème de la crème" of Parisian Hotels—a great location with many Swiss license plates on the Ferraris, Bentleys, and Rolls Royces parked at the curb. The next day we flew to the Riviera and the Hotel du cap Antibes, (equivalent to Georges V, but facing the Mediterranean). This was followed by several nights at Chateau de là Chevre d'Or, a small but opulent hotel in Eze with spectacular views of the Côte d'Azur.

We spent our remaining honeymoon days driving north across Europe and dining and sleeping each night at others of the great hotels in Italy, Switzerland, Liechtenstein, Austria, Germany, and, finally, Amsterdam—from which we flew home.

We had a great party with friends in San Francisco after our return, and my mother flew down from Spokane to join us. It was quite a bash. Later, I made a DVD of images and music reminiscent of the trip plus the party. We still watch it perhaps once each year to relive our travels.[14]

Once we were back, picking an architect and a general contractor to build our Sonoma house was a priority. In our stack of images, we may have had 100 different houses. When we went through them, only one architect was represented more than once and he, Bill Turnbull, had been the architect for three. Fortunately, his

---

[14] We continued to travel the world together, particularly after 1996 and the sale of Transcisco.

office was in only a few blocks from mine. He had been one of the four collaborators who created Sea Ranch, an exquisite development on a bluff overlooking the Pacific Ocean about 100 miles north of San Francisco.

Bill took on the assignment and spent hours on our lot, with his dog, conceiving a unique home of multiple levels with views of Sonoma and the North Bay. He did a great job. Bill wanted us to use one particular contractor to build the house, which was saltbox style with shingle exterior walls, cedar shake roofs, and Douglas fir interior walls plus hardwood floors. Roland Friedrich did a superb job in building the house. We also used him more than thirty years later to remodel our downtown Sonoma condominium. He has become a very good friend.

What was supposed to be a weekend home soon became our primary residence. We loved it. In the beginning, I commuted to San Francisco on and off for years. Later, when I was doing venture capital, involved with both Russia and pro bono activities in Sonoma, I could function in almost any place that had access to the internet.

It was a great party house, and we had many family weekends for Joyce's kids and family over the years, often playing in pétanque tournaments, a game somewhat similar to bocce ball.

A couple of years ago we sold that "house on the hill," and moved to our remodeled condo a few blocks from Sonoma's historic plaza. We soon discovered something we missed earlier when visiting the condo.

While our new views were not the panorama we had from the hill, we can look west from our living room (and outside deck) to see the tree we were married under.

When asked, we now tell people we moved to Sonoma thirty-four years ago. That is the longest either of us has ever lived in one place. We consider ourselves Sonoma folk and have built our lives around this wonderful small community of friends, volunteers, and interesting people. We have been reasonably active in the community and since our condo project[15] is adjacent to a cemetery, our next move is likely only a block or two away.

---

[15] Since we moved in, I've taken to calling our Cobblestone condo project God's Waiting Room!

Chapter Six

Professional Lease Management (PLM), PLM Railcar Maintenance, PLM International, Transcisco Industries, and Soviet-Finnish-America Transport (SFAT)

I've been workin' on the railroad . . .
—*"Levee Song" in 1894 Princeton Songbook*

Between 1981 and 1996 I was CEO of the same company (with different names) on three separate occasions. Each time, I was asked to come in to solve a significant problem. That would get done and I would resign to move on to another endeavor. Later, a new Professional Lease Management (PLM) problem would arise, and the board chair would call and again ask me to come back to solve it. For me, it was one of the most interesting experiences of my career. At the end of the third stint as CEO, in 1996, I sold the company to Trinity Industries, America's largest railcar builder and maintainer.

The main force behind PLM and Transcisco was Mark Hungerford. I had met him socially in the 1970s through one of Karen's colleagues when she worked in Ronald Reagan's California political operations.

Mark was something of a boy wonder from Montana. He grew up in Billings, was selected to be a delegate at the Boys State Program that brought boys together to train them in the structures, legislation, court proceedings, and other aspects of local government. Mark was selected to be the leader of the Montana group. He was a star.

After college, Mark became a stockbroker helping clients make investments. We met socially, played tennis and were casual friends. Later he went on to form investment syndicates where investors owned their own railcars that were managed by PLM. PLM then formed partnerships that bought transportation assets, such as railcars, and leased and managed them on behalf of the partners.

In a brilliant flash of entrepreneurial insight, Mark perceived a remarkable opportunity after the Arab Oil Embargo of 1973 arose. Most were fearful for the future when the embargo caused soaring gas prices, long lines at gas stations, dramatic inflation, and a major economic downturn. To my knowledge only Mark perceived this unique and important opportunity.

At the time, many American public utilities burned petroleum products to generate electricity. With the embargo, those products were in short supply and prices were headed for the sky. America decided the future fuel for these utilities would be coal. All over the United States, utilities built new coal-fired power plants. That meant they also needed to get the coal from the mines to their plants. At the time, railroads had fallen on hard times—most of them could not afford to buy the huge numbers of new railcars needed to haul the coal. It meant the utilities could and would buy their own large fleets of coal cars. Those cars would move in mile-long consists (groups) of cars, carrying coal from mines in Wyoming, Montana, West Virginia, Ohio, and other states to power plants all over the United States.

Mark knew all this. He also knew that if utilities allowed the railroads to perform maintenance on their cars, it would be very expensive, and union work standards (the number of hours required to do a task) were loose. The parts were heavy, but the work was not highly technical. A younger group of non-union employees could be hired and trained to be much more productive than existing railroad crews. A lot of money could be saved.

Mark conceived of a new startup company to be formed within PLM. He would approach the utilities, tell them they could maintain their own coal cars, and he would build the necessary repair shops while also hiring, training, and supervising all of the work. He would tell them he could do it but in order to raise the money he would need fifteen-year "take or pay"[16] contracts with each utility to build the facilities.

Mark was very articulate and a good salesperson. Still in his early-to-mid-30s, he chartered Lear jets and other aircraft to barnstorm the Midwest, often calling from the air to set up a last-minute meeting with utility executives. As a marketing approach it was very smart, and many

---

[16] "Take or pay" refers to a particular kind of contract where a vendor must purchase substantial assets and have a trained labor force on call at all times, in order for necessary work to be done. The customer must either take the work in to be done or pay for the availability if they do not use it. Such contracts are common in the energy sector where overhead costs are high.

executives took the call and arranged to meet with Mark on short notice. This was surprising in a world where public utility executives were among the most conservative businessmen in the United States.

Once Mark had several utilities in Oklahoma, Iowa, and other states ready to sign contracts, he used the same techniques to approach construction firms to build the required facilities. Among them, one of America's largest construction companies, Morrison Knudsen based in Boise, Idaho, got the call from Mark and agreed to meet with him. Gene Armstrong, a very senior Morrison Knudsen vice president, bought the sales pitch and agreed to begin construction on a large plot of land near Alliance, Nebraska.

The shop would be built just a few miles from one of Burlington Northern's large railcar repair shops. PLM's facility would be able to take in and park up to two unit-trains (200 coal cars), inspect the cars from one train, cut out the cars needing work, and replace them with previously repaired cars and then return that train to service. That sequence would continue nonstop from train to train over the years. Meanwhile, PLM would post all the work done into spreadsheets for future reference.

Eventually when Mark ran out of money to complete the Alliance facility, he went "hat-in-hand" to Gene Armstrong. Smitten with this young "go-getter," Gene immediately helped Mark get the financing to complete the shop.

Mark was a great visionary and salesperson. He was off to the races. PLM would be paid a negotiated amount for every mile every coal car moved. This involved large spreadsheets identifying every part of a railcar, expected miles before replacement or repair, and much more. But like many models, "God (or some say 'the devil') was in the details." As soon as the financial results began to arrive, it was clear that something was wrong. The losses were mounting. The guy they hired to run the operation was let go.

I knew Mark. Others close to him knew both of us and they told him he should hire me and then get out of the way. We came to an agreement with my getting stock options on 14 percent of the PLM stock. I began to dig in and soon learned the place was out of control. I asked the CFO to tell me what we should expect to make or lose that first month I was there. He said we would break even. When those results came in, we had lost $100,000. Lesson One: the CFO does not always make reliable forecasts.

About that time, I learned Mark was trying to sell the company. Perhaps it reflected his fear of a failure, but later, I found out Mark had a penchant for needing large sums of money. When I registered my anger over being recruited after having given up pursuit of other opportunities only to likely have PLM sold out from under me, he confessed that he needed $500,000. I never did learn the full truth behind his need. I called it "The Monster." I told him I would find him the $500,000 to buy stock from him, but he would no longer be CEO. Later, we might return "the keys" to him but not before everyone who participated had gotten back their money.

He readily agreed and we went forward. Lesson Two: Mark could prove very unreliable.

About that same time, Mark asked me to join him for a meeting at Ford Motor Credit in Detroit. They had become a major source of financing for Mark's railcar repair operations, and they were concerned. I sat next to Mark as we did the introductions after which they asked Mark how it was going. Mark said it was going very well. I chose not to say anything but was astonished. Lesson Three: Mark lied with impunity.

I was able to enlist others of the PLM senior management team to participate in the $500,000 stock purchase loan by borrowing full recourse loans from PLM's local banker in San Francisco. I was lead investor, we signed the agreement, and I took over as CEO. I never embarrassed Mark, nor did I move him from his corner office, but I ran the place and listened to Mark when he wanted to talk.

One thing I learned over time was that Mark often knew when he had screwed up, and I was something of an older brother to whom he would confess. We had several airplanes we used to get quickly to and from remote locations like Alliance, Nebraska; Miles City, Montana; Waycross, Georgia; or Sioux City, Iowa. Mark would either ask to visit a facility or hitchhike when I was going. In the privacy of the small plane, the problem would emerge.

One such problem involved Mark getting angry with a senior PLM manager. In that anger, he shouted "You're fat and your wife is ugly." That insult ultimately cost PLM $250,000. Lesson Four: Mark's temper could be costly.

I also quickly learned the only way to handle him was to match him stroke for stroke. I remember one long drive I was making to Lake Tahoe when Mark called complaining and screaming about something. I screamed back and after several rounds of this, we hung up. Lesson Five: I never let him cow me. I could yell louder and longer.

I also learned that when things cooled down, we could talk. One such time, he suggested lunch away from the office. We were both voracious book readers. I arrived to find him reading a book. I queried him about the book and asked if he liked it, and with that, all the rancor was gone.

Immediately after I joined PLM, I tightened up the financial controls. I demanded more conservative forecasts, and I literally took the general ledger home to look at all the accounts and entries over the last year or so. One entry indicated that Bob Dehlendorf (Arcata's CEO known to both Mark and me) owed $100,000 to PLM. I asked Mark to go after the money. I still have in my office a note Mark penned to me on October 28, 1981, which read: "SLP—I'm in touch w/Dehlendorf. Thanks. Nothing to report yet. MCH."

About a month later, I spoke to Bob. He told me he had already paid Mark the $100,000 some months before.

Lesson Six: If Mark told you it is raining, open the shades and look out the window to check the weather.

There are more such stories, but please understand, I am not telling these stories to say Mark was simply immoral, dumb, dangerous, or anything of the sort. He was a truly visionary entrepreneur. He was a gifted public speaker and salesperson. He was charismatic, commanded loyalty from many employees and customers, and his creativity was a delight. He would often have a very different take on a situation than most people and often his insight was the best. You could not paint Mark simply as black or white. You had to take both the good and the bad; but in the process, it was wise to be skeptical.

Much later, I learned Mark was bipolar. He knew it, but never shared that with me. Several friends let me know and Mark's wife, Katy, confirmed it. She said he refused to take medication that he felt dulled him.

After a few months at the helm at PLM, the railcar maintenance operations began making money. George Tedesco, our VP sales, ten years my senior and a former salesperson of Pullman Standard Railcar Company, became a friend and confidante. He did a great job in bringing in more business. When we put out the word we were looking for acquisitions, it not only stopped rumors we might fail, it also led to opportunities.

One of those involved a huge coal car repair yard and facility in Bill, Wyoming, owned by a competitor. It was losing money and we were able to buy it for something like $400,000. It was a steal. It was adjacent to the Black

Thunder coal mine, the largest open pit coal mine in the United States, and it served a number of our largest utility customers.

Soon PLM began to syndicate tax shelter partnerships at a time when inflation and the tax benefits made such investments wise for many investors. We would be the general partner, using the investors' money to buy the railcars (and later a mix of trailers, containers, aircraft, and other transportation equipment), and lease them to major corporations for which leasing was preferable to ownership. We managed the assets and used stockbrokers to sell the investments to their clients.

While Mark played a vital role in pursuing equipment leasing partnerships and had been doing much the same on a small scale before he went after the railcar maintenance business, much of the success from the more recent efforts could be attributed to Charles Kremer. I had met Charles before I joined the company. He was hired as Mark's assistant. He was Jewish, British, and if I recall properly, a chartered accountant who had traveled the world. He met and married Naomie, his talented artist wife, and had worked in various jobs before joining Mark. Mark was interested in exploring whether a business could be created to retrofit Cessna 421 aircraft with turboprop engines. He asked Charles to check it out and asked me to help, albeit on a pro bono basis, and I did.

As I would come to know Charles, I came to realize he was one of the brightest and best arbitrageurs I would ever meet. He had an instinctive feel for situations where two parties saw different values in the same situation (or assets). He then found opportunities to serve that disparity in perceived valuation to the benefit of both parties and PLM as well. He was also a close approximation to the British actor Hugh Grant for his looks and wonderful sense of humor. Over the years, he became a very good friend and still is.

Building the business of equipment leasing partnerships mostly fell to him, with Mark more akin to a chairman of that part of the business while Charles, aided by others, was the CEO reporting to me. My role was to oversee the efforts, occasionally as a "brake" to help us reduce risks. But between Mark, him, and me, Charles was the entrepreneur who built the business. He did a superb job. Between 1972 through 1996 that business, which we named PLM International,[17] raised over $1.7 billion of equity for investment in railcars, aircraft, marine containers, shipping vessels, and refrigerated trailers.

Ultimately, we also renamed the railcar maintenance side of the business, PLM Railcar Maintenance Company, which was later changed to Transcisco Industries.

Over the first six years we managed to turn PLM around. When I joined in August, 1981, we ended up that first year losing $3.5 million. By the time I resigned that first time in 1987, PLM had become two American Stock-Exchange–listed companies with combined profits of $5.5 million.

---

[17] In 1983, PLM International became a separate publicly traded company.

When I left PLM that first time, it was to set up a small boutique venture capital partnership (Deucalion Venture Partners). That story will be covered in a later chapter.

Transcisco Industries Bankruptcy and Soviet-Finnish-America Transport (SFAT)

Six years later, in early 1993, I got a call from Transcisco's chairman (Gene Armstrong) asking if I would consider coming back to serve as CEO. It was a long story, but the company was bankrupt. Mark had become enamored of passenger rail services using vintage cars to make such trips appealing.

Twice, Joyce and I had traveled from London to Venice on the Venice Simplon Orient Express (VSOE).

In 1977, James Sherwood, founder of Sea Containers, had purchased two vintage train carriages at a Monte Carlo auction. He thought he sensed heightening interest in sophisticated travel. He added and refurbished another thirty-three or so cars to take passengers on the

EBRD
European Bank for Reconstruction and Development

HAKKA
Finnish construction firm

SFAT
Soviet-Finnish-America Transport

TUSRIF
The U.S. Russia Investment Fund

USRF
U.S. Russia Fund

VSOE
Venice Simplon Orient Express

overnight trip leaving London in the early afternoon, crossing the English Channel by boat to France, or, in later years, using the Chunnel to travel under the Channel. In France, passengers usually changed to the vintage cars, dressed for a sumptuous dinner, and slept as the train crossed the Alps en route to Venice.

In 1987, Mark, his wife, Katy; George Gibbons, the COO of Oklahoma Gas and Electric and his wife, Lou; George Tedesco and wife, Dorothy; and Joyce and I took the Gibbons on the VSOE to Venice to honor George on the occasion of his retirement.

Despite rumors that VSOE was losing money, Mark thought it was great. He decided to copy the idea in beautifully restored vintage cars that would initially offer service between San Jose, California, and Reno, Nevada. It would be launched providing transportation for snow skiers who would ride from several stops in the Bay Area and be dropped off in Truckee, California, where they would be bussed to their ski lodge accommodations. A few days later, they would return home reversing the journey.

The big money was up front, buying and refurbishing the cars. They were beautiful. Joyce and I enjoyed a free introductory trip with other "friends of Transcisco" before the service began.

Unfortunately, Mark's timing could not have been worse. The economy went into recession in 1992, and that year proved to be a drought year with little in the way of rain or snow. Not many people were heading to the slopes on Friday nights for the weekends. Transcisco was bleeding cash, and Mark was not capable of solving the problems. The banks were mad and the board had no confidence in him when he would blow his top and anger creditors, vendors, and employees.

I got the call, had completed making most of the original Deucalion venture investments, and had some time to try to clean up the Transcisco mess. In the process, I also inherited the title of vice chairman of Soviet-Finnish-America Transport (SFAT) the Russian tank car idea I had pitched to AMTORG and the Russians in 1985. Mark had successfully pursued the idea after I left. Just before I left, I had arranged for the Finnish company HAKKA to visit our shops in the United States as a possible partner if PLM pursued the idea. Mark continued with them, plus Russia's Ministry of Rails (MPS)[18] and its Ministry of Petrochemicals. The ownership split made sense. The Ministry of Rails had 40 percent of the stock, the Ministry of Petrochemicals 25 percent, Transcisco had 20 percent, and HAKKA had 15 percent. It was a good deal on all fronts.

SFAT licensed the technology from Transcisco to retrofit their old tank cars with pie-shaped false bottom plates in the bottom of the old cars. This allowed steam to flow under the cars' contents rather than around the outside, heating the contents much more quickly by convection, circulating the oil from bottom to top and back down inside the car. It allowed a car filled with frozen oil

---

[18] The railroads in Russia are vitally important for transportation. Therefore they are universally known by the Russian acronym MPS.

from Siberia to be unloaded after a day of steaming rather than a week for conventional tank cars.

For MPS, this nearly doubled the productivity of their fleet. They did not need to buy new tank cars at a time when the Russian economy was nearly bankrupt.

The Russians were pleased, but more investment capital was needed. At that point I approached the Russian enterprise funds which were newly established by the U.S. government to assist in the transition from a failed "command" economy to a "market" economy. The enterprise funds seemed incapable of considering this kind of financing. That was tragic because this should have been a perfect deal with U.S. technology being used to help Russia and make a profit for the enterprise fund as well.[19]

In any case, drawing on the "good offices" of Otto Karl Finsterwalder, a Transcisco director and Viennese banker with Credit-Anstaldt Bank, I was introduced to Ron Freeman, the No. 2 person at the European Bank for Reconstruction and Development (EBRD). It had been set up to help finance major investments in Russia and Eastern European countries as they migrated to market economies. When the SFAT story was laid out for them, EBRD liked it and provided $42 million of financing for SFAT.

Using that money, SFAT built a fleet of 5,000 retrofitted tank cars to transport petroleum to Tallin, Estonia, where SFAT would be paid in hard currency as

---

[19] There is a touch of irony in all this. In 2001, I joined the board of The U.S. Russia Investment Fund (TUSRIF) and, in 2006, became its chairman. I still am. That will be the subject of a later chapter.

soon as the petroleum was loaded onto the oceangoing ships used to transport the oil to the buyers. In addition, SFAT had nine river tankers to haul oil on Russia's waterways, and for a reason I never figured out, SFAT's CEO decided we also needed a passenger boat that would transport 100 people or more on the Russian rivers. We used the boat for board meetings.

Matching Russians and Finns Toast for Toast

One of my early lessons about Russian and Finnish culture occurred over board dinners during my numerous trips to attend SFAT board meetings in Russia, Finland, Cyprus, and on our passenger ship while traversing the Volga River.

Typically there were eight to ten of us including directors, senior staff, and a translator. At every dinner, each of us would stand at least twice to deliver a toast after which the glass of vodka in front of us was to be downed in a single swallow. All of the toasts were highly effusive and complimentary of another colleague at the table.

At times the drinking continued after the toasts. I will never forget the evening when the restaurant told us they had just run out of vodka. At that point, we called it a night. Never before or since have I ever been told that a bar has run out of vodka!

In any event these were something of a test of manhood as well as the embodiment of the sense of comradery among our "comrades."

I have lost touch with my Russian colleagues from that era, but I still communicate with and see Pertti Happonen, the Finn I had first allowed to tour our rail car shops in America before my meeting with AMTORG and before SFAT was created.

SFAT was making very good money with profits that were roughly 30 percent of gross revenues. SFAT Chairman Valery Butko (the No. 2 person at MPS); Alexander Zablotsky, the Ministry of Petrochemicals board member; Vladimir Kuzin, SFAT's CEO; and Pertti Happonen, the HAKKA director, all insisted we open an office in Cyprus. I agreed. All revenues (entirely in hard currency) would be sent to, invested, and managed by that office. Funds would only be transferred to Russia to pay bills when they came due. In short, they all thought if the money went to Russia, it would be grabbed. Cyprus, a longtime protectorate, crown colony, and later, a territory of Britain, was thus part of one of the first three countries (Britain, Italy, and Japan) to recognize the Soviet Union after the 1918 Revolution. As a result, there were long ties between Russia and Cyprus and funds could flow freely. Moreover, Cyprus had superb computer and communications facilities so the SFAT fleet could easily be managed from those offices.

The caution of the chair and other directors was vindicated in two ways. First, when the Russian government grabbed the money in SFAT's Moscow bank accounts, there was almost no money in them. A week later, we had set up new accounts and resumed paying our bills.

Further, when the then mayor of Moscow (Luzhkov) attempted to grab the SFAT shares owned by MPS on the specious grounds that the Ministry was domiciled there, I approached a young staff member at the Russian consulate in San Francisco. I told him of the threat and that if it happened MPS would no longer support SFAT and with that, the business would likely die, much to the detriment of Russia. He agreed and we wrote a four-page letter to Anatoly Chubais, then the head of privatization in Russia.[20] Chubais intervened and Luzhkov backed off. In 1994, Harvard Business School wrote a twenty-four-page case on SFAT for use in teaching. They did a great job in describing the history, the issues, and the people that were involved. The four-page letter to Chubais (mentioned above) was included in the case. Those interested in reading the case can email me at spease@vom.com and I will respond with a PDF version.

Those days in the 1990s, Russia was a spooky place with hundreds of kiosks selling beer, cigarettes, and other products on streets and street corners all over Moscow. Buildings were grubby, windows were dirty and broken, streets were potholed, cars and buses were parked overnight along the major thoroughfares. Traffic cops would signal for drivers to stop. When they did, the issue

---

[20] Later, I had a chance to thank Chubais over a San Francisco USRF sponsored breakfast at which he spoke. (Amusingly, Chubais introduced himself as "the second most hated man in Russia"—Gorbachev being first. Everyone laughed.)

was how long the driver would be away from the car. The longer the time, the larger the bribe.[21] It was a way of life.

In those days security was considered essential by our CEO, Kuzin. He was well aware that our success and profits were widely known. We might be vulnerable. He arranged for me to be met in the baggage area on every trip. I would be taken to the car where I would meet the driver and the armed security guard, and they would take me to my hotel.

In a period when so many Russia ventures were failing, we (SFAT) were doing well, and typically when I got home, I was debriefed by U.S. government representatives interested in my trips and my reflections.

Later, I got a call from another U.S. government representative who told me she was interested in the Russian consulate employee (Sasha) who had helped us avert the Luzhkov effort to grab the SFAT shares from the Ministry of Rails. She asked if I would consider inviting him and his wife to our Sonoma home where I was authorized to offer him U.S. citizenship. I told her I would do it, but in light of the arrest of Aldrich Ames[22] and the death of

---

[21] Russian police were on the take. Being pulled over meant a ticket that would have to be paid. It would take time and cost money. Everyone knew, it was simpler to pay the cop. The longer it took, the more the cop wanted. Later, because the government was embarrassed by the reports in Western newspapers, the Kremlin outlawed the practice.

[22] Aldrich Ames was a high-level, thirty-one-year CIA agent, convicted of espionage in 1994. He had identified more than ten top-level CIA and FBI sources of information who were reporting on

Russians who had been cooperating with the CIA and FBI, I was skeptical he would accept the offer and he did not.

Our families became good friends. They came to our Sonoma home three or four times during the remainder of their San Francisco posting, and we often dined with them in Moscow after he returned home. I also visited them in their new Moscow home a couple of times. Their son also took a liking to our granddaughter, Caitlin, as a possible pen pal. For many years, they called us on the Fourth of July and Christmas. He also introduced USRF to one Moscow organization that we worked with.[23]

One consequence of SFAT's healthy earnings was that they turbocharged Transcisco's return to profitability. Still, the sharks and others were trying to take advantage of the bankruptcy estate. One was an attorney for some shareholders. He submitted unjustifiably large bills for the

---

Soviet activities. All of the Russian sources were executed after being lured back to the U.S.S.R.

[23] After 2012, Sasha and I had a breakfast at my Moscow hotel. Over the course of the conversation, he skeptically asked about USRF's motivations for its work in Russia. I told him our hope was that a successful Russian economy would spur closer relations between our two countries with more entrepreneurs helping Russia develop while operating their businesses internationally. He suggested we might harbor some less altruistic intentions. I told him that was not true.

After the Sochi Olympics, Russia grabbed Crimea and also occupied the Donbas in southeastern Ukraine. I was among many Americans who had close relationships with Russians startled by the immediate ending of the friendships. I reached out to Sasha on several occasions to no avail. We have not spoken or exchanged emails since then. It is a sad ending of our friendship, but also completely understandable. His family were apparatchiks and his father was formerly a Soviet military attaché.

estate to pay. We fought him and our attorney, Craig Prim, did a superb job. When the shareholder attorney was challenged, he told the court that Lincoln's Gettysburg address had some parallels with his own work.

Lincoln had spent months working on one of the shortest major speeches ever delivered. The attorney said he had spent many hours on his work and it, too, was superb. That was not so. Craig Prim stood up in court and said, "But Judge, Lincoln never asked the South to pay for it." The courtroom broke out in laughter. The bad guy lost the bulk of his claim.

We sold the vintage railcars, added more maintenance business, and included our portion of SFAT's earnings in our own statements. We were doing well. Bill Bryant, who had worked with me at Arcata, was "doing railcar deals" for us based on his intimate knowledge of the business. He had worked with Mark before I joined PLM. In one superb transaction, he discovered that the Burlington Northern had unused coal cars. He saw an opportunity to lease the cars with an option to buy them. He then found a buyer. He immediately completed the lease and simultaneously bought and re-sold the cars. Transcisco pocketed a $3 million profit.

Given these results, we were able to settle with creditors and emerge from bankruptcy with our shareholders still owning 95 percent of the stock. They and the board were very pleased.

So, fifteen months after taking over as CEO for the second time, in March of 1994, I told the board it was time for me to get back to my venture capital partnership. I also made a recommendation to the board of a superb younger candidate to replace me. Instead, they picked an older person who had been in the container leasing business.

The Last Rodeo

In January 1995, the Transcisco board chairman called again. Their choice for CEO had not worked out and they wanted me to return.

Over the following twenty months, we fought and won a proxy fight for control of the company, thwarted an unwanted tender offer made by a crook, and refinanced the company substantially reducing interest expense and debt.

Over my last two stints, we had taken the business from break even with a $3.9 million net worth to annual profits of $12.5 million and a $29 million net worth.

In September, 1996, Transcisco was sold to Trinity Industries (NYSE) for $46 million. That was fifty times its market value in January of 1993 when Transcisco was bankrupt.

Two Important Lessons

On reflection, I learned much during my stints at PLM and its various progeny and challenges. But not obvious in my previous comments are two important changes in my perception of my own skills and abilities.

First, I had always discounted any idea of myself as being creative. I was the "block and tackler" who poured over the problem, identified and thought through the alternatives, and came to the best answer. Creativity was not an arrow in my quiver.

But, during my first stint at PLM, I inherited a $5 million lawsuit filed by the Pillsbury Company against our various companies, officers, and directors (including me). It was a complex case for which I believed we had a solid defense, yet that did not mean we would win. I led the negotiations and understandably, there was a good bit of pressure.

I will never forget driving down Columbus Avenue in San Francisco one morning on my way to work. I was thinking about the dispute and, at a stoplight, an idea flashed into my mind. It was not yet a complete solution, but I had hit on the notion that we might be able to settle the dispute for $1.75 million, all of it paid for from tax benefits. A few minutes later, I explained the idea to Herb Montgomery, our CFO, and James Dawe, our chief counsel. They completely agreed. I went to Pillsbury and described exactly what we were prepared to do and why. (I did not want them to later say they had legal or other problems with my proposal.) They said they were completely satisfied with the idea, and we wrapped up the settlement. I came away with an altered view of my own abilities. I had proved to myself that I could be, and in this case was, quite creative. It was a very important lesson.

The second lesson concerned my talents as an entrepreneur, an aspiration I had long held. It was a slogan painted on the side of some Kaiser Industries vehicles ("Find a need and fill it"), an expression actually coined by Ruth Stafford Peale, the wife of the Reverend Norman Vincent Peale who wrote *The Power of Positive Thinking*.

My early entrepreneurial ideas, such as making unique and colorful neckties from drapery materials, came to nothing. But at PLM I came to know a great deal about railcars and railroads, and I oversaw development of an invention by Richard Loevinger, whose business we had acquired. As described earlier, his invention was a new way to heat tank cars by inserting steam heated false bottoms into tank cars.

At the same time, I had greater insight to the Soviet Union and its problems than most laymen. I knew petroleum was the major source of hard currency that kept the country afloat. Their economy was sliding and they lacked funds to replace their aging tank car fleet that transported petroleum from Siberian wells to Tallin, Estonia. The cars might take a week to get to Tallin and by that time the petroleum could be completely frozen in winter, or at least would have thickened over the course of the trip. It could take another week to heat up and unload the contents. As mentioned earlier, our convection-heated cars could be unloaded in about a day. That would dramatically improve the productivity of the fleet and speed the flow of hard currency to the Soviets.

In like fashion, I knew the two best ways to pursue such an opportunity was with Finnish or Austrian partners because both countries were Western but had long histories in dealing with Russians.

Those were the insights that led to my invitation of the Finns to tour our car repair shops in the United States when they called to ask if we would consider it. Those two facts also led to setting up the Moscow meeting with AMTORG during our 1985 honeymoon.

It was a solid example of knowing enough about an industry and technology (railroad tank cars) and a problem (Russia's need for hard currency and the deficiencies of their fleet).

Ultimately, those entrepreneurial insights led to the creation of SFAT and its major contribution to the value of Transcisco Industries.

Perhaps I, too, had the insights and experience to count myself as an entrepreneur.

Chapter Seven

Deucalion Venture Partners, Venture Capital and Its Present Scale

*You can't expect to hit the jackpot
if you don't put a few nickels into the machine.*
—Flip Wilson

This chapter tells two related stories. One is about Deucalion Venture Partners (DVP), a venture capital partnership I formed in 1987 and ran for roughly thirteen years. The second is about the emergence and evolution of the venture capital industry. But in order to tell you the Deucalion story, I need to first provide some basic background on the venture industry. Later in this chapter I will more fully discuss the history and evolution of venture capital.

In the 1970s and 1980s, venture capital emerged in a big way and transformed the financing of startups and early-stage companies in the United States—and later in many other countries as well. There had always been private equity investing, particularly by wealthy investors, many of them with long experience in finance, but all of that would be eclipsed by venture capital. While there may have been thirty to fifty U.S. venture partnerships in 1980. By 1990 there were 650. Deucalion was one of them.

Wishing to spur economic growth during the 1970s and 1980s, the U.S. government enacted major tax law changes lowering tax rates for capital gains. This made such investments much more attractive. In addition, during those years, regulatory changes allowed pension plans to invest in venture funds. That significantly increased the amounts invested in such funds. Finally, the remarkable success of some very profitable high-growth technology startups, such as Fairchild Semiconductor, resulted in a huge surge of interest in venture capital partnerships and a dramatic rise in investible dollars.

In like manner, compensation packages for CEOs and founders of new ventures became more generous. Whereas in the 1960s a new CEO might hope to get stock options on 4 percent of a company's stock (the state of California, for example, promoted a standard of "fair, just, and equitable" for such stock option awards), in the 1980s and 1990s, new startups typically provided much more generous awards if you were a founder or added substantial value to an early-stage company.

Most venture capital firms adopted the "carried interest" approach for partner compensation. It followed sixteenth- and seventeenth-century models in which ship captains would earn a 20 percent share of the profits from the goods "carried" on transoceanic voyages. Seventeenth-century whaling ship captains earned similar shares of a whaling expedition's profits. Later, early nineteenth-century, American oil and gas partnerships did much the same, as have real estate partnerships in more recent times.

Thus, typically, 20 percent of the partnership's profits have gone to the venture capital general partners in addition to the 2 percent annual fee earned on the assets being managed. Later, a few venture firms with superb track records were able to earn as much as 30 percent of the profits.

Most startup investments failed or underperformed and there were more losers than winners, but if you were a venture capitalist, you only needed one or two successes for total results to be excellent and partner awards to be very large. Kleiner, Perkins, Caufield & Byers first venture fund invested in Genentech, Tandem Computers, and one or two other successes while others of its investments were mediocre or failed. But the home runs made the partnership an immense success spurring yet more interest in investing in venture partnerships.

Deucalion Venture Partners (DVP)

As described in an earlier chapter, my longtime friend Frank Caufield was an early venture capital pioneer as one of the four founding (general) partners of the legendary firm of Kleiner, Perkins, Caufield & Byers. I learned much from him and was intrigued. I had been doing some small-scale venture investing on the side and did well, so I decided I would try to set up a small $5 million boutique fund as a one-man band in 1987.

The investors included Frank Caufield, Charlie Crocker, Tom Ford, me, and twenty-five others. PLM also invested.

There is something to be said for the idea that venture investing is a career for dilettantes. You have to be willing to explore industries and situations in which you have little experience, and you must quickly master what you need to know and do in each unique circumstance to be successful. In the process, while you know that in any portfolio of perhaps 10 investments—just to pick a number—one or two will turn out very well and two or three will do fine. You also know the rest will fail or do poorly. That said, venture investors generally believe every check they sign for a new or follow-on investment will do well. They believe that despite the fact that they also know that it's not true.

You also have to establish a source of potential investments—so-called deal flow. In my case, deals came largely from my investors, advisors, and friends; and as in many circumstances, one deal follows another. A lot of time is spent at the beginning digging up deals, doing due diligence on the ideas, the industry, and the people: evaluating their experience, their integrity, their strengths, and their weaknesses.

My first deal was mostly a bust. A clever inventor had a device to convert a conventional residential oven into a convection oven. It cooked food more quickly and more evenly with a uniform temperature. (We branded it the Zephyr, meaning "a soft gentle breeze.") The foodies really loved the idea and so did the retailers. It looked like a sure winner, and we invested in the first round in late 1987. But the "sell-through" proved very difficult. Beautiful packaging and retailer displays could not offset customer fears that self-installation of the product would be unsafe and there was no practical way to have someone standing next to prospects to explain how simple and safe it was.

Ultimately, that and general ignorance about convection ovens led us to "show and fair" marketing (sometimes called "demonstration marketing"). It is used when a very convincing salesperson operates a booth at a show or fair and attracts prospects around the booth so he or she can explain the product's benefits and show how they are delivered. Sales are made on the spot and the customer walks out with the product in hand.

We began working (and later merged) with Nationwide Marketing. It had a product that allowed customers to buy food in bulk at stores like Costco, divide it into smaller portions, and then wrap and vacuum seal all of the portions giving them much longer shelf life. The product was branded as the Food Saver. Originally, it could not sell itself on a retail store floor, but it was very successfully sold in fairs by good salespeople using demonstration marketing. Later it also sold on cable television, which became a great place to use demonstration marketing to reach much larger audiences. In the process, many prospective customers were quickly educated and, with that, the product began to sell well in retail showrooms.

No one was able to make the Zephyr a success, but the Food Saver was. While we did not get all of our money back, the Food Saver royalties we received returned two thirds of our investment. Today you can find Food Savers in any Costco and at other retailers or online.

Our second deal did better. I met David Berliner, a Jewish Mexican, over a dinner at Frank Caufield's home. David met Frank while bailing out Paul Cook's bad deals below the border. David was a Ph.D. physiologist, very smart, and a senior scientist on the Mexico-based staff of Syntex, one of the very early developers of birth control pills. David relocated first to Utah and later to Palo Alto when Syntex ultimately decided to relocate from Catholic Mexico to the United States where public attitudes were expected to be more accommodating toward this form of birth control.

David's knowledge of biology and chemistry was extensive. He met a team of Ph.D. biologists who were developing techniques for inserting genes into living organisms to help recipient organisms deal with pests or diseases. Perhaps one day in the future, the technology might also be used to develop pharmaceuticals. This was state-of-the-art biotech in its day. The CEO and board originally named the company BioSource and Deucalion first invested in late 1987. Interestingly, one of the best vectors for transferring preferred genes into other organisms came from tobacco. As a result, R. J. Reynolds took a big interest in the company, invested in it, and provided access to their farms and facilities to develop and test the vectors.

It was a fascinating idea, and with R. J. Reynolds as an investor, *Fortune* magazine did a feature story on the company and its brilliant young scientists.

The company went through great successes and failures. I invested in it over more than four years (1987 to 1991) in its different rounds of fundraising. I served on the board and received stock options, which I transferred to the partnership.

The company later changed its name to Large Scale Biology and went public at $17 per share. When we got out of the investment, our $447,849 investment was worth $4,632,927. Not a home run, but a ten-times return on our money was pleasing.

Siva was a company that could destroy (incinerate) hazardous waste, a major issue in the late 1980s. It did get off the ground, but not very far. Our $408,333 ended up yielding only $51,269 in royalties over the years.

Lease Partners had Neil Brownstein, a very smart and prominent venture capitalist who served as the lead investor. He thought I could add value based on my PLM experience in transportation asset leasing. I invested $251,925 but soon found my experience was irrelevant and the company was a poor judge of the value of its collateral. On more than one occasion when a leasee defaulted on the lease payments, Lease Partners found the underlying assets had little value. I wrote off the entire investment.

Erox and Pherin were two more ventures championed by David Berliner, drawing on his physiology and chemistry expertise. They arose from his interest in human pheromones and the existence of the little-known vomeronasal organ in our noses that sensed the pheromones. Quoting from a *Medical News Today* article:

A pheromone is a chemical that an animal produces which changes the behavior of another animal of the same species. Pheromones, unlike most other hormones, are secreted outside the body, and they influence the behavior of another individual. Many people do not know that pheromones trigger other behaviors apart from sexual behavior in the animal of the same species.

David recruited biologists to synthesize the chemistry of an attractant that might generate sexual interest in humans and, in his tests, he developed confidence it would work.

The first user for David's pheromones was a new company we named Erox. Deucalion invested in 1988 and 1989 and I served on the board. We retained one of the leading "noses" in the perfume industry to formulate a fragrance into which we would incorporate the pheromones. A leading designer was retained, and he created a unique and beautiful bottle for the perfume. (I still have one in my office.) We also recruited Pierre de Chamfleury, who had previously served as general manager of Yves-Saint-Laurent Parfums in Paris. Erox became a publicly traded company in 1993 and when we sold our shares, our $152,400 investment was worth $785,418.

The second application for David's pheromones involved a possible therapeutic use in treating social anxiety and depression. Pherin is still a private company. Despite David's death some years ago, it continues to be funded by drug developers who believe the products are, or will be, safe and efficacious. We will see. This is more likely to be among the "living dead," meaning a venture investment that continues to exist (now for nearly 30 years) but never succeeds or dies. The $72,600 we invested in 1991 was written off years ago, but I am still asked periodically to vote on certain company matters, which I do.

Real Estate Research Company (RERC) should have been a good investment since it involved real estate information. Its founder, a very smart and successful real estate investor, made a fortune converting a large warehouse on the New Jersey side of Hudson River into "back-office" space for Wall Street firms. It would save them serious money by paying much lower lease amounts to house their administrative staff.

Unfortunately, RERC hired too many people too quickly and was slow to generate revenues. I wrote off the entire $1 million investment.

Landbase was another wipeout. It contemplated building a library of geographic information but was unable to generate revenues. That one cost $291,385.

Applied Imaging was a decent investment. The original company had two genetic engineers who used techniques to identify the genes involved in certain kinds of ailments and hoped to produce and market equipment to do such work. It was more difficult than they expected but Applied Imaging acquired their technology making us shareholders in a company that had developed, made, and marketed automated image analysis systems. Its equipment was used by cytogenetic laboratories for prenatal, cancer, and other genetic testing in international markets. When we sold the publicly traded stock, we received $785,418 from our $525,079 investment.

Datis, our last portfolio investment to be sold, proved more successful. It was a spin-off from the Northern California Hospital Association and was led by the association's former president, Mark Collins.

Datis collected information on patient discharges from all hospitals in selected states. The information included the zip codes of all patients (but no patient names or identifying information), the name of the hospital and its zip code as well as the diagnostic data and procedures that each patient received. It represented a complete market analysis, zip code by zip code, of all patients, ailments, and procedures. The reports gave each hospital a tool for knowing the total numbers for each kind of procedure in their market, that hospital's share, the number of patients they got from people who lived closer to other hospitals, and the number of people from their market area that became patients elsewhere.

Datis was very well led by Mark and his team. When it was sold in 1993, we received $1,367,466 for our $279,361 investment. Collectively when all the investments were sold, we grossed $9,010,632 from our $4,089,990 invested in the companies.

The venture industry entity that collected results on all venture capital partnerships ranked us in the upper 25 percent of all VC partnerships formed in the mid-to-late 1980s. Not too bad for a first timer operating "solo," but also not spectacular.

There was one wrinkle, however, that the industry group could not take into consideration in their ranking. Namely, when PLM went bankrupt, its chairman, Gene Armstrong, called. They had invested $1 million in the partnership and wanted to be bought out. I told him that we were nearly fully invested and did not have $1 million. I told him, however, that I would contact my advisors and see if they were prepared to support me offering $400,000 for PLM's $1 million investment. He said, "Yes, he would accept that amount." And we did that deal.

In effect, it meant that each limited partner received a benefit from their pro-rata share of the $600,000 discount that PLM forfeited to them. Said differently, each remaining limited partner got a 12 percent bonus in the value of his or her interests from the 60 percent discount PLM had surrendered to Deucalion Venture Partners.

Next?

As Deucalion Venture Partners came to a close, I decided I would not raise a successor fund. There were several considerations. While an upper 25 percent ranking would provide credibility for a first time VC's results when stacked up against others, the thing I liked least about the work was the almost inevitable task of having to report on investments that did not work out.

I do not know of any VC who ever wrote a check to invest in a company he thought was likely to fail, but the industry results show most investments are losers or total busts, with one or two excellent outcomes. The overall results are dandy. And you are always enthusiastic when you write those checks and share that perspective with your limited partners, but when some of the "eagles" turn into "turkeys," you hate to report the bad news.

Moreover, I had been well rewarded for my work at PLM, did fine with my profits from Deucalion Venture Partners, and I was interested in serving as a director of The U.S. Russia Investment Fund (TUSRIF) while perhaps also doing some research and writing about disproportionate Jewish achievements.

Evolution in the Venture Industry

There is one other aspect of my experience with venture capital that I find interesting. That is, I believe the era in which I participated, made money, and learned much is probably over. Namely, I liked the size and scale of the companies I invested in as well as those I ran. I wanted to run my own show, earn enough money that I could tell any difficult people who tried to control me to "go to hell" and I did not want to be pigeonholed or get slotted in a particular job or industry. I wanted variety in my life and for it to be interesting. I also hoped to make a mark, but immense wealth never appealed to me.[24]

---

[24] My friend David Nitka once said, "the perfect business to own and operate has $5 million in revenues, $1 million of profits, and two employees . . . but perhaps that is one employee too many!"

These days almost no major venture capital firms do smaller deals. Such investments are mostly financed by so-called "angels," typically individuals who operate in specific places—often a particular city or area where they work with other "angels." Many of them made the money they now invest from their success as entrepreneurs. Returns are good but rarely exceptional. Interest in such deals by major VCs is limited. One reason is that there is so much money to be had by the large and successful venture capitalists with great track records. Their goal is to invest large sums to create huge companies and whole new industries. At that scale, the money to be made is enormous.

Why this is so arises from the evolution of private and venture investing from the end of World War II to now. From 1945 to the late 1960s, most startup investing was done by wealthy individuals and families such as the Rockefellers, Vanderbilts, Whitneys, and Warburgs. In addition, General Georges Doriot, the Harvard Business School professor mentioned earlier in Chapter Two, founded one of the first two venture firms, American Research and Development (ARDC) and J.H. Whitney & Company. In 1957, ARDC invested $70,000 in Digital Equipment Corporation (DEC) which grew to be worth $35.5 million after DEC's 1968 public offering. It was one of the first "home runs" in venture investing.

Whitney had been investing since the 1930s often partnering with his cousin, Cornelius Vanderbilt Whitney. Over time, they broadened their investor groups to include

ARDC
American Research and Development

CFE
Center for Entrepreneurship

DARPA
Defense Advanced Research Projects Agency

DEC
Digital Equipment Corporation

DVP
Deucalion Venture Partners

ENIAC
Electronic Numerical Integrator and Computer—the first digital computer

ERISA
Employment Retirement Income Security Act

SBIC
Small Business Investment Companies

UCLA
University of California Los Angeles

USAID
The United States Agency for International Development

USRF
The U.S. Russia Foundation for Economic Expansion and the Rule of Law

institutions and other wealthy investors. Minute Maid orange juice was one of their successful investments. They sold to Coca Cola.

A vitally important stimulant for venture investing was the creation and development of "research universities" coming out of the end of World War II. Technology was seen as vital for the defense and economic development of America and the West. Basic research was done at universities such as UC Berkeley, UCLA, Cal Tech, MIT, and others. And when the Soviets launched Sputnik and we thought we were "behind" in the Space Race, the research done in those research universities helped us regain the lead and put the first humans on the moon. In like manner, the Defense Advanced

Research Projects Agency (DARPA) was charged with helping develop emerging technologies for use by our military.

In 1957, Fairchild Semiconductor was created as a division of Fairchild Camera and Instrument. Sponsored by Arthur Rock, a well-known fundraiser for technology startups, Sherman Fairchild listened to an impassioned presentation by Robert Noyce. Noyce envisioned using silicon as a substrate for an integrated circuit. Fairchild was very impressed. At its core the new division consisted of its eight "traitorous" founders[25] who had resigned from William Shockley's Semiconductor Laboratory to form the new company. In addition to Noyce, among the eight were Gordon Moore, Eugene Kleiner, and Jean Hoerni.

All of them, including Rock, became industry legends, and Noyce's 1959 invention of the first monolithic integrated circuit on a chip of silicon has revolutionized high technology. In 1946, the first digital computer named Electronic Numerical Integrator and Computer (ENIAC weighed 30 tons. It was 100 feet long, 10 feet high, and 3 feet deep. Today our cellphones, iPads and personal computers are far more powerful and cost almost nothing compared to ENIAC.

This is the reason we call it "Silicon Valley," and its chips are the heart of why today we have those cellphones, personal computers, GPS, and much more. With support

---

[25] So-called by Shockley, the Nobel laureate who recruited them all but proved to be an impossible boss. They rebelled and Arthur Rock helped them.

from Rock (who in 1962 formed a venture capital partnership with Thomas J. Davis), Noyce, Moore, Andrew Grove, and Les Vadasz would form Intel in 1968. Rock would later invest $57,000 (at nine cents a share) to buy 640,000 shares of Apple and serve on its board. Gene Kleiner would become a founder of Kleiner, Perkins, Caufield & Byers.

In 1958, the Small Business Administration licensed Small Business Investment Companies (SBICs) to help finance small companies. Clearly, our government wanted to encourage and provide financial support to small business.

In the 1960s, a few new venture capital firms were established in Northern California. They adopted the compensation model where limited partners paid annual management fees of 1 to 2 percent of total capital raised to the general partners plus a carried interest that paid 20 percent of the profits to them as well.

Draper and Johnson was formed in 1962, Sutter Hill Ventures in 1964, and Sequoia and Kleiner, Perkins, Caufield & Byers in 1972. Kleiner Perkins raised $8 million from limited partners for its first fund, and it scored big with Tandem Computers and Genentech.

The troubles and economic slowdowns of the 1970s served to prod efforts to promote entrepreneurs and start-ups. It was a difficult decade with Nixon's resignation, the Vietnam failures, stagflation, malaise, and a stock market crash in 1974. That same year, the Employee Retirement Income Security Act (ERISA) prohibited corporate pension funds from "certain risky investments" such as investments in private companies. Only later (in 1978) did the Labor Department reverse itself and allow pension funds to invest in private equity. Economic growth continued to be slow; there was a broad sense that the government needed to do even more to stimulate entrepreneurship and economic growth.

Ronald Reagan defeated Jimmy Carter in 1980 and Congress began to sponsor legislation to stimulate the economy. In 1980, the Bayh-Dole Act (or Patent and Trademark Law Amendments Act) was enacted. It stimulated commercialization of government and university sponsored research and a sharing of the profits with the inventors and the universities. Almost immediately, Stanford set up an office to encourage its technologies to be licensed. This caused entrepreneurs and venture investors to look for new ideas at those universities.

As discussed earlier in this chapter, one tax benefit for venture capital and private equity general partners is "carried interest" treatment for 20 percent of profits paid to the partners. As noted earlier, the gains are taxed at capital gains rates. The Internal Revenue Service affirmed this tax treatment in 1993 and again in 2005.

In 1981, the Kemp-Roth tax cut bill was passed, lowering capital gains tax rates from 28 to 20 percent. This made high-risk investments more attractive.

Founded in 1966, the Kauffman Foundation, with its endowment of $2 billion, is a legacy arising from the success of one entrepreneur, Ewing Marion Kauffman. The foundation's mission is to help individuals attain economic independence by advancing educational achievement and entrepreneurial success. They do this through philanthropic grants to organizations that support entrepreneurship and bolster the education of children and youth. It is the world's largest not-for-profit supporting entrepreneurship.

Kauffman, a superb salesperson, formed Marion Labs in 1950 after two years when his earnings from commissions at a pharmaceutical company paid him more than the salary of the CEO. The first year they cut his commission, and the second year they cut his territory. He decided it was time to go out on his own.

He began with no proprietary products, merely buying products in bulk from a large pharmaceutical company, repackaging them in his basement at night, and selling them during the day. In his first year, total sales were $39,000 and the profit was $1,000. He was a superb entrepreneur, and he treated his employees generously. Over time he developed a family of proprietary products. By 1959 sales were $1 million; he took the company public in 1965. By 1988 Marion Labs had revenues of $930 million, and when Kauffman merged it with Merrell Dow Pharmaceuticals, he created more than 300 millionaires.

From inception his foundation was intended to be innovative and change people's lives for the better. He strongly supported education and saw building enterprises as a way to realize an individual's promise while creating jobs and building the economy.

I had personal experience with the Kauffman Foundation after our Center for Entrepreneurship (CFE) in Russia adopted many of its training programs. The United States Agency for International Development (USAID) so liked the approach that they adopted our model, based on Kauffman's in other countries they supported.

As suggested earlier, successes among the major venture capital firms spurred immense interest by pension funds and investors to become limited partners. Kleiner Perkins went from raising $8 million in 1972 to $15 million in 1978, $55 million in 1980, $150 million in 1982, and on and on. It simply kept growing. As of this writing, Kleiner Perkins has now raised $9 billion for its nineteen partnerships, made 1,308 investments, and had 306 exits.[26]

My point is scale. The coming together at this time of the development of new technologies and the companies that commercialized them, along with tax law and regulatory changes that spurred the enormous growth of limited partner investment have created an investing environment that has been simply phenomenal.

As innovation and entrepreneurship flourished particularly from the 1990s on, governments around the world realized this was the engine of growth and employment. There was worldwide interest in free

---

[26] In this context, exits refer to the sale of the stock, either because the company is sold outright or because public stock can be sold.

enterprise and individual initiative. Entrepreneurship and private enterprise proved to be critically important in moving a billion or more people out of poverty in most of Asia—particularly in China when Deng Xiaoping adopted programs to reform China's economy.

Couple that with the emergence over the last forty years of remarkably talented entrepreneurs—Steve Jobs, Elon Musk, Jeff Bezos, Paul Allen, Bill Gates, and others—who have built companies valued in billions. We have all benefited from much of what they have created and achieved. Their companies now launch their own rockets to take astronauts to the Space Station. They hope to return to the moon and perhaps, before long, get humans to Mars.

From 1945 to 2010, missile and space technology was the domain of the United States and foreign governments as well as huge aerospace engineering firms such as Boeing, Airbus, Lockheed Martin, and others that had been in the business for half a century or more. Since 2000, Musk, Allen, and Bezos have all built companies that have exceeded much of what those pioneers achieved. It is a stunning story of human achievement.

At the same time, this huge scale means that unless you have an idea for a business that might quickly grow to $100 million or more, you probably should seek your money elsewhere.

The world has changed, and the kind of life I aspired to is becoming a thing of the past. I would not change it for the world, but I am very happy I reached my maturity when there was room for someone with decent skills who could build, run, turn around and otherwise be involved in businesses that afforded me the opportunity to have a huge variety of experiences.

A codicil: I recall well when Monsieur Thomas Piketty went after the inequities of wealth around the world. He attributed much of it to inherited wealth that spanned the generations and the investment returns on their assets. My own conclusion is that he may be partly correct about the disparities but he is completely wrong about the cause, at least in the United States. At the time, I was doing research for my books on Jewish achievement (see Appendix I). I carefully studied the Forbes 400 for the years I worked on the books. The constant fact about the 400 was not the continuity of old money. Instead, it was by far about new wealth created by entrepreneurs. Nearly all of America's richest have gotten their wealth in their own lifetimes.

Piketty is simply misinformed. In the United States it has been the culture, opportunities, and people who have reached for the gold rings and gotten them further. His analysis of low income/net worth people fails to include government transfer payments they have received. The data show those lower quintiles have had large gains in total income that appear to have contributed to lower levels of labor force participation[27].

More recently I am also moved by the speed with which the United States pharmaceutical industry developed

---

[27] Phil Gramm and John Early, "Income Equality, Not Inequality, is the Problem," *Wall Street Journal,* August 29, 2022.

COVID vaccines. Two men, both foreigners,[28] who did their work largely in and from the United States where most of their funding was raised, have led those endeavors.

One of my points is that we should not villainize successful high achievers. They accomplish much that benefits us all. Instead, we should encourage more of what they aspire to in terms of human achievement. We should not discourage what they do because they are successful.

Nonetheless, it is important to be mindful of Lord Acton's famous insight that "Power corrupts and absolute power corrupts absolutely." In this regard, I differ from America's more recent approach to monopolies (based largely on whether consumers are injured by having to pay higher prices). Thus I believe that when a company becomes immensely powerful, we should praise the success but split it up into smaller entities. That does not destroy values, it divides that value among smaller entities which, in turn, provide more opportunities for multiple new leaders to take over and successfully build the various progeny while reducing the absolute power of the preceding entity and its leader who, if he wishes, can move on to start and build something else.

As I was finishing this chapter, the *Economist* magazine on November 21, 2021 ran a feature story titled, "Adventure Capitalism: The Venture-Capital Industry Is Being Supersized. Good." It is very well done and could be said to support much of the last half of this chapter.

---

[28] Stephane Bancels, CEO of Moderna, was born in France. Pfizer CEO Albert Bourla was born in Greece.

Introduction to the Russia Chapters

My Russia Involvements—2001 to date

My initial Russia experiences between 1985 and 1996 involved SFAT, a for-profit joint venture between two Russian ministries (railways and petrochemicals), a Finnish construction company, (HAKKA) and a publicly traded U.S. railcar maintenance company (Transcisco Industries). It was a memorable and very profitable experience for all concerned.

In the 1990s Russia's economy was devastated. Communism had failed. There was rampant chaos and corruption. And yet, when Yeltsin resigned in 2000 and turned the presidency over to Vladimir Putin, there were reasons for cautious optimism. Putin's early steps helped reduce corruption, reform and simplify taxes, and promote privatization while stabilizing and building the economy.

ഇ ഇ ഇ

The following chapters on Russia focus on my pro bono involvements in Russia since 2001, with three U.S. government-funded NGOs and with USAID, the federal agency overseeing much of America's foreign aid and development assistance (including the enterprise funds). All three NGOs worked to help Russia migrate from a communist "command economy" to a free enterprise "market economy."

Chapter Eight *covers The U.S. Russia Investment Fund (TUSRIF), a U.S. government-sponsored venture capital fund established in 1995. It invested*

$330 million in forty-five startups and early-stage Russian companies. It also helped train Russians in how to start, finance, and build early-stage companies. Most of them became profitable and created many jobs. When TUSRIF's investments were sold, they yielded $615 million.

Chapter Nine *covers the Center for Entrepreneurship (CFE). It was created by TUSRIF in 2001 to promote and encourage entrepreneurship. In the process, CFE partnered with public and private Russian organizations to help build Russia's small business sector.*

Chapter Ten *describes the U.S. Russian Foundation (USRF) created by TUSRIF in 2008. It was funded with half of the proceeds from the sale of TUSRIF's investments. Its mission is to make grants in support of Russia's economic expansion and the rule of law.*

Chapter Eleven *focuses on the relationship of the three NGOs with USAID—in particular, the relationship between TUSRIF and USAID.*

Chapter Twelve *describes selected remembrances from my experiences in Russia and with Russians, while also covering several late-breaking events.*

Over time, as Putin consolidated his power, corralled the oligarchs, took control of the media, and curtailed free speech and free elections, the earlier optimism died. By the time he returned to power in 2012, democracy was in retreat, the economy was stalled and his ambition to restore a Russian empire led, almost inexorably, to the 2022 invasion of Ukraine. That is the situation we face now.

Chapter Eight

The U.S. Russia Investment Fund (TUSRIF)

Chance favors the prepared mind.
—*Louis Pasteur*

The Enterprise Funds

A little-known but successful American initiative following the collapse of the Soviet Union was the creation of ten enterprise funds in support of eighteen former Warsaw Pact countries. They were funded with $1.2 billion of United States taxpayer money to help those countries transition from their failed "command" economies to "market" economies.

Most enterprise funds functioned like venture capital partnerships using their money to help start new ventures or fund early-stage companies. In support of entrepreneurship, they also trained locals in the skills to finance and support such ventures. Some enterprise funds went further, investing in infrastructure projects such as the international airport in Albania. This illustrated the so-called "dual mandate" to make successful investments, while also supporting initiatives to help the countries build institutions that would advance their growth and development.

> **AFL-CIO**
> American Federation of Labor-Congress of Industrial Organization
>
> **AMTORG**
> AMTORG Trading Company, short for *Amerikanskaya Torgovlya* in Russian
>
> **FLEER**
> Fund for Large Enterprises in Russia
>
> **PAEF**
> Polish American Enterprise Fund
>
> **PAFF**
> Polish American Freedom Foundation

A few funds had significant problems, but when the investments made by all ten enterprise funds were liquidated, the proceeds totaled $1.7 billion. Roughly half of that was later set aside to fund permanent non-political NGO foundations that to this day continue their support to these countries.

One would be hard pressed to name another U.S. government program that did its job so well. It made a $500 million profit, developed successful companies, returned perhaps $500 million to the U.S. Treasury, and created successful progeny that continue to carry on their work more than thirty years later—a small Marshall Plan as it were.

The Polish American Enterprise Fund (PAEF) was first. It was proposed by President George H. W. Bush in April, 1989, and established in 1990 with $240 million of United States funding. Its distinguished board of directors included diplomat Zbigniew Brzezinski, AFL-CIO president Lane Kirkland, and GM Chairman John F. Smith Jr. The chairman of Dillon Reed, John P. Birkelund, chaired the fund. After liquidating their investments, they established the Polish American Freedom Foundation (PAFF) which is currently endowed with $281.4 million.

PAFF is headed by the former Polish ambassador to the United States, Jerzy Kozminski. It is a remarkable success with a mission to level the education playing field in Poland, emphasizing Poland's rural communities.

The original Polish enterprise fund created and left behind eight successor private equity funds that have now raised more than $2.5 billion to invest in Poland. The foundation and the enterprise funds are very much appreciated by the people of Poland.

In like manner, the Albanian-American Enterprise Fund (AAEF) was originally funded with $60 million. It established the American Bank of Albania and invested in forty Albanian companies that have contributed more than $1 billion to the country's economy while creating 5,000 jobs. The fund also invested significant amounts in the modernization of the Mother Teresa-Tirana International Airport. Today, this enterprise fund still has

> **AAEF**
> Albanian-American Enterprise Fund
>
> **EBRD**
> European Bank for Reconstruction and Development
>
> **KGB**
> Committee for State Security in Russia
>
> **RAEF**
> Russian American Enterprise Fund
>
> **RERC**
> Real Estate Research Corporation
>
> **SBIC**
> Small Business Investment Companies
>
> **SFAT**
> Soviet-Finnish-America-Transport
>
> **TUSRIF**
> The U. S. Russia Investment Fund
>
> **USAID**
> United States Agency for International Development

assets of $79 million and its endowed foundation has $214.5 million.

I well remember a meeting of enterprise fund leaders in Washington, D.C., a few years ago where then Kauffman Foundation President Carl Schramm politely nudged the United States Agency for International Development (USAID) to publicize this good work and use it as an example to spur the creation of more enterprise funds.

The U.S. Russia Investment Fund (TUSRIF)

In Russia the situation was different—practically and politically more complex. Rather than one fund, in 1993-94 the U.S. government set up two—the $100 million Fund for Large Enterprises (FLEER) and the $340 million Russian American Enterprise Fund (RAEF). The arrangements and two boards of directors proved unworkable and, in 1995, they were merged and renamed The U.S. Russia Investment Fund (TUSRIF). It was first chaired by former Secretary of the Treasury Michael Blumenthal.

As you may recall from Chapter Five, I visited Russia during my 1985 honeymoon and met with AMTORG officials to discuss my idea of creating a Russian railroad tank car business consisting of retrofitted tank cars to move petroleum and petrochemicals. In 1993, when I returned as CEO of PLM/Transcisco, I also inherited the position of deputy chairman of the board of Soviet-Finnish-America Transport (SFAT), the business I had promoted to

141

AMTORG. I already knew a good bit about Russia and much more about railroad tank cars. Between April, 1993, and October, 1996, when I sold Transcisco, I had made thirteen trips to Russia to attend SFAT board meetings.

That was why I had approached RAEF and FLEER in the early 1990s seeking financing for SFAT. They appeared incapable of evaluating and acting on our proposal. As a result, we got $42 million from the European Bank for Reconstruction and Development (EBRD) and built a successful company.

In a 2000 conversation with Frank Caufield, I mentioned my experience in approaching RAEF and FLEER, which occurred before he had joined the TUSRIF board. "Endlessly fascinating," was Frank's perspective on Russia and a major reason for his serving on that board. After graduating from West Point, he served in military intelligence while stationed in Europe and learned much about Russia before returning to the United States to attend Harvard Business School. Like Frank, I too found my involvement in Russia endlessly fascinating. He suggested I consider joining the TUSRIF board, and he set up a meeting for me with then chairman Pat Cloherty. (She had succeeded Blumenthal in 1998.) Because of my direct experience in SFAT and venture capital, she immediately offered me a seat and, after sleeping on it, I accepted.

At the time, my views about serving on the TUSRIF board were positive. Having been highly critical of the U.S.S.R. for nearly all of my life, my more recent experiences had changed my outlook. I was optimistic about Russia and Vladimir Putin.

Boris Yeltsin had replaced Mikhail Gorbachev after a failed August, 1991, coup attempt. He was later elected president of Russia when the U.S.S.R. dissolved. Yeltsin lasted eight and a half very troubled years as the economy went into a tailspin. Putin, who had served as a KGB foreign intelligence officer for sixteen years, resigned that position in 1991 to pursue a political career in St. Petersburg. In 1996, he moved to Moscow to work in the Yeltsin administration and served briefly as director of the Federal Security Service (FSB), the successor of the KGB. He was appointed prime minister in August, 1999. When Yeltsin decided to resign on December 31, 1999, he appointed Vladimir Putin, age 47, to be the acting president. (Later, in 2000, Putin was elected.) He was young and a fresh face, and he embarked on a series of reforms including simplified tax laws and continued privatization of the economy.

During his first eight years as president, the economy (GDP) grew 72 percent and real wages tripled, in no small part because oil and gas prices increased 500 percent.[29] He adopted a 13 percent flat tax, reduced profits taxes and pushed for new land and civil codes. Poverty dropped by more than half. His efforts helped reduce the need for businesses to keep two sets of books and with

---

[29] Over a Moscow lunch with a Russian economist, we shared a joke about Putin's hubris in those times: "Born on third base, he thought he hit a triple."

that, it seemed there might be a bit less corruption. With the economy improving, the streets were cleaner, the buildings in better repair and the incidence of paying bribes to traffic cops declined. Mikhail Khodorkovsky and others were successfully privatizing natural resource-based companies and making them more efficient. The Russians I knew were more upbeat, so I was generally optimistic.

At the time, I accepted the attitude of America's foreign policy establishment that the migration from a command to a market economy would help Russia, create wealth, and perhaps promote some measure of freedom and financial independence for its citizens. Russia was beginning to develop a middle class, perhaps migrate toward democracy and become a "normal country."[30] If so, Russia might be a much less dangerous antagonist of the West. What was not to like? I would work with some very interesting Russians and Americans while learning a lot and seeing more of the country. I might also be able to help in that effort.

The TUSRIF directorship was—and still is—a pro bono position; but earlier, the State Department had decided they wanted investment professionals to serve on the enterprise fund boards, so the offer included first-class air travel and hotels along with service as a director. At this writing, I am in my twenty-first year at TUSRIF and have been its chair since 2006. It is my eighteenth year with the

---

[30] The term "normal country" was commonly used in Russia and the United States to express the hope that the country would become more democratic, entrepreneurial, and economically diversified.

Center for Entrepreneurship (CFE) in Russia, and my fourteenth year with The U.S. Russia Foundation for Economic Expansion and the Rule of Law (USRF), which I served as co-chair from 2008 to 2018. Working with those three boards was effectively a full-time job in many of those years. My wife, Joyce, once chided me, suggesting I should "consider serving on boards that that paid fees to directors."

From 2001 to 2006, I was simply a TUSRIF director and chairman of its Compensation Committee, and from 2003, I was also a director of CFE.

> **APAX**
> Alan Patricof and Sir Ronald Cohen's venture fund name
>
> **CTC**
> Story First Communications (a broadcasting radio and television company)
>
> **DPEP**
> Delta Private Equity Partners
>
> **INTH**
> Russian television broadcasting company
>
> **OPORA**
> All-Russian nongovernmental organization of small and medium businesses

Pat Cloherty and TUSRIF

Pat Cloherty and her staff had built an interesting portfolio of investments. Her background was in venture capital in the United States, where she was a partner with Alan Patricof. Alan was a successful New York venture capitalist I met in the early 1970s when, as a New York "snowbird," he was in Florida checking out prospective investments (such as REDI) during the winter months. Alan set up APAX, a venture capital firm in 1972. Pat was a successful APAX partner. She had also served as deputy administrator of the Small Business Administration (SBA). Later, she advised the George H. W. Bush administration on how to revamp the SBA's Small Business Investment Company program.

Frank likened her to "Auntie Mame" for her ability to walk in and take control of a room. She invited Nancy Pelosi to attend a TUSRIF board dinner in Washington, D.C., and like Pelosi, Pat spoke as much with her hands as she did with her mouth. She was something of a force of nature.

TUSRIF's structure was a bit complicated with a subsidiary partnership, Delta Private Equity Partners (DPEP), contracted to manage the investments. She and her professional investment staff were partners in DPEP but also employees of TUSRIF.

By the time I joined the TUSRIF board in 2001 it had already made thirty-nine of its forty-five investments. Some were quite impressive. For example, TUSRIF:

- Helped set up INTH, an early Moscow radio and television broadcasting company, which it sold for fourteen times its investment.
- Invested in CTC Media, another early-stage media company. It was sold for more than three times its investment.
- Helped establish the laws for the mortgage industry in Russia and set up a successful

mortgage company that was later sold to the French bank Société Générale, realizing 1.3 times its investment.
- Set up a commercial bank that became the first issuer of VISA cards in Russia and was later sold to GE Capital for $100 million—four times its book value.
- Established one of Russia's first equipment leasing companies, Delta Leasing, which it sold for a 57 percent gain.
- Created the first new hotel in St. Petersburg since the Revolution, the Radisson Royal on Nevsky Prospect (the city's main street). TUSRIF sold it for a 53 percent gain.

The $328.9 million granted to TUSRIF generated $614.8 million in total investment reflows,[31] a respectable outcome in what became an increasingly difficult political environment in Russia after 2011.

One wise choice Pat made was to avoid large Russian companies, especially those in natural resources, minerals, and metals such as steel and aluminum. Those would simply place TUSRIF in oligarch territory. It would be dangerous to be an American organization competing with oligarchs who might play rough, and it might come with substantial risks of corruption. TUSRIF was required to comply with the U.S. Foreign Corrupt Practices Act.

---

[31] Reflows is a rarely used term for the proceeds from selling an investment.

Pat quickly made many important connections. Before heading out to Russia, she had served on the board of the Kauffman Foundation and worked with Carl Schramm, its CEO. Later that would help us when we drew upon the foundation's entrepreneurial training programs to establish the Russian Center for Entrepreneurship (CFE). She also served as president and chairman of the National Venture Capital Association.

In accordance with the "dual mandate," (invest successfully while helping a country develop its economic infrastructure), she founded CFE, which became one of the foremost entities in Russia training prospective entrepreneurs and helping them network. Later she helped bring Ernst & Young's Entrepreneur of the Year award program to Russia.

She got to know most of the significant venture capitalists and Russian government officials involved with small business and entrepreneurship. One of them was Sergey Borisov, a successful entrepreneur who built a chain of Moscow gas stations before Putin asked him to serve as president of OPORA, the officially sanctioned Russian NGO. It was the most significant organization working with small-to medium-sized companies all over Russia.

She also got to know Charlie Ryan, one of the most successful Americans to run a Russian investment bank and a venture capital fund. Drew Guff was another American doing much the same. Michael Calvey was the third, and he was a close friend of Ryan's. More recently, Calvey became an unfortunate victim of harsh treatment, including prison and later house arrest, because of an investment dispute.[32] He had been very successful, bringing more than $3 billion of investment capital to Russia and was generally considered a remarkable venture investor. None of that mattered when he ended up in a dispute with a "connected" Russian over a business deal.

Pat could also be a good judge of talent. Among her hires was Kirill Dmitriev, a Ukrainian who came to the United States as a teenager and was able to get into Foothill College near the Stanford Campus. Two years later, he transferred to Stanford and graduated with high honors. From there, he went to Harvard Business School, graduated again with high honors (a Baker Scholar). From there he joined Goldman Sachs and later McKinsey. Pat recruited him, and he did a very good job before leaving to work with some wealthy and prominent Ukrainians and Russians. More recently, he was appointed to head up the newly created Russia Direct Investment Fund. With its major foreign investment partners, it is very prominent. In that job he frequently deals directly with President Putin. He is also the person who led the effort to develop Sputnik V, the Russian COVID vaccine.

Pat also did a superb job in creating and publishing *Taming the Wild East: New Russian Entrepreneurs Tell Their Stories*. Published in 2004, in both Russian and English, it was a compendium of twelve biographies and stories of entrepreneurial successes. It celebrated the successes of

---

[32] I thought Calvey's relationships with prominent Russians and Americans, including some close to Putin, might protect him, but it did not.

TUSRIF, but it also inspired Russians with what they could achieve in pursuing their own entrepreneurial endeavors.

Pat was active in the U.S. Russia Business Council as well as the Russian American Chamber of Commerce. She became friends with Bill Browder, founder of the very successful Hermitage Fund. I met Browder over a dinner Pat sponsored shortly after I joined the board and I made a successful investment in his Hermitage Fund.

But my views of investing in Russia began to sour when, in October of 2003, Mikhail Khodorkovsky was arrested after landing on a private flight from Moscow to Siberia. Heavily armed Russian security forces had surrounded his plane and arrested him. He ended up serving ten years for tax fraud and other crimes. Following that he was rearrested and tried for a different crime. He was only released just before the 2014 Russian Olympics when an influential German (Schröeder?) suggested to Putin it would be wise to let him go. My skepticism arose in part from the fact that Khodorkovsky had been considering running for Russia's president. I had made money investing in Russia, but after Khodorkovsky's first trial, I began to liquidate my Russian investments.

Similarly, Browder who early on had cordial relations with the Kremlin, eventually crossed swords with oligarchs and with Putin. In November, 2005, he was barred from entering Russia. Later, in June, 2007, twenty-five Russian Interior Ministry officers raided the Hermitage offices in Moscow and the offices of Browder's American law firm Firestone Duncan.

Browder's Russian attorney Sergei Magnitsky later discovered major corruption in Russia's Interior Ministry and in the Russian bankruptcy process. Russian authorities seized the records of Browder's Russian companies—which were closed after they had paid all their taxes. Using the seized records, the Russians transferred ownership of the companies to an ex-convict, created fictitious losses, bankrupted the businesses, and then used the fictional losses to fraudulently claim and collect $230 million in tax refunds from the Russian government (and people). Magnitsky was arrested and, in mid-2009, he died in jail. Browder subsequently wrote the very popular book *Red Notice*, which chronicled his history in Russia and led to passage of the Magnitsky Act in the United States.

In 2008, Pat was awarded the Order of Friendship from President Putin. She is one of very few Americans to ever receive that honor.

Over time, however, the TUSRIF board and Pat began to face ever more serious differences over a number of major issues. The board consisted of smart, highly experienced directors and the disputes became ever more heated.

One issue involved bonus payments made to staff members. As chair of the compensation committee, I saw those problems up close. In addition, a CEO was terminated and lost the carried interest he might have earned from his share of long-held portfolio investments that he had helped originate and oversee.

A board committee Pat established to advise on plans for the proposed new foundation (to be endowed with proceeds from the sale of TUSRIF's investment portfolio) found major differences between her vision for what should be done and theirs.

In addition, an anonymous letter received at the office of a U.S. senator alleged corruption and self-dealing at TUSRIF. Pat felt the letter should be ignored. The board insisted it be addressed, so they commissioned an investigation led by outside attorneys. Months later, the attorneys issued a "Special Report" that was shared with USAID. It cleared TUSRIF, its employees, and board.

Finally, there was a problem concerning large bonuses paid to DPEP partners to reimburse them for taxes due on investments that had not yet been sold.

Ultimately all these issues were resolved, but Pat was very unhappy.

In March, 2006, Pat resigned from the board and her position as CEO. I was asked to take over and accepted. In the end, she stayed on with DPEP managing the portfolio until she turned the managing partner reins over to Charlie Ryan.

Pat remained well thought of by USAID for all that she had accomplished and for the way she interacted with them. As chair, I spent time responding to USAID inquiries and in the process developed rapport with USAID and State Department staff, who came to also understand the position of the TUSRIF's directors. That perspective became even more widely appreciated at State and USAID after a Washington, D.C., dinner when Pat was very upset.

In short, Pat was much like Mark Hungerford with whom I worked at PLM and Transcisco. Both Pat and Mark could be brilliant as well as difficult. Moreover, they both were justifiably confident in their own decisions and style. They were often not of a mind to admit they might be wrong. But Pat proved remarkable in the way she ultimately came to grips with the situation.

At one point, perhaps five years ago, I received an email from her saying she was over it. We had set up some small dinners in New York where four or five of us would go to her favorite restaurant when we and Pat were all in town. She seemed to enjoy that. In addition, we made arrangements for her to be honored by the U.S. Russia Business Council at a dinner attended by perhaps 150 people involved with the council—including the senator whose office had received the letter alleging corruption at TUSRIF.

I do not really know what changed her perspective. I had never seen such a complete "180" in my life, but I know it continues to this day. We still swap emails and war stories from time to time.

But most important, when you add it all up, Pat simply did a superb job. It reinforces my point that complex and talented people are not all black or all white. They are human and deserve respect both when they are right and when they are not.

Chapter Nine

The Center for Entrepreneurship (CFE)

Волко́в боя́ться — в лес не ходи́ть

*Old Russian proverb that translates as
"If you're scared of wolves, don't go in the woods,"
which Russians take to mean,
"Nothing ventured, nothing gained."*

As discussed in the last chapter and as part of the USAID "dual mandate" for enterprise funds, the Center for Entrepreneurship (CFE) was established in 2002. It was set up by Pat Cloherty, drawing on her relationship as a former director of the Kauffman Foundation.

In 2001, she recruited Victor Sedov, then a TUSRIF director, to become CEO. Victor, born and raised in Russia, holds both a Russian and an American passport. Earlier, he had set up a service business introducing Russians and Americans who were interested in importing goods, cross-border transactions, and potential licensing and franchising arrangements. His English was very good. He had stage presence and contacts in Russia that would prove helpful.

CFE's mission was to support and promote innovation, training, development of entrepreneurs, and the creation of new enterprises that might make profits and generate jobs in Russia.

At first I was skeptical. It seemed to me to be a bit like a "self-improvement boondoggle" that sounded appealing but did little beyond spouting generalizations and maxims to those who would listen. It was probably late 2002 or early 2003 when I was invited to join that board and at this point, I am still considered a director.

Early on, I met many of the successful entrepreneurs Victor recruited to join the CFE board or serve as an advisor. Mostly, these were people who wanted to "give back" and they did it by serving on the CFE board, telling their stories, mentoring younger entrepreneurs, and assisting with the networking process. Some appeared in videos that ran on Russian television to encourage more Russians to think of starting their own businesses. As noted in the prior chapter, in 2001 Pat produced a book *Taming the Wild East: New Russian Entrepreneurs Tell Their Stories*. It was 136 pages of entrepreneur success stories, and it was very well written. A few of the entrepreneurs are described below.

Sergey Vykhodtsev began starting companies when he was a student at Moscow State University and at Stanford. He had a degree in chemistry and was mostly known for his food companies including Bystrov (instant porridge), Velle ("an outlandish juice"), and Invite (instant juices). In 2008, he won the Ernst & Young Entrepreneur of the Year award and, in 2012, he launched the Student Entrepreneurship Award (GSEA) in Russia. He served with me on the CFE board and, unfortunately, he died of cancer much too young. His funeral at Moscow's Cathedral of Christ the Saviour filled nearly all of the thousands of seats. He is greatly missed.

Andrey Korkunov began his career as an engineer making rockets and missiles for Russia's allies. I may be wrong, but I think he was a graduate of Bauman, Russia's most prestigious technical university. When the Cold War ended, he migrated to business, importing a wide range of products, some of which were food. He became fascinated with Italian luxury chocolates. In 1999, he created A. Korkunov, his luxury chocolate company that now controls 75 percent of the Russian market for high-end chocolates. When he sold control to Mars, they paid $300 million for 80 percent of the company. He continues to support and mentor Russian entrepreneurs.

Anna Belova has a Ph.D. in economics and a degree from the National Research University in Moscow. She was a principal consultant with Booz Allen and Hamilton. As deputy minister for railways, she privatized much of the ministry's extensive rail operations. She was chair of the Russia Venture Company (a 30-billion-ruble fund of funds), and was involved in the launch of Vimpelcom, Russia's largest mobile phone company. Among her very long list of remarkable achievements, she was also deputy chair of CFE's board.

There are many such stories and people I met in Russia. They helped convince me CFE was needed to help develop and promote entrepreneurship and innovation.

Over time CFE built many partnerships and sponsorships with other organizations described below.

- OPORA is Russia's state supported NGO for small and medium-sized businesses. Its membership consists of roughly 400,000 entrepreneurs who live in all eighty-five of Russia's regions. Its focus is on legal protections for businesses, support for their financing, encouragement of business leaders, and promotion of dialogue between those business leaders and representatives of federal, regional, and local governments. Sergey Borisov, an early head of OPORA, also served on the TUSRIF and USRF boards.
- Agency for Strategic Initiatives (ASI) is also a state-supported NGO whose supervisory board is chaired by President Putin. Its aim is to improve Russia's business environment. In that work, it coordinates interaction with authorities. Among the members of ASI's supervisory board and its experts are: Putin; Herman Gref, president of Sberbank (Russia's largest bank); Alexander Kalinin (now president of OPORA); Rustam Minnikhanov (president of the very entrepreneurial Republic of Tatarstan); Igor Shuvalov (chairman of VEB.RF, Russia's large and important development bank); Maksim Reshetnikov (Russia's minister of economic development; Sergey Sobyanin (mayor of Moscow); and Anna Belova.
- Delovaya Rossiya is another NGO that represents entrepreneurs doing business in "non-commodity" sectors of the economy. It too promotes dialogue between civil society and government agencies to encourage development of Russia as "a democratic

country integrated into the global economy with a modern and an up-to-date diversified economy." It has 2,500 members and sixty offices. Its former president, Boris Titov, is Putin's handpicked ombudsman for the small business sector.
- The Union of the Organization of Business Angels of Russia brings Angels together and encourages their direct investment in startup companies.
- The Russian Association of Business Education is comprised of over fifty business schools and commercial centers. It is also open to state and commercial enterprises. It focuses on the training of professors of business as well as Russian businessmen and businesswomen.
- The Union of Entrepreneurs of Novgorod Region works with that region's government and its local entrepreneurs.

CFE has also had significant support from the Russian Ministry of Economic Development; the Moscow City government; Skolkovo, the Russian Agency on Youth Affairs; the Russian Microfinance Center; Ernst & Young, and others.

CFE's original training modules covered every aspect of entrepreneurship from writing business plans to accounting, finance, marketing, sales, production, and other functional topics. OPORA long considered CFE the foremost organization providing such training.

These days, CFE's most popular training programs include:

- *Startup Huddle* which brings together entrepreneurs giving them a forum to make a pitch for their business idea or plan in a friendly, nonthreatening environment. They get feedback that helps them refine the pitch before they ever have to give it to a VC or prospective investor. Each presenter gets six to eight minutes for his or her pitch followed by twenty minutes of Q&A. The meetings also build relationships among the entrepreneurs and government representatives as well as vendors interested in working with them.
- *ScaleUp* brings together entrepreneurs with only a few years of experience in their own businesses. They work with their peers and professional trainers to creatively think through steps to significantly enlarge their businesses and make them more profitable. Such training can encourage getting the basics down cold, marketing effectively, outsourcing everything that is not essential, managing social media, delegating authority and responsibility, and hiring the best people. The training strongly encourages a mindset for growth.
- *Global Entrepreneurship Week (GEW)* has been funded since its inception by the Ewing Marion Kauffman Foundation. Every November GEW engages more than 10 million people from nearly 200 countries around the world. While most are entrepreneurs, it is also focused on getting more people to consider becoming entrepreneurs–

especially youth who often make up a large proportion of the unemployed in many countries. In Russia, GEW engages both government and the private sector. Its events are attended by over 180,000 Russians every year. Of them, more than 7,500 meet in Moscow. Attendees who have not started a venture can learn about the process and see if it is something they might want to pursue, and if so, how to do it. CFE has been the sponsor and organizer of the program in Russia.

CFE has also produced videos featuring successful entrepreneurs who are interviewed, and their stories are told on television in the service of developing greater interest in those who may become attracted to starting their own businesses.

Over its twenty years, CFE has interacted with tens of thousands of Russians, and during the pandemic, it began to take many of its training programs online.

More recently, in 2021, USRF, CFE's major funder, has concluded that the costs are too great. That topic will be described more fully in the next chapter.

Chapter 10

The U.S. Russia Foundation for Economic Advancement and the Rule of Law (USRF)

No good deed goes unpunished.
—*Variously attributed to Dante Alighieri, Billy Wilder, Clare Booth Luce, Andrew Mellon, Oscar Wilde, and others.*

On July 15, 2006, the White House issued a press release announcing "support of the United States for further development of an independent entrepreneurial sector in Russia, rooted in the rule of law, which can contribute to the modernization of the Russian economy. To this end, the United States government endorses creation of the U.S. Russia Foundation for Economic Advancement and the Rule of Law (USRF)."

As TUSRIF approached completion of its liquidation process for selling off its investment portfolio, its next task was to put together plans for the U.S. Russia Foundation to be proposed to the Bush administration through USAID and the State Department.

There were many points of view about what we should do and who would serve on that board. We began discussions with Tom Adams. He was the State Department's coordinator for Europe and Eurasia.

Tom was instrumental in suggesting new candidates to serve on the board. He "encouraged" me to talk with former ambassador to Russia James (Jim) Collins. Jim is a

Harvard College graduate with a master's degree from Indiana University's Russian and East European Institute. He and his wife, Naomi, also studied at Moscow State University. He served as second secretary at the Moscow embassy from 1973 until 1975 and as ambassador from 1997 to 2001.

Tom also recommended Stephen (Steve) Biegun, who had served on the National Security Council reporting to Condoleezza Rice who was President Bush's national security adviser. Steve was also close to Senator John McCain and had been national security advisor to Senate Majority Leader Bill Frist.

Finally, Tom also recommended I talk with federal judge Michael Mihm, who had long worked with prominent Russian judges. All three were remarkable individuals with much greater Russian experience than my own.

We asked all three to join the board, and I asked Jim—who had said he would like to play a significant role—if he would consider serving with me as co-chair. They all said yes.

They joined Karen Horn, a John Hopkins Ph.D. economist who was the first woman to head a Federal Reserve Bank (of Cleveland) and who had served on the TUSRIF board since 1995. She also served on the boards of prominent American organizations such as Eli Lilly, Simon Property Group, Norfolk Southern, and the Rockefeller Foundation. In addition, the board included Frank Caufield, me, and Jenne Britell, a Ph.D. historian who was GE Capital's CEO for Central and Eastern Europe, had been an advisor to the Polish and Baltic enterprise funds, and a director of numerous major U.S. companies.

Later, they would be joined by: Paul Magnuson, a sitting federal judge with significant Russia experience; John Beyrle, a very popular recent U.S. ambassador to Russia; Craig Kennedy, previously the CEO of the influential German Marshall Fund; Tom Firestone, a former federal prosecutor with significant Russia experience; Susan Eisenhower, President Eisenhower's granddaughter, who married a prominent Russian, lived in Russia for a time, and is a well-known policy analyst and writer; and Greg Rigdon who has a Russian Studies master's degree from Princeton and is president of content acquisition for Comcast Cable.

Jim was a superb person to serve as co-chair. He is a highly experienced foreign service officer and a bona fide "old Russia hand." He knows Russia intimately as well as the "ways of D.C." and how to communicate with people on the Hill, at the State Department and at USAID. One of his first tasks was to develop the specific language that would constitute the new foundation's mission statement and be incorporated into its grant agreement from TUSRIF—which already had its own "grandfathering" grant agreement from USAID. Jim did an excellent job and USAID agreed with his written mission statement.

USRF's first board meeting was held on March 20, 2008, to establish the organization and elect members. A second meeting, on April 16, added Mike Mihm to the board and authorized three of us to choose between two finalists for CEO.

We used Heidrick & Struggles, a well-regarded professional search firm, to help develop candidates for the CEO slot. Jim knew both finalists quite well. Ultimately, our pick was Mark Pomar, who, like Jim, was a bona fide "old Russia hand." From 1975 to 1982, Mark taught Russian Studies at the University of Vermont and received his Ph.D. in Russian history and literature from there in 1978. From 1982 to 1983, he was assistant director of Russian Service at Radio Free Europe/Radio Liberty, a director at the Voice of America, and executive director of the Board for International Broadcasting. He also did on-air interviews, including one with Aleksandr Solzhenitsyn.

Mark, Jim, and I spoke at length about our approach and our focus. At the time, we were aware of negative perceptions of USAID in Russia. Many Russians thought USAID was condescending ("We know best.") and likely working against Russia's best interests. Perhaps incorrect, our perception was that USAID had been very specific about what each grantee was to do. Almost all grants tended to be projects with a budget, a beginning, an end, and a requirement for detailed records and approval processes.

A few years later, in 2012, the Kremlin would shut down all USAID activity in Russia after the United States had already expended $3.5 billion in support over the years following the collapse of the Soviet Union.

Our approach would be different. Rather than push our own ideas, we chose to solicit ideas from Russians about what they would like us to do. We would invite their input and would only consider ideas we thought would be good for both Russia and the United States. Moreover, we would treat grant recipients like partners rather than as supplicants.

> **CEELI**
> Central and Eastern Europe Law Initiative
>
> **CFE**
> Center for Entrepreneurship
>
> **EURECA**
> Enhancing University Research and Entrepreneurial Capacity
>
> **GEN**
> Global Entrepreneurship Network
>
> **ITMO**
> St. Petersburg Institute of Technology, Mechanics and Optics

We learned that both Mike and his colleague Paul Magnuson, also a sitting federal judge, had cordial relations with Russia's General Jurisdiction Court and the Council of Judges. Later they also developed a relationship with the Arbitrazh (business) Court, which was very reform-minded at the time. In Russia, there was also great interest in learning about American bankruptcy law because Russia contemplated introducing its own personal bankruptcy code. From inception, Sid Brooks, a federal bankruptcy judge, provided that support and served on USRF's Rule of Law Committee. The opportunities looked attractive as a base for our rule of law efforts.

In like manner, the Center for Entrepreneurship (CFE) had operated in Russia since 2002 and was well regarded by OPORA and leading entrepreneurs who thought CFE's training programs were excellent. CFE would be the initial base of our "economic expansion" activities.

Jim knew that the Russian Academy of Sciences and Russian research universities were beginning to integrate some activities and were looking for ways to commercialize their intellectual property.[33] Russians were superb inventors of important new technology but had a poor record in building businesses that used it.

Jim also knew Yevgeny Zvedre, the science and technology attaché at the Russian embassy in Washington, D.C. Together they talked about what might be done to help Russian universities commercialize their intellectual property.

In the process, we suggested they explore what the 1980 Bayh-Dole Act had done to pursue similar goals in the United States.

Ultimately, this led to a major new USRF program: Enhancing University Research and Entrepreneurial Capacity (EURECA). Initially, it brought together two Russian universities and American partners. The first was the University of Nizhny Novgorod which we partnered with the University of Maryland, College Park, and Purdue. In the second, St. Petersburg Institute of Technology,

---

[33] Russia's long history of failures to commercialize scientific breakthroughs is superbly chronicled in Dr. Loren Graham's book, *Lonely Ideas*. We invited him, and he spoke at a USRF board dinner.

Mechanics and Optics (ITMO),[34] was partnered with UCLA.

Another aspect of EURECA was roughly fifty-fifty shared financing. In the initial two-year program, USRF committed $3.34 million and Russian universities committed roughly $3 million, much of it provided by the Ministry of Education.

Later Jim would learn that young Russian post-doctoral economists would be very interested in learning about and doing research work outside of Russia. Initially, our Yegor Gaidar Fellowship Program in Economics and Public Policy provided them with opportunities to work with U.S. government institutions, think tanks, universities, and others engaging in collaborative research. The Russians gained international experience and exposure and were able to broaden their network of collaborators.

To stimulate even more programming ideas from Russians, we set up a "Small Grants" program that provided for grants of up to $100,000 to Russian entities wishing to propose innovative programs for USRF to consider. In its first year ninety-seven grant applications were received, of which nineteen were selected. Among them we worked with Intel, the Higher School of Economics, Junior Achievement, the Institute of Law and Public Policy, OPORA, the Committee of 20 (a women's group), the Russian Microfinance Center, and others.

---

[34] More recently, ITMO was recognized as one of the 100 best universities in the world—the only Russian university so honored.

Things were going well. We had a small staff in Moscow who supported the operation, and we were generally well regarded, particularly in our first few years.

U.S. Russian Relations Worsen

In December 2011, United States-Russia relations worsened when Secretary of State Hillary Clinton criticized Russian parliamentary elections, characterizing them as dishonest and unfair. Putin responded that she had given a signal supporting political demonstrations in Russia and he suggested the U.S. State Department views were the same as hers. In effect, he said, she was supporting regime change. Things became even more complicated in 2012 when Putin announced he would again run for president and later win 63 percent of the vote. It meant he had a new six-year term as president and perhaps even more after that. Then, when former President Medvedev was re-appointed prime minister, Andrei Fursenko, the Minister of Education and Science, who supported EURECA, was not reappointed to the Medvedev cabinet.

Major street demonstrations brought out thousands of Russians to protest the cynical way Putin, having already served two terms as president from 2000 to 2008, returned to power in 2012. It added to the tensions, and the Kremlin's criticism of the United States became shrill. While in Moscow for meetings in 2012, I found out my picture had been shown on TV1, the main television channel for government commentary. It was not meant as a compliment.

Everyone began to put their heads down. We carried on as before and in January, 2013, we invited Russian ambassador Sergey Kislyak to attend our Los Angeles board meeting, and he did. Over drinks after dinner, I had a chance to ask him about the importance of fracking[35] about which Russia had been quite critical. My point is that, at the time, he was still comfortable coming to a USRF board meeting and participating in the discussions.

EURECA first came under attack in Nizhny Novgorod with the school's administration taking a defensive 180-degree turn. A class on entrepreneurship they earlier said should be mandatory for all seniors was canceled. Scott Blacklin, a former president of the U.S. Chamber of Commerce in Russia, was jailed in Nizhny Novgorod for two weeks and then deported. The Russians said his lecture at "a university" was incompatible with his visa. Kendrick White, an American who held a senior position at the university and who was married to a Russian, quickly became a "non-person." He lost his job and his status at the university. Our efforts at that university wound down to nothing.

---

[35] In response to my question, Kislyak responded, "a flash in the pan." I still chuckle. He had given me "the party line." Later, at a U.S Russia Business Council meeting, I asked leading petroleum and energy expert Daniel Yergin, about it. His response was clear. "Many fracked wells play out more quickly than conventional wells, but there are an immense number of locations and wells to be fracked." A flash in the pan it is not.

At some point, the Arbitrazh court system came in for major criticism and its leadership was removed. Its connection with USRF was gone. Our judges and staff quickly made a shift. While the bankruptcy dialogue continued, we took steps to respond to Russian interest in reforming its approach to teaching in its law schools. Russia had a long history of teaching law through assigned reading and lectures by law professors. There was no case method instruction as is used in many other countries, nor was there any practical training in the day-to-day activities of being a lawyer, such as setting up a practice, trying a case, etc. Some Russian law schools wanted to explore partnering their law schools with ours to explore new ways of teaching. The Rule of Law Committee pivoted quickly to set up such programs. It also began to work with foreign training organizations such as the Central and Eastern Europe Law Initiative (CEELI) in Prague that offers a full curriculum of programs to train lawyers (including Russians) in such areas as human rights law.

In 2012, Russia began to enact "foreign agent" laws requiring Russian NGOs receiving money from foreign sources to be labeled "foreign agents." Selected foreign NGOs in Russia were voluntarily leaving the country or being declared "undesirable" and being shut down. While we studied the issue with counsel and thought through contingency plans, over most of 2015 we were not labeled "undesirable" or "a threat to the security of the Russian State," which would force us to shut our Moscow office.

On August 31, 2015, we received word that Mark Pomar, our CEO, had been detained at Moscow's Domodedovo airport and denied entrance to Russia. Later that evening he was fortunate to catch a plane to London. As it turned out, he was told he could not return to Russia before 2025.

In October of 2015, I was asked to represent USRF at the Fort Ross Annual Conference that brings together perhaps 75 to 150 Russians and Americans for meetings to talk about common issues. I was to speak about USRF programs in Russia, and I shared the dais with Alexander Stadnik, minister counselor and Russian trade representative at Russia's Washington, D.C., embassy. He spoke just before I did and, among his initial comments, he said he was quite concerned about the deteriorating relationship between our two countries. Following those comments, he went on to express high praise for the EURECA program, saying it was one of the most important things happening in Russia. After the event he came up to thank me in person for my comments.

In November, 2015, John Beyrle and I were in Moscow and had lunch with a prominent Russian well known both inside and outside of the country. He suggested that we should check our CEO's Facebook page. John was able to look it up that evening before I did, and he called me alarmed with what he saw. A day later when I was back in the United States, I too saw what John had seen. I knew Mark was not a big fan of the Kremlin, but I was surprised he had posted his critical comments on

Facebook. When I spoke to him later that day, he said he thought his Facebook comments were private. I told him that was incorrect, and with that he tendered his resignation. As it turned out, the November, 2015 trip to Moscow was my fiftieth—and probably my last—trip to Russia.

On December 4, while vacationing on a cruise to Antarctica, I got an email from Sergey Guriev, a prominent Russian who left the country after disagreeing with the second conviction of Mikhail Khodorkovsky. By then, Guriev was the chief economist at EBRD. He wrote to tell me USRF had been designated "undesirable," and Russia's prosecutor general had said, "Its activities will be banned as its activities present a threat to the foundations of Russia's constitutional system and state security."

Our Pivot

Fortunately, we had already laid out a plan for what we would do if forced to shut our Moscow office. We provided generous severance for our staff members based on their length of service. They had all done good work and they had nothing to do with why our Moscow office was shut down.

Of them two, Gennady and Yegor, were LGBTQ men who earlier had been targeted by a media campaign based on two-year-old recorded telephone conversations between them. Selected parts of those conversations were released to Russian media to embarrass and intimidate them. Yegor had never told his family he was gay. Moreover, Russians accused USRF of allowing our LGBTQ staff to abuse young Russians. That was complete nonsense. It simply never happened. The purpose was to discredit us and intimidate the two men.

Because we knew both had performed honorably and well and would be villainized and probably find it impossible to get another job, we told them that if they wished, we would bring them to the United States to work in the proposed USRF Washington, D.C., office. We could not promise them a job for an unlimited time, but initially we would hire them and work with them to get temporary or permanent resident status. Gennady got the gold ring—he was quickly issued a green card that allows him to remain in the United States indefinitely. He lives in the D.C. area and is still on the USRF payroll. Yegor's is a separate story. It will be covered later in this chapter.

We carried on with our major programs.

Our rule of law programs continued with the Russian and U.S. law school partnerships focused on improving teaching methods and curriculum. We also continued working with European groups such as the Central and Eastern European Law Initiative (CEELI) and others that have long trained Russian attorneys on such matters as civil rights. In addition, USRF hired Yulia, a Russian-American female attorney, who did a superb job in support of our rule of law programming. She not only kept up the momentum but made the programming stronger. In addition, our bankruptcy work continued on an ad hoc basis with bankruptcy judge Sid Brooks.

We did much the same with EURECA's UCLA-ITMO partnership. It continued, and at one point the ITMO rector and some of his senior staff came to UCLA for continuing work in support of their joint efforts. The rector was what I call a "standup guy." He sent a personal note to Mark when Mark was barred from returning to Russia lamenting what the Russian government had done.

CFE also carried on, but it was a more complicated transition. Originally, USAID had said we might be able to write checks to fund CFE from the TUSRIF escrow account (since TUSRIF was not an "undesirable" organization in Russia). That escrow account would immediately be reimbursed by USRF. Just before we were set to begin doing that, a call from USAID said their legal counsel nixed the idea. He thought it might "look bad." Instead, we arranged for the Global Entrepreneurship Network (GEN) to become the funder. We would make the grant to them, and they would support CFE.

GEN was the perfect intermediary. Jonathan Ortmans is GEN's founder and CEO. He is one of the world's leaders on entrepreneurship. His career in such matters began with the Kauffman Foundation. When Kauffman began to have issues with grants outside of the United States (due to the founder's expressed wishes in his bequest), Jonathan set up GEN in Washington, D.C. He still receives some funding from Kauffman, and he has built GEN in his own entrepreneurial way. He was already on the CFE board—earlier he was an adviser to then President Obama on the subject of entrepreneurship. He hosts conferences all over the world bringing thousands of people together in different locations to support such work. Usually this is because many of the world's countries believe economic growth is critical to their country's future. Among those conferences was one in Moscow, at which Putin asked to be invited to speak. I attended a GEN conference in Bahrain that had 4,300 attendees from all over the world.

In short, we carried on.

Having accepted Mark's resignation, Jim and I took over as interim co-CEOs and managed to "keep the lights on through 2016."

We retained a professional search firm to assist us in finding a new CEO. They unearthed a number of solid candidates, and the search committee winnowed the number down to two, both highly qualified. In the end, the board selected Celeste Wallander, who joined USRF as president and CEO on February 1, 2017. Celeste, fluent in Russian, had an impressive background in Russian studies at leading universities including a Ph.D. in political science from Yale. She served as deputy assistant secretary of defense for Russia, Ukraine, and Eurasia, and most recently was special assistant to then President Barack Obama as well as senior director for Russia and Eurasia on the National Security Council.

She immediately set out to locate a Washington, D.C., office for USRF and build a qualified staff. She inherited two longtime D.C.-based employees plus the two LGBTQ Russians. In addition, she added four or five more staff members and set up an intern program for young students interested in Russia.

The team also built an excellent website (https://www.usrf.ru/) and she began to systematize the process for soliciting grants, recommending grants to the grants committee and board, as well as monitoring and evaluating the outcomes of completed grants. It was a substantial upgrade from the pragmatic approach she inherited, which was much more oriented to working in partnership with grantees and drawing on agreed-upon key performance indicators (KPIs), and spending versus budgets as measures of performance. Her system was much more detailed and disciplined, albeit more of a formal grantor/grantee relationship than the partnership KPI and spending-versus-budget approach we had used.

The new CEO was encouraged to work closely with the board and grants committee as we refined our strategy in light of the constraints of being named "undesirable" and no longer having a Russian presence. We also actively pursued European NGOs whose efforts in Russia were complimentary to our own. She was effective in those efforts in part because she knew many of the major players.

She also encouraged a more systematized approach to budgeting and categories of programming and a preference for formalizing USRF as a perpetual foundation. Previously, we had chosen not to be "perpetual." Instead, we (and we believed the George W.

Bush administration) preferred that we retain our flexibility. That is, we kept the option to "spend down" the endowment if we believed that might be a more effective use of the money.

The new approach followed the perpetual endowment model. USRF developed and modeled different financial projections for investment income and different levels of administrative and grant spending.

Soon, USRF budgeted its efforts between three or four major domains of programming with equal budgeting allocations for each of them.

Out of the strategy update and budgeting exercise we began to be selectively more active in civil society grants. With input from John Beyrle and Jim Collins, we hired a very capable former Russian employee at the U.S. embassy in Moscow (now living in the U.S.) to oversee our programming in that sensitive area of our work.

We pursued ways of restoring significant American expertise about Russia because that kind of knowledge has declined precipitously after the end of the Cold War.

One topic on which the board began to have differences was CFE. That is, economic expansion is clearly one of USRF's two major priorities. (Our full name is The U.S. Russia Foundation for Economic Expansion and the Rule of Law.) The language is a carryover from TUSRIF and the original USAID grant agreement of priorities set for all enterprise funds and their progeny.

For some directors, the existence of CFE from 2001 most clearly represented a major program that could continue and become ever more successful. Over the years, it had literally touched tens of thousands of Russians, had a distinguished board of directors, and was highly regarded by USAID and many others.

For other directors, however, there was a sense that the new CEO deserved the opportunity to put a new stamp on the economic expansion programming and that the amount of money required to keep the Center for Entrepreneurship (CFE) going crowded out the opportunity to launch new economic advancement programs. It was all made somewhat more complex because a few USRF board members believed it would be wise to "encourage" the founding CEO of CFE to claim victory for what he had built and for CFE to then recruit new leadership, which we did.

The differences of opinion were exacerbated by the fact that those with the most relevant experience—such as Charlie Ryan, one of America's two most successful venture investors in Russia; Frank Caufield, one of America's premier venture capitalists; Karen Horn, a Ph.D. economist, Federal Reserve Bank head, previous board chair of CFE, and a director of many Fortune 500 companies, as well as myself—with my SFAT, venture capital, and TUSRIF experience—were all strong supporters of CFE.

While the CEO and all of the USRF directors were impressive, none, except for Jenne Britell who headed GE Capital in Central and Eastern Europe had ever created or financed a startup, met a payroll, or dealt with a business crisis.

Efforts to involve those with less experience by encouraging them to attend CFE events and board meetings received expressions of interest in learning more, but there was no follow-through on their part. When specific opportunities were presented, they passed.

The grant process was becoming ever more disciplined. As noted previously, from inception, the Center for Entrepreneurship (CFE) was managed by defining key performance goals (KPIs) for each year, tracking performance against those goals and against the overall budget. That approach no longer satisfied the new disciplines. For example, any budget variance of more than 10 percent in any line item (of which there were twenty-five or more) had to have prior approval by the USRF staff in D.C. CFE's supporters pointed out such tight control was impractical and inappropriate for a $3 million a year small business operating in Russia, especially during the COVID crisis.

CFE was an ongoing business rather than a USAID-styled "project" with a beginning, a defined duration, and an end, such as a conference. CFE was eight time zones away from Washington, D.C., operated in a different language, was required to follow Russian accounting standards, and had to be able to quickly respond to circumstances, such as COVID. Later these differences of opinion welled up to ever sharper differences of views. Also tragically, USRF was reducing or eliminating opportunities for grantees to come to its board meetings to present and discuss their results. Board members were to trust the staff and rely only on their advice and opinions. This was an approach I never used as CEO of any organization. I always spoke directly to all key customers, employees, partners, and vendors. I refused to be constrained by having to completely accept information only from "direct reports." I learned much more my way.

More Complexities

A second issue also became significant and was discussed a bit earlier in this chapter. The judges leading the rule of law program very much wanted to staff their efforts with a Russian lawyer operating in the United States. It was a reasonable request and as mentioned Yulia, a Russian-American attorney, was hired and she did an admirable job.

What made it difficult was that until early 2018, that role had been handled by Yegor, one of the two LGBTQ Russians. At one point, I contemplated whether or not there might be an opportunity for either or both of them to raise significant sums from successful American gays, such as Peter Thiel, to develop new programming in support of LGBTQ people in Russia.

I arranged to speak with Masha Gessen, a very prominent Russian journalist, author, translator, and activist dissident who is non-binary and now resides in the United States. She has written many influential articles published in *The New Yorker, The New York Times,* the *New*

York Review of Books, The Washington Post, the *Los Angeles Times,* the *New Republic, Harpers,* and many others. I asked her if she thought there were things in Russia that USRF could do to support the LGBTQ community. She was immediate and very direct: "Steven," she said, "don't waste your time. There are only three things you can do for Russian gays. First, hide them. Second, get them out of Russia; and third, help them find a job. As long as the current regime controls Russia there is nothing else worth doing."

Given that unhappy advice and the reasonable wishes of the judges, the best course of action would have been to find another way to support Yegor.

Complicating the situation further, some challenged whether or not the arrangements with Gennady and Yegor were really a USRF obligation (a contract) since they were never made in writing. Attorneys were consulted. Having taken courses in business law and having had experience with verbal agreements, I wrote a memo laying out the specific understanding and how it came about. I knew there is such a thing as a binding oral agreement. My co-chair agreed with my characterization of the circumstances and the agreement. He too, thought that was the deal. The argument evaporated.

USRF might have approached Yegor's friends in Russia for advice and support as well as the USRF co-chairs and other members of the board. Instead, when Yegor expressed concerns about the legal credentials of his replacement, he was informed there was no job for him

Yegor feared being forced to return to Russia, but those concerns fell on deaf ears. When told there was no job for him and he was escorted out of the office he felt he had no option but to commit suicide. He attempted to kill himself shortly thereafter.

A number of us organized to talk to him after he was released from the hospital and we (USRF) later subsidized his employment at a different NGO. He knew we supported him. He is now in line for possible permanent asylum in the United States or a green card and has expressed immense gratitude for what was done to help him. As noted, we have helped support his compensation, but at this writing, the green card/asylum is not resolved.

In 2018, Jim and I stepped down as co-chairs. Years before, when I had told the board Jim and I might step down, I suggested John Beyrle and Steve Biegun might replicate our co-chair approach. Jim and I stayed until mid-2018. By then, Steve was in the process of becoming America's pro bono special emissary to North Korea. He could not be USRF's co-chair. We asked John Beyrle to take it on by himself. He agreed.

In 2020 and 2021 the CFE issue ripened. The death of Frank Caufield helped alter the equation. By the end of 2021, the board chose to adopt a new policy saying its board members who served on CFE's board could not vote on CFE matters. The original paradigm was always that it was important to have USRF directors serve on the CFE board to oversee its activities. Moreover, many of us in venture capital partnerships have served on the boards of portfolio companies we helped finance. Full disclosure usually solves such problems.

There were other questions for which we commissioned a KPMG forensic audit that CFE passed. From inception through 2020, CFE had been funded with grants totaling $28.6 million. Now it was over.

From its inception in 2009 through the end of November, 2021, USRF spent a total of $57.7 million on all of its grants. TUSRIF spent another $12.8 million for a total of $70.5 million. By then, USRF had received $152.5 million from TUSRIF and despite having spent $58 million on grants its total endowment had grown to $174.3 million.

In late 2021, the CEO resigned because she was nominated for a senior position in President Joseph Biden's Department of Defense. A highly qualified replacement, Matthew Rojansky, who is a well-known and respected expert on U.S.-Russian affairs, was selected and he became CEO on January 10, 2022. I have great confidence he will do a very good job.

Chapter Eleven

Working With USAID

I'm from the government and I'm here to help.
—*President Ronald Reagan*

Generally, TUSRIF and USAID worked together well. They appreciated what we were doing and how we did it and they very much liked our programs such as CFE. We worked with some superb staff members such as Richard Johnson, Steve Eastham, and David Cowles, but there were times when relations with USAID were "challenging."

I deserve some of the blame. First, I was the person who replaced Pat Cloherty, who many at USAID thought was great. I was also the guy who said the entire proceeds of TUSRIF's portfolio liquidation should be preserved for use in Russia (more on that later).

We also had issues with some forms of technical assistance USAID wanted TUSRIF to do. One difficult subject involved grants intended to "level the playing field" by providing financial support to offset the extra costs incurred by portfolio investments operating in Russia. The theory was that Russian companies faced unique difficulties that penalized their earnings. USAID felt TUSRIF should offset those penalties with various kinds of support. It is a gray area. This was made clear to me one day when the senior audit partner at TUSRIF's outside auditors told me the result was to subsidize (reduce) expenses and inflate profits.

The standard for such grants, how much and how to do them, was a judgment call. The auditor believed the grants "goosed" earnings, thereby making the company's stock and stock options more valuable when the company might be sold with its inflated earnings. If you were a TUSRIF or DPEP partner, your carried interest could be enhanced while a buyer might later experience lower earnings than expected. It was a valid issue but not one USAID wanted us to push. At one point I suggested we footnote the financial statements to document and explain the accounting, but that proposal did not fly.

At one point, I began hearing stories about USAID's unhappiness over Mark Pomar's compensation. No one asked me. Later I heard more of the same. One day in a meeting when John Beyrle, a USRF director, was with me, I was finally asked. I explained that the problem was the Federal Form 990 filings that TUSRIF was required to submit. I said the very high 990 figure included not only Mark's base pay and any bonus, but in addition, we were required to include all kinds of "benefits." At the time, Moscow was the world's most expensive city in which to live so the rent for his apartment was very high. I added that his base pay was lower than that of the CEO of the German Marshall Fund and the head of the American Chamber of Commerce in Moscow. Both were comparable slots. I said that if USAID in Russia had to provide the same 990-styled information for the head of its Moscow operation, it would have to add to his base salary and any bonus, the value of his U.S-government-provided Moscow housing, his car and driver, his kids' schooling, his health benefits, the cost of his life insurance, his family's home leave travel expenses, the cost for preparing his tax returns and many other such "fringe" benefits, the total would be reasonably close to that of Mark Pomar. Had they asked me earlier, we could have avoided the confusion. The issue went away—if only for those who understood the math.

Another issue concerned management fees paid to TUSRIF/DPEP. Namely, with USAID's support, TUSRIF collected management fees based on the total of the original $100 million in grant for FLEER as well as the $328.9 million TUSRIF grant. Such funding was generally received only when money was needed for a particular investment or expense. My recollection is that over time, TUSRIF received no more than $328.9 million in funding. Said differently, and I may be wrong, but I do not believe TUSRIF ever received any of FLEER's $100 million grant money nor any of its investments to oversee, yet management fees were paid based on the $440 million total figure.

As mentioned previously, when TUSRIF was liquidating its portfolio and planning for the future foundation, there was a question about how much of the liquidation proceeds should go to the foundation. Poland's enterprise fund began the process for all enterprise funds and, in that case, USAID and the Polish fund agreed that half the proceeds would go back to the U.S. Treasury and the other half would go to a new Polish foundation. But that was not a legal requirement.

Our position was that Russia is larger and more important to the United States than Poland—both for good or for ill. Russia has parity with the United States in nuclear weapons and boomers (submarines armed with nuclear missiles). Our legal counsel suggested returning the money to the U.S. Treasury would get "lost in the rounding," but if managed by the foundation, it could make a significant difference.

When we took the position that it should all go to the foundation, USAID and State were unhappy. Our counsel told Senator Richard Lugar, then chair of the Senate Foreign Relations Committee, of our position, Lugar completely agreed with us. He put a "hold" on any demand for the use of those funds. Thus, the residual half of the liquidation proceeds would not go to either the foundation or the Treasury until there was a final resolution acceptable to all of the significant parties—including TUSRIF. In the years since, "the Hill" (Senate and House), the "administration" (White House, National Security Council, the Office of Management and Budget (OMG), and others) plus various D.C.-based NGOs and TUSRIF, have never been able to agree. Matters are difficult to resolve in today's partisan times in Washington, D.C., and with the heightened tensions between the United States and Russia.

Further, the money has one subtle and very interesting feature. It is something I discovered only after we refused USAID's request that we write a check for $35 million to the United States Institute of Peace, which promotes nonviolent conflict resolution worldwide. We refused out of concern Russians might think of it as a hostile political act. We said we would write a $35 million check to USAID, and they could in turn pay the same amount to the Institute of Peace. USAID never explained why that was not acceptable. Greater candor would have encouraged a better working relationship.

Only after we retained a former USAID attorney to help us with a different matter was it explained. In essence those dollars were no longer USAID grant dollars that could be returned to USAID and reused by them. These were "reflows" (money that came from selling the portfolio investments). That meant the TUSRIF board had to agree and sign the check to the Institute of Peace. USAID was not happy we had said no, but they dropped their request.

Finally, there was another subtle wrinkle that mattered. Namely, in the parlance of D.C., "It doesn't score." That meant that if TUSRIF grants part or all of the escrow money to another NGO and that decision is approved by USAID, the administration and the chairs of the four relevant committees on the Hill, it does not require further congressional action. But if we were to pay it back to USAID, they must return it to the U.S. Treasury. Any subsequent claim for its use will be "scored." Namely, it will require new legislative action. Thus, money that does not score has much greater flexibility. USAID has had many ideas about uses for such funds that would serve its priorities and placate NGOs who could use the money. But the bottom line is that TUSRIF's board would also need to agree and sign those checks.

All of this led to some lengthy conversations in which USAID proposed to have TUSRIF use the money in Russia, but in ways that would generally be determined by them. Our board did not want to be put in a position of being responsible for decisions it did not make. There was a hint of "bait and switch" in the approach that, once again, might have benefited from more candor at the start.

At one point a senior USAID representative suggested that USRF might be shut down for foreign policy reasons. It was a thinly veiled threat that we disregarded, since with two former ambassadors to Russia on our board, we felt we, too, had some clout. The issue went away.

On a more positive note, several years ago Ambassador William Burns, former ambassador to Russia, then Under Secretary of State for Political Affairs, and now director of the CIA, attended part of a TUSRIF/USRF board dinner in Washington, D.C. In his remarks, Burns generously thanked the boards for their valuable work. About that time, I also received a USAID Certificate of Appreciation for "Extraordinary Service." It still hangs on my office wall.

In 2016, USAID retained an outside evaluation firm to audit the enterprise funds. The firm's 2017 report gave TUSRIF good marks for its performance both financially and for its dual mandate efforts including the creation and operation of the Center for Entrepreneurship plus

TUSRIF's small-business lending program, its microenterprise loans, its auto and mortgage lending portfolio investments, and its $34.3 million dollars of technical assistance that went to various Russian entities and companies. The entire report can be accessed using the link: https://pdf.usaid.gov/pdf_docs/PA00STKC.pdf.

In 2014, USAID also asked us to prepare a "Final Report" covering TUSRIF's history from 1995 to 2014. We did so and delivered the 32-page printed and PDF versions to them. It is available through me as a PDF file on request to spease@vom.com.

As of late 2022, TUSRIF continued to exist. It has distributed $152.5 million to USRF. Another $153.7 million remained in an escrow account earning money. As in the past, TUSRIF and USAID continued to have ongoing conversations about the lack of agreement in D.C. as to how to put that money to a good us. Like everything in D.C., there was no agreement. The escrow remained.

But we did know TUSRIF had done its job very well.

Chapter Twelve

Russia Remembrances and Updates

Don't give in to Putin or give up on Russia.
—Steve Biegun, USRF board member,
former Deputy Secretary of State, and a former
member of the National Security Council

Perm 36 and Memorial

In September, 2012, about twelve USRF board members and staff toured Perm 36, the only remaining Russian Gulag[36] prison camp out of the hundreds that existed from 1918 to 1960. Perm 36 continued to operate until 1987. The rest had been abandoned or demolished.

Located in the Urals and built in 1946, it was designated a "strict regime" and "special regime" camp for incarceration of "especially dangerous state criminals." It was grim with prisoners barely surviving the long freezing winters with temperatures generally ranging from 5 degrees Fahrenheit to 21 degrees below zero.

Our guide knew the history well. For political prisoners, mostly dissidents and "refuseniks" such as Natan Sharansky, Perm 36 remained open until 1987.

---

[36] An estimated 1.2 to 1.7 million Russians died in the camps between 1918 and 1956. To my knowledge the best book on the system and its horrors is Aleksandr Solzhenitsyn's *The Gulag Archipelago*.

We were accompanied by several young Perm State University students. They told us that although it was only a few hours' drive from the university campus, they had never heard of the camp nor did they know it existed before our trip.

In 1994, Perm 36 was preserved by the local branch of Memorial, the Russian historical and human rights organization. Memorial's first chairman was Nobel Peace Prize winner and nuclear scientist Andrei Shakharov, who worked side by side with his wife, Yelena Bonner, as outspoken supporters of human rights.

Ironically, Perm 36 was taken over in 2015 by Russian and local government officials opposing Memorial's description of Stalin's hardline rule in creating and operating such camps. The Russian government entities were resurrecting Stalin as a hero and Memorial's depiction could not be tolerated.

In December, 2021, Russia's Supreme Court ordered the closure of Memorial—one of Russia's oldest and most prominent civil rights NGOs. In court, the prosecutor labeled Memorial a "public threat," saying it was "in the pay of the West to focus attention on Soviet crimes instead of highlighting its "glorious past."

The Price for Some Russians Who Served

Over the years, eleven or more Russians served on the boards of TUSRIF, CFE, or USRF.

This does not count a prominent Russian female attorney who chose not to serve over concerns about possible adverse consequences for her high-profile legal practice. Another impressive Russian woman headed the Moscow office of a major American software company. She attended one meeting before stepping down for similar reasons. The third (a successful female entrepreneur) simply chose to fade away as the Kremlin became ever more hostile to Americans.

Still, we were blessed with very honorable and important Russians who joined and were active on the boards. For some however, there was a price to be paid.

One Russian attorney worked to build links between American and Russian lawyers and judges. He was accused of corruption by the Russians. Perhaps the charges had validity, but most likely they did not. He served time in jail and lost his job at a government agency.

Another well-known Russian attorney headed Russia's Securities and Exchange Commission. He is featured in Bill Browder's book *Red Notice*. Browder credits him as a very honorable man who blocked a corrupt and highly dilutive stock offering that would lose $87 million for investors in Browder's Hermitage Fund. He was a very good USRF director who ultimately felt it best to step down. "Too risky" was his explanation.

A very thoughtful woman—so small I nicknamed her "The Sparrow"—ran an NGO devoted to helping Russia's youth. She had also played a prominent role in the Kremlin for a couple of years before she joined the USRF board. At USRF, she helped American board members better understand the culture and thinking of average Russians—often drawing on survey data provided by Levada, Russia's foremost public opinion survey company.

Ultimately, the Kremlin made her life very difficult. She was hassled by airport security when departing on international trips to attend our board meetings. Her son was pulled over while driving in Moscow; the cop asked him about his mother. When he objected, they took him to police department to be interrogated.

In another incident, she and I met at a Marriott hotel in Moscow to discuss USRF business. We used the fifth-floor lounge accessible only for certain hotel guests and preferred Marriott customers. Shortly after we began our conversation, two men came in and sat down at the next table. I noticed she quickly appeared to become uncomfortable. When she confirmed her discomfort, I suggested we leave and she said yes. We narrowly evaded the two men who followed us by switching elevators at the last minute.

Life can be very difficult for those who fail to toe the party line.

The Invasion of Ukraine and USAID Escrow

In recent months the world has changed. Vladimir Putin has a long history of pushing the envelope to advance his vision for restoring the Russian empire. His constant message to his people has been that they are tragic victims of the Western nations who do not appreciate their historic greatness and who have conspired against them.

In a "special military action," launched February 24, 2022, Putin took his biggest risk ever in an effort to quickly return Ukraine to the Russian orbit. Instead of immediate success, his army got bogged down with major losses of men and material. Moreover, he revived Reagan's paradigm of Russia as an "Evil Empire." The horrific actions taken against Ukraine and its civilian populations—including women and children—may well backfire. Finland, a new member of NATO solely because of the invasion, shares an 830-mile border with Russia, part of which is only 250 miles from St. Petersburg. That is much closer than Ukraine's border.

To date, Ukraine has repulsed most of the Russian attacks. The West has come together to support Ukraine and perhaps further strengthen its own alliances. An estimated 700,000 to 1 million mostly young Russians have fled their country since the invasion and the recent call-up of additional forces. This further weakens Russia's high-tech sector, and with that, its future economic potential.

Within days of Russia's invasion of Ukraine, USRF and TUSRIF held board meetings. A USAID representative encouraged us to consider making a proposal to USAID that would support Ukraine with a $100 million grant to their Western NIS (Ukraine) Enterprise Fund.

On March 1, 2022, the TUSRIF and USRF boards jointly stated their position on the USRF website.

The U.S. Russia Foundation condemns the Russian government's unprovoked and unjustified war against Ukraine and we stand with the Ukrainian victims of this cruel aggression. To support a sovereign and democratic Ukraine, the boards of TUSRIF and the U.S. Russia Foundation have voted unanimously for a resolution recommending to the Executive Branch and Congress that $100 million of TUSRIF's escrowed funds be immediately redirected to the Western NIS Enterprise Fund,[37] an organization devoted to helping the Ukrainian people.

We also stand with the brave Russian people who continue to speak out against the Kremlin's invasion of Ukraine. The board reaffirms the U.S. Russia Foundation's commitment to continuing our support for Russians who seek a different and peaceful future for their country.

We also saw this as a potential opportunity to resolve TUSRIF's 13-year escrow, now totaling $153.7 million. At their meetings, both boards voted unanimously to support a proposal TUSRIF sent to USAID on March 16, 2022. If approved by USAID, the administration, and the Hill[38], it will result in a $100 million grant to the Western NIS (Ukraine) Enterprise Fund, plus a $53.7 million grant to USRF. Shortly after, TUSRIF would shut down, ending its 27-year existence.

---

[37] The Western NIS (*Newly Independent States*) Enterprise Fund is the counterpart to TUSRIF and USRF for Ukraine. It can help rebuild the country.

[38] A "Congressional Notification" (CN) would be sent to the four chairs of the committees with jurisdiction. Any chair could block, or place a "hold" on the proposal, but if all four sign off, or if they choose not to respond at all, in two weeks the proposal will automatically be approved.

A month later, having received no response from USAID to our proposal, we nudged them in a follow-up letter. That led to a May 11, 2022, meeting in Washington, D.C., with senior USAID leadership. On May 16, 2022, they asked USRF to prepare and deliver a complete description of its already functioning Emergency Grant Program and a description of USRF's future plans in light of the Russian invasion. Four days later, on May 20, 2022, USRF delivered the 14-page response to USAID.

On August 8, 2022, five months after we made our proposal, we finally heard back from USAID. In a series of virtual and telephone conference calls, we were told USAID would not be able to support our proposal for $100 million to Ukraine and $53 million to USRF. Russia was simply too toxic. Instead, USAID said they might be able to support a $7.5 million grant to USRF plus a $146 million grant to Ukraine. It was not immediately clear why $7.5 million might fly, but they said USAID would support it. At the next meeting we suggested the $7.5 million proposal reminded some of us of the old joke that ends, "We have already substantiated what you are. Now we are merely dickering over the price." We made the case for more money to support a perpetual USRF endowment. We also noted USAID wanted and needed the TUSRIF board support and signature on the checks. A few weeks later, a CN went to the Hill proposing $18 million for USRF and $135 million for Ukraine.

We decided to hold off on printing this memoir hoping we might soon have a final go/no go decision.

Some weeks later we learned "holds" had been placed on the CN. Negative attitudes about Russia, a lack of congressional understanding of our history and our proposal—plus inter-party politics—was stalling our proposal.

In November, 2022, as USAID worked to get the holds lifted on the Hill, they asked USRF for assistance to overcome congressional skeptics who knew next to nothing about USRF's history, its efforts since the invasion, and its plans going forward. Matt Rojansky, USRF's CEO, took the lead and did a superb job of explaining: 1) our emergency grants program helping Russians that have fled the country with almost no money and who need immediate help; 2) USRF's support to Russia's independent media that have fled the country and continue to cover the war and its horrors from outside Russia; and 3) our support of civil society organizations within and outside Russia working to help those whose rights are under attack. All of these are part of the USRF mission.

The skeptics were impressed. In early January 2023 we got word the holds had been lifted and with that, USRF will proceed to grant the Ukraine Enterprise Fund $135 million and USRF $18 million.

When that is completed, likely by the end of January, 2023, TUSRIF will be dissolved after its 37 years of existence.

I am proud TUSRIF chose to retain all of its reflows—*for good or for ill*—so that Putin's invasion will have triggered the beautiful irony that most of the money will help rebuild Ukraine's entrepreneurial sector. In addition, USRF will be able to continue supporting those Russians within and outside the country that want their country to end its failing and horrific invasion. All of this will be a notable and worthy outcome for all those who have long served on a pro bono basis The U.S. Russia Enterprise Fund (TUSRIF) and the U.S. Russia Foundation (USRF).

Terminated Employee

In the previous chapter I discussed the unfortunate handling of Yegor, one of two LGBTQ Russians we brought to the United States in early 2016. This followed Russia's demand that we close our Moscow office and the social media vilification of the two men.

Yegor was initially employed by USRF in its Washington, D.C., office, but before he received a green card or asylum, he was terminated. He was terrified he would be forced to return to Russia where he would be unemployed and at great personal risk. That resulted in his suicide attempt. We intervened and USRF subsidized his employment at another NGO.

In late October, 2022, our immigration attorney told us she expects Yegor to receive his green card by mid-2023. With that, he can remain in the United States and pursue employment with any organization he chooses. We will support him in that effort. We are very pleased that he will be able go on with his life in the United States.

My Personal Perspective on Russia

It may seem surprising, but despite my long history in Russia, I never learned the language. In the early years, I relied on serial translations. Later, with a device similar to a hearing aid, I could hear a simultaneous translation. As a result, there was never a pressing need to learn the language. It was never a barrier.

In retrospect, the price I paid for not taking the time to learn Russian was that I could not converse with Russians who did not speak English, nor could I truly enjoy some Russian music or read its classic literature and Russian language newspapers and magazines.

I visited Russia fifty times over a period of 37 years. Despite the probability I will not be returning again, it has been a marvelous part of my life. I loved the time there and the experience. I conceived of and helped build a successful business (SFAT), chaired Russia's Enterprise Fund, served on the CFE board, co-chaired The U. S. Russia Foundation and still serve on its board. I made wonderful friends, saw much of the country (including a trip on the Trans-Siberian Express from Irkutsk/Lake Baikal to Vladivostok), and toured its major cities. I saw Russia's unique architecture and scenery, attended its Bolshoi Ballet in Moscow and at the Mariinsky in St. Petersburg, and I listened to great Russian music at concerts. I fell in love with the Red Army Choir's version of "Kalinka," and worked with impressive colleagues of which I was the least qualified.

I would do it all over again.

PHOTOS

AMTORG Meeting
Steve Pease 4th from Left
Moscow | April, 1985

Sasha, Joyce, Natasha, Yvgeny, and Caitlin
Moscow | June, 2003

Ambassador James (Jim) Collins, Steve,
Frank Caufield, and Naomi Collins
Washington, D.C. | November, 2016

Steve and Joyce
at George W. Bush Inauguration
Washington, D.C.
January, 2001

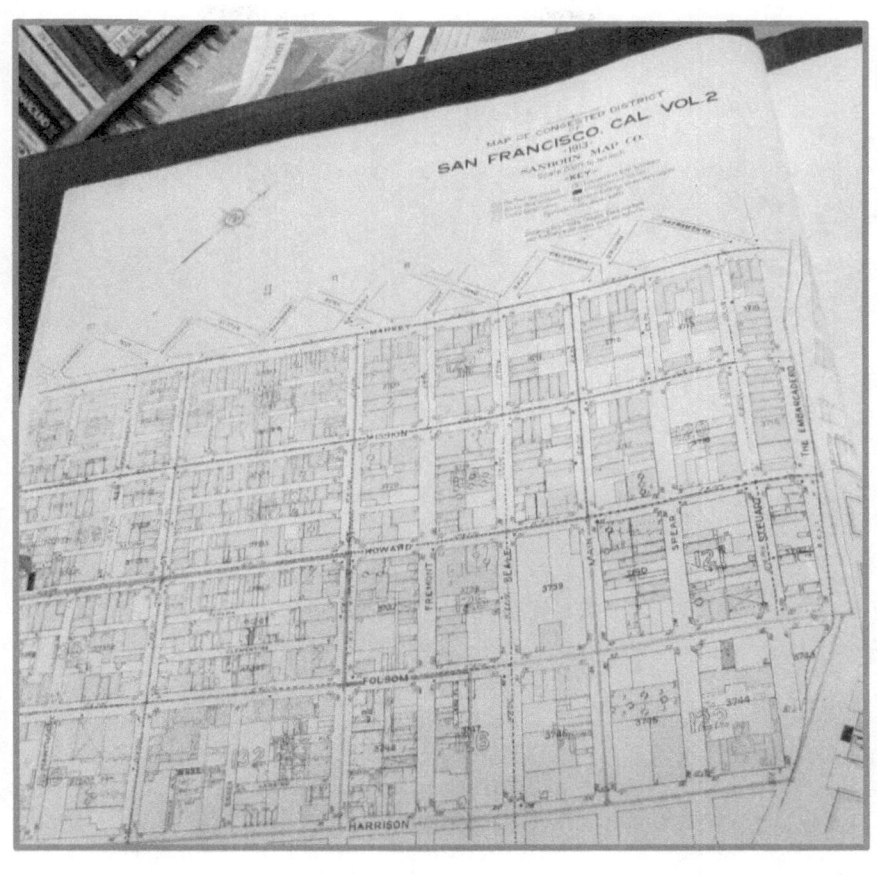

Sanborn Map Company
One page from the San Francisco Atlas

**Captain and Joyce
Summer, 2002**

**Steve and Joyce in Greece
October, 1982**

**Sunrise over the Sahara
September, 1995**

**Steve in the Sahara
September, 1995**

**Joyce in the Sahara
September, 1995**

Steve in Machu Picchu
March, 1997

Steve in Torres del Paine Park, Chile
March, 1997

Happy Shepard (my maternal grandmother),
Raymond Shepard (my maternal grandfather),
Leroy Pease (my father), and Ruth Pease (my mother)
Christmas, 1940

High School Graduation | June, 1961

My Mother | Ruth Pease | Age 55

Michael Stansbury heading to Harvard Law School
and Steve to Harvard Business School
August, 1965

Mother's Day | 2021

Back Row (L-R) Lisa Sorem, Jonathan Sorem, CJ Sorem, Andrew Calhoun, John Calhoun, Bernadette Calhoun, Maggie Sorem, David Auerbach, Juliana Sorem
Middle Row (L-R) Minh Tham, Thao Nguyen, Joyce Pease, Caitlin Jolicoeur
Front Row (L-R) Kevin Calhoun, Thanh Tham holding Argo, Steve Pease, David Sorem

Chapter Thirteen

Writing About Jews[39]

*Russians and Jews,
Pease, you can really pick 'em!*
—*Lucy Merello Peterson*[40]

The Golden Age of Jewish Achievement

Asked why he, a Gentile, was donating $1 million to the Aish Ha Torah's World Outreach Center in Jerusalem, successful American entrepreneur John Kluge responded: "Last year I turned eighty. At my birthday party, I realized 85 percent of my friends are Jews. I have always admired the Jewish people and their contributions to humanity and to civilizing the world. What Aish Ha Torah is doing to reconnect Jews with their heritage, to strengthen their roots, and to educate them about their values, enables the Jewish people to continue to be able to play their incredibly valuable role in history."

My research, writing, and speaking about Jews over the past fifteen years or so hardly compares with Kluge's generosity, but it arises from a similar impulse: recognition

---

[39] A good bit of this chapter, and in the later appendices, includes text, which though edited, essentially reprises parts of *The Golden Age of Jewish Achievement* and *The Debate Over Jewish Achievement*. With apologies for a seeming shortcut, I decided "I could hardly have said it better myself!"

[40] Lucy Merello Peterson produced TUSRIF's *Final Report* and edited *The Debate Over Jewish Achievement*.

of many rich and rewarding friendships, appreciation for the immensely valuable role Jewish people have played over their 4,000-year history, and an effort to explore their achievements and the culture that brought them about.

I was born and raised as a Presbyterian in Spokane, Washington, a fairly conservative Eastern Washington town. My mother was a member of the First Presbyterian Church and, because of that, so was I. In my early grade school years, she usually took me to Sunday school and then to the church service that followed.

I was unaware of any synagogue in town and only had a few Jewish friends and acquaintances through my high school years, but I read a lot about World War II, the six million Jews destroyed, and the creation of Israel.

I thought what the Jewish people had been through in the Holocaust was simply horrifying, and I admired their scrappy creation and defense of the state of Israel. In college, Larry Levy was our Jewish sophomore class president when I was vice president. He was a great guy, smart, and fun to be around.

At Harvard Business School, my first-year roommate, Michael Tarre, was Jewish, and he told me that when he was a Harvard undergraduate, Jewish students were 30 percent or more of his class (despite being only 2 percent of the United States population).

As a management consultant, I had an impressive and amusing Jewish colleague, David Morrisroe, who later became the chief financial officer of Cal Tech when Harold Brown, also Jewish, was the school's president and, as noted earlier, our South African client, Norman Herber, was also Jewish and was a fascinating guy.

Bottom line: I was never anti-Semitic. I had a positive view of Jews, but my knowledge was not deep. I thought the ultraorthodox dress, kippah, kosher food, davening, and some other parts of the dress and customs of some Jews were unusual. I never attended a service at a synagogue, and I liked my Jewish friends but we rarely discussed Jewish history or culture.

That changed in the 1970s, when I began to work with Dick First, REDI's Jewish founder and CEO. I liked him a lot and knew I would learn much about running a business from him. As noted in Chapter Five, I became close to David Nitka who reported to me but was probably 15 years or so older than I was. As I noted in Chapter Three, his parents had immigrated to Palestine from Poland, and David fought in the war to create the State of Israel. Marty Zuckerman, our Jewish VP of Marketing, reported to me, and through him, I was responsible for ten to twelve "one call close" Jewish salespeople who were very good at their jobs and well paid. I acquired a couple of Jewish-owned companies for REDI and in the process, worked with two Jewish Skadden Arps attorneys—one of whom (Ted Kozloff), like David Nitka became a lifelong friend.

During those years I obtained a much deeper understanding of Jewish history and culture. It was not as though I was learning the equivalent of a degree in Jewish studies. It was not an academic exercise, but instead, a more personal exposure and experience for me. And it was a pleasure.

With my expanding number of Jewish friends, my extensive reading, and my experiences, I began to develop an intuition that Jews were disproportionately high achievers as compared to their percentage of the population as a whole. I saw it in Dick and David's entrepreneurial skills and Jim Freund's and Ted Kozloff's legal talents. I loved Rodgers and Hammerstein's musicals, Leonard Bernstein's *West Side Story*, and Barbara Streisand's voice. I was astonished by Einstein's relativity, thankful for Salk and Sabin's polio vaccines, learned Milton Friedman's and Paul Samuelson's economics, and was amazed by Sandy Koufax's pitching, and George Burns's delightful humor.

It was then that I first began to think that if I could find lists of history's highest achievers in domains such as academics, science, literature, entrepreneurship, Nobel Prize winners, and others (and if I could identify the Jews on those lists), I would find Jews in disproportionate numbers among them. Generally, however, such lists were few. Even if I could get or make the lists, it would be very difficult to identify the Jews. I had neither the time nor the resources to do the work (I had to pay the mortgage). So I tabled the idea.

In the late 1990s and early 2000s, I began to have some discretionary time. Over a period of roughly twelve months or so I tried to help Charles Kremer and David Lacagnina see if we could sell their company, Salestar.

Ultimately, we concluded it would not be as valuable as we had hoped and I stepped back from that effort.

The gift I got back was time. I had to help my ailing mother. At the same time, the internet was beginning to flourish and become a revolutionary tool for research and communication. All of a sudden, without leaving home, I could do meaningful research about high achievers by perusing indexes of obituaries, reading the articles and often confirming who was and was not Jewish. Guidestar's website helped in tracking down philanthropic foundations and major donors, and without too much effort, I could find out who among the Forbes 400 were Jews.

What I thought might prove interesting turned out to be much more significant than that. It was astonishing. As it unfolded before me, I began to conclude Jewish people were the most important high achievers of at least the last 200 years and perhaps much longer. Almost no one knew that.

The Measure of Their Achievement

For those who have not read my book *The Golden Age of Jewish Achievement* or its companion volume *The Debate Over Jewish Achievement* (a synopsis largely taken from the first book) may be helpful in understanding why I make these bold assertions.

The brief table that follows is a tiny sample of what I discovered in my research. Hopefully, it provides a feel for the significance of the disproportionate achievements of Jewish people. Appendix I (reproducing a two-page table from the front of *The Golden Age*) provides a much more extensive analysis of the huge numbers of domains in which Jewish people have excelled like no other group. It is also worth browsing in support of the argument.

As context for the table below, it is helpful to know that there are roughly 13 to 15 million Jewish people in the world. In contrast, the population of greater Los Angeles is 18.7 million. In a world of 7.9 billion people. Jewish people are so few in numbers (less than two-tenths of one percent of the world's population) that in a room of 1,000 people representing the world's people, only two would be Jewish. A comparable sample from the United States would count only 22 Jews among 1,000 representative Americans. It is useful to keep that in mind as you look at the table below and the much more comprehensive one in Appendix I.

The table below lists thirteen kinds of distinctions. For example, the first line looks at Nobel Prize winners from inception of the prize to the time my first book was published. The adjacent column says, given the number of Jews in the world (or in the United States) and the number of Nobels that had been awarded, Jews should have won fewer than 2 (1.8 to be exact). As shown in the next column, they actually won 181 Nobels and, in the column after that, the total is 101 times what we would expect. Finally, the table shows that they have won 23 percent of all Nobel Prizes ever awarded. It is a phenomenal performance.

Sampler of Golden Age Jewish Distinctions				
Distinction	Should be or Have Won	Are or Did Win	Multiple of Expected	% of All
Nobel Prizes	1.8	181	101	23%
E.B. Great Inventors	0.6	13.7	22	5%
Ivy League Students	2,380	24,000	10	21%
Ivy League Presidents	0.2	4	20	50%
John Bates Clark Medal	0.6	20	32	67%
Pulitzer Prizes non-fiction	1	25.5	25	51%
Kennedy Center Honors	3.2	41	13	26%
Symphony Conductors	4.2	66	16	33%
Academy Award Directors	1.7	31	18	37%
CEOs of Major Companies	1.5	16	11	22%
Forbes 400	8.3	126	15	31%
Bus Week Philanthropy 50	1	19	19	38%
Ladies Hm Journal 50 Women	2.1	20	10	20%

Further examination shows they are, or were, 21 percent of all Ivy League students and half of the Ivy League presidents when the book was published. Today, they are five of the Ivy League's eight presidents, rather than just four.[41] They have won more than half of all Pulitzer Prizes for nonfiction ever awarded, 26 percent of the Kennedy Center Honors, 37 percent of all Academy Awards for Best Director, and they are 31 percent of the

---

[41] Lawrence Bacow became Harvard's president on July 1, 2018.

Forbes 400 wealthiest Americans. I could go on, but a look at Appendix I tells a more complete story.

The Achievements of Jews in Shaping Our Industries and Our Lives

There is a second way one can take a look at Jewish achievements. It is not statistical but it is analytical, more personal, and it is just as striking.

When considering the impact of Jews on shaping America and the way we live, it may help to know they first arrived in 1654, one (Jacob Barsimson) was an employee of the Dutch East India Company, and twenty-three more came in a group from Brazil. All twenty-three were Portuguese Jews fleeing the Spanish Inquisition. Jewish numbers remained small, but one of them, Haym Solomon, is thought to have been the prime financier of the Americans in the Revolutionary War. He was never repaid for his loans.

Between 1880 and 1924, roughly two million Jews arrived in the United States, most from the Pale of Russia where they were being persecuted. They were mostly illiterate because of the lack of schools in the Pale. Within one or two generations, their huge emphasis on becoming literate and getting an education resulted in Jews becoming 22 percent of the Harvard student body by 1922. Their education and Jewish culture made them capable of creating and operating businesses.

Out of this history has evolved a huge number of different ways in which our personal and business lives have been positively influenced by Jewish entrepreneurs, scientists, entertainers, academics, and others. These stories cannot all be covered here. The tiny sample in the next three paragraphs will be more fully told in Appendix II.

Consider, for example, the fact that every major Hollywood movie studio except United Artists was created by or largely shaped by Jews, as were NBC and CBS. Of the three original radio and television broadcasting networks, only ABC was not started by a Jew, but Leonard Goldenson bought the company seven years after its founding and ran it for forty-five years. Today those three major networks have been joined by Viacom and Comcast, both created by Jewish families.

Jews pioneered the ready-to-wear garment industry and, in 1885, they owned all but seven of New York's 241 garment factories. Names like Levi Strauss, Ralph Lauren, Calvin Klein, and Donna Karan are just a few contemporary representatives of that legacy. Of the four pioneers of prestige cosmetics—Helena Rubenstein, Elizabeth Arden, Estée Lauder, and Charles Revson (Revlon)—only Elizabeth Arden was not Jewish. More than half of America's department store chains were started or run by Jews, including such greats as Macy's, Federated Stores, May Company, Bloomingdale's, Filene's, Saks, Abraham & Straus, Neiman Marcus, Bergdorf Goodman, Sears, and in London, Marks & Spencer.

No group of people in the world could match their performance. As noted previously, the above descriptions are only an introduction to the many industries, companies, unions, philanthropies, and other institutions Jews have created and led. Many of the rest are discussed more fully in Appendix II.

Exploring Whether to Write One Book or Two

I began to share those insights with my Jewish friends. A few already had a sense it might be the case, but most were as surprised as I was. My friend Ed Stolman had gotten to know Rabbi Harold Kushner, author of *When Bad Things Happen to Good People*, and Ed shared my research and lists with him. Rabbi Kushner was interested and offered to talk with his agent and publisher about the idea of writing a book. He also asked the most intriguing question. "Steve," he said, "why do you think this happened?" Answering that question made the work even more interesting and more important.

Michael Larsen, a San Francisco literary agent, was holding small seminars in Marin County where ten to fifteen prospective authors could present their ideas for a book. So, in 2003, I attended one of his seminars and made my "elevator speech" describing my idea. He was impressed. He told me I did not even have to be a great writer for the idea to result in a successful book. I signed up, and we worked together for a year or more to make it so. In the process, he coached me on drafting a proposal to publishers.

We both knew I had much more to do including completing the research, compiling the lists, preparing the exhibits, outlining the chapters, and writing the bios that would make the book more interesting than a series of spreadsheets with a few pages of observations.

Michael was a secular Jew. He knew the New York publishers very well and was optimistic. He wanted strong biographical stories of the high achievers. He occasionally wanted me to exchange one story for another (Einstein, for example, rather than Richard Feynman, who became my lead bio for the science chapter), but I did not do so. We got along well and met periodically to review our status.

After five or six months, he began to share with me the limited interest he was getting for the proposal. Nonetheless, I was still marching ahead; I completed the various lists and began the bios. I was fortunate to have friends who liked what I was doing. They were very interested and willing to help. Les Vadasz, Intel's fourth founder, was very close to Andy Grove (the third Intel founder). Les read my draft profile of Grove and was very helpful. Michael Sonnenfeldt introduced me to J. J. Goldberg, then publisher of *The Forward* who shared the "second generation immigrant" theory of Jewish success.

Michael also set up a phone call with Richard Pine as an alternative candidate to Michael Larsen when Mike was not getting a positive response from publishers. Richard and I spoke, and I summarized the book. At the time, he was the agent for Rabbi Joseph Telushkin, an excellent author of numerous books. When I finished, he said, "Steve, I get it, but I cannot be your agent." He did not elaborate. Later I learned Rabbi Telushkin disliked the idea of such a book. He was not the first or last to have that view. My good friend Danny Kaplan searched for other people who might support the book and made calls on my behalf.

I struck up a relationship with Steven Silbiger who had written *The Jewish Phenomenon*. He told me that he had been scheduled for an interview on NPR. Just before it was to happen he was told it was canceled. He explained that a wealthy Jewish donor to NPR had told them he would withdraw his financial support if Silbiger was interviewed.

At some point, Michael had one publisher who might have interest, but it quickly went away. After more than a year of working with Michael, I concluded he was striking out and there were long odds that he would be able to line up a good publisher. I knew there were many Jews who liked the idea and supported the effort.

At the same time, however, for a variety of reasons there were other influential Jews who hated the idea. I already knew Rabbi Telushkin disliked it very much and hoped I would simply stop. I met with the head of Judaic studies at the University of Southern California, who was very gracious as he explained that anti-Semitism was cooked into the basic attitudes of Christians starting with Judas. His belief was it all extended into fundamental ideas held by each religion that made them sharp enemies of the other. My book would only make it worse.

It was never said directly to me, but I think perhaps some Jews thought I was trying to profit from selling the book to Jews who wanted the affirmation provided by a

Gentile saying nice things about them. Others might be put off by the notion that a Gentile would suggest he knew so much about Jewish history and culture.

One of the most telling incidents arose from the call I got from a prominent San Francisco Jew who wanted to come up to Sonoma to meet me. He came and asked if I would be the keynote speaker at the upcoming Israel Day celebration in the city. I told him I would be happy to be so honored but it was possible he would have to retract the invitation.[42] In fact, a couple of weeks before the event, he called to tell me that was the case. He asked me to attend anyway. I found I had been replaced by a speaker talking about solar energy. At the event, I received gratis a dark blue metal water flask with the words "The Gift of Israel" written in white on the outside. It still lives in our refrigerator and it chills the water wonderfully.

The good news was that self-publishing was just beginning to get significant attention. That attention was only enhanced by the growing popularity of Amazon.com, where books could be sold without the patina and marketing talents of the major publishing houses. I decided to use "Deucalion" as the publisher. The corporation was created in 1980, served as my employer of record since then as a turnaround CEO and later, as a venture capitalist. Now

---

[42] Later, my friend Ed Stolman, who introduced me to Rabbi Harold Kushner whose blurb "A book to strengthen one's pride in being Jewish." graced the cover of my book, invited me to a dinner party at his house. Sitting across from me was the prominent Jewish woman who had headed up the Israel Day event. Neither of us mentioned the invite or the retraction.

Deucalion would take on a new assignment as my publisher.

Around that time, I read Lawrence E. Harrison's book, *Culture Matters*, and I introduced myself to him. He became a close friend. He and Samuel P. Huntington together edited a series of influential essays that they brought together into the book with a subtitle that delivered the heart of their message: *How Values Shape Human Progress*. And, I never would have expected it, but Larry was a Boston Jew.[43] When the manuscript was done, I sent him a copy and he responded with a blurb that began: "This is a hugely important book. Not only does it document Jewish achievement in compelling, fascinating detail, it hits the nail on the head in explaining that achievement is the consequence of Jewish cultural capital—values, beliefs, and attitudes—that drive progress. And it makes it crystal clear that those values, beliefs, and attitudes are available to all—Jews and Gentiles alike."

I genuinely believed what I had learned about the Jewish record of human achievement was astonishing, and I had some worthwhile and solid responses to Rabbi Kushner's vital question: "Steve, why do you think it happened?" I thought those answers might provide lessons for all of us about the nature of human achievement and how to nurture it. So, I marched ahead.

---

[43] Harrison is not a Jewish name. Larry told me that someone, most likely an immigration officer, assigned the family that name when they arrived in the United State. I have never heard of anyone else who is Jewish with that family name.

I probably spent two or three years of nights and weekends doing the writing. I thought what I wrote was decent but realized I might be giving myself way too much credit, so I decided to find out what would be recommended by a "macro-editor," (namely a big picture editor who can not only wordsmith, but also can suggest more fundamental changes to create a better book). In early 2008, I introduced myself to Michael Denneny, a very good New York editor and asked if he would consider editing the book. He asked for a copy of the manuscript, and I sent it. In early March, he responded saying he was "remarkably impressed," that I had "done a superb job of research, organization and presentation," and that the bios were "so well written and interesting that I enjoyed them immensely." He finished, saying, "I don't think you need an editor, you need a good book designer," and he recommended Deborah Daly. I was on Cloud Nine.

Deborah took it from there. She did the fonts, the layout, designed a handsome cover, including the image. She encouraged me to do a comprehensive index, which I did. She also had family in the printing business and recommended we use them both for the galleys and final printing. I did. She was a superb one-stop shop.

Before we would complete the final hard copy and paperback books I had to seek out "blurbs" for the front and back covers and expected it might be difficult for an unpublished author to get much response. I was surprised and pleased to get ten people to provide them, including friends as well as Sir Martin Gilbert, Winston Churchill's official biographer; Charles Murray; and Kirkus Discoveries. With that behind us, we were ready to go to press.

The official release date was December 2009, and by that time we had hard copies and paperbacks in the Amazon fulfillment warehouses, the book's website was live, and I had a PowerPoint presentation ready for book talks. We were "good to go." Then on January 11, 2010, I got a delightful surprise. I did not know it, but Larry Harrison had sent a copy of *The Golden Age* to David Brooks, who gave it a very favorable mention in his *New York Times* Op-Ed column that featured my book along with Dan Senor and Saul Singer's new book, *Start Up Nation: The Story of Israel's Economic Miracle* that described the immense technological and economic success of Israel.

Almost immediately the phone rang asking if I might be available in Los Angeles to be interviewed by Brad Pomerance for Jewish Life Television.[44] Another call asked if I would speak at Congregation Shearith Israel in Manhattan, New York's oldest synagogue. I was also invited to speak at San Francisco's Commonwealth Club.

But perhaps the most interesting of the twenty to twenty-five events where I spoke was my presentation at the Jewish Book Council event for authors held at the Lincoln Park Synagogue at 50 East 87th Street in Manhattan. There, perhaps fifty authors of books about Jews would each have two minutes to address roughly 400

---

[44] Available at:
https://www.jewishlifetv.com/videos.php?id=1&play=513

leaders of Jewish community centers and synagogues responsible for inviting speakers to appear at their events for books and authors.

I did not know how long it would take me to walk to the synagogue, so I left my hotel early and got there about fifteen minutes before it was to begin. None of us could enter until they were ready for us. Almost immediately a woman, also an early arrival, showed up and we spoke. Of course, I asked her about her book, and she asked me about mine. Her story was much more interesting than mine. When we were both invited to speak at a Jewish community center in La Jolla, California, a few months later, we had a chance to renew the acquaintance, one which has ripened into one of the close friendships in my life.

Marilyn Berger Hewitt told me that her book *This Is a Soul: The Mission of Rick Hodes*, involved a Jewish American doctor who worked at the Mother Teresa Clinic and other hospitals in Addis Ababa, Ethiopia. She had been told he was something of a modern-day saint, and she wanted to find out if that was true or not. If it was true, she would write the book. Her background made her perfectly qualified to do it. After graduating with a master's degree from the Columbia School of Journalism, she had been a reporter for *Newsday*, the *Washington Post*, and *The New York Times*. She also worked for *NBC News*, hosted a public television news program *The Advocates*, and anchored *The Nightly News* on public television's station, WNET, in New York. In 1979, she married for the second time. Her husband was Don Hewitt, who set up the televised Nixon-Kennedy Debate and, in 1968, created the *60 Minutes* program that he led for thirty-five years.

Marilyn flew to Addis Ababa, got a hotel room and, over a period of about two weeks, she got to know Rick Hodes quite well. She concluded he really was a remarkable human being, and she would write a book about him. Technically employed by the Jewish Distribution Committee, a leading Jewish humanitarian organization, he was hired to medically assist the airlift of 14,400 Ethiopian Jews from Ethiopia to Israel in twenty-four hours. Later, volunteering at the Mother Teresa Clinic and other hospitals, he pursued another calling: helping young Ethiopian kids with spinal problems (mostly scoliosis) as well as tuberculosis of the spine and other medical ailments, including cancer and heart disease.

Very late in her visit, she decided to walk back to her hotel, and noticed a young beggar sitting in the middle of the sidewalk. He looked as dignified as any kid in a dirty green shirt could look, with his hand held up seeking coins that would buy him dinner. She said Rick had taught her enough to do a "drive-by diagnosis" and she recognized that he probably had tuberculosis of the spine. She walked back to the clinic and asked Rick if he would come take a look and see if he agreed. Rick confirmed her observations and said, "We can help him." As it turned out, the kid had been abandoned by his family and he caught his first gold ring when Marilyn spotted him and would ask the foremost spinal specialist in Ethiopia to diagnose and arrange for surgery to heal him. With that, Rick would also, in effect, adopt him.

Marilyn returned home, told Don about "Danny" the 7-year-old boy she had seen (and thus saved). She also kept thinking about him and after speaking with Don, she called to ask Rick if she might be allowed to bring him to the United States where he could meet Don. Rick said yes and soon, in spring of 2009, Danny arrived in New York, and was taken to Marilyn and Don's seventeenth floor co-op apartment on Central Park West in Manhattan. He stayed with them for a few months before his return to Addis Ababa, but Marilyn kept thinking about him. She was smitten.

She began to study adoption and found out it might be possible in the United States. She talked to Rick, who liked the idea, and by the spring of 2012, she was before the family court judge who asked Marilyn if she promised to love and take good care of this bright and very handsome Ethiopian child. As Marilyn tells the story, when she responded with "Yes!" the judge broke into tears.

One night in Manhattan when I was with the two of them and Marilyn was in the kitchen, I told Danny I thought he had caught the biggest gold ring I had ever heard about. First, by having Marilyn save his life in getting Rick Hodes to arrange for surgery to heal his tuberculosis, and then by coming to America to be adopted by Marilyn, live in a seventeenth-floor co-op with views of Central Park, and be admitted to some of the best schools in New York.

As you might expect, *This Is a Soul* became a very popular book, and on her book tours she managed to raise substantial donations for Rick and his clinic. She is frequently in touch with him.

I love Danny and Marilyn's story and am delighted to have Marilyn as a good friend. I have never earned a thing from my two books, but I have been handsomely rewarded in the friends and stories that came from researching, writing, and talking about both books. By the way, Danny entered college this last fall. He has his Jewish mother to thank for nudging, encouraging, and helping him get through the difficulties of being a teen growing up in New York.

After the Jewish Book Council event, I was invited to speak at the Greater Detroit Jewish Community Center in Bloomfield, Michigan. When I was getting set up to make the presentation the room began to fill. Soon, I had an audience of about 225 people. It proved to be a friendly crowd. The woman attending from the Jewish Book Council told me as I was leaving the hall, "You really convinced them." Indeed, in the plus-or-minus twenty-five events, I never had a hostile question nor did any person say he or she was not pleased with what I had said. They liked it and they bought books.

The Debate Over Jewish Achievement

Early in presentations of my first book, I immodestly said *The Golden Age* is the most comprehensive book ever written to document the astonishing record of Jewish disproportionate achievements. Thirteen years later, that is still true. The book's 622 pages and 61 exhibits document their remarkable achievements and stories. Only in 16 pages, near the end of that book, did I provide my responses to Rabbi Kushner's question: "Why are Jews such high achievers?"

Typically, when discussing why disproportionate Jewish achievements mattered, I would explain that as a kid, I could not swim in the public swimming pool at Comstock Park in Spokane. Polio was rampant and no one wanted to die or live the rest of their life in an iron lung. I told everyone that it was two Jews, Jonas Salk and Albert Sabin, who created the vaccines that eliminated polio in most of the world. Salk's was first in 1955 when I was 12. I stood in line at grade school for my vaccination, and when that was repeated around the United States, the scourge was ended.

In the years following the release of *The Golden Age*, major advances in genetics continued to be announced almost weekly as the cost for sequencing our three billion base pairs of genetic code dropped dramatically and the volumes of genetic data being collected and analyzed exploded. That work was germane to analyzing what roles genetics and culture may play in shaping us.

Several major genetic discoveries were made in those years. One was epigenetics, which demolished the long-held theory that genetics are constant and don't change from generation to generation. While the genes themselves may be largely stable, epigenetics allows some genes to be turned on or off and up or down largely because of environmental circumstances. Those epigenetic changes have already been proven to be capable of carrying on for at least four or five subsequent generations.

Further, the notion that only one or a few genes shape our physical characteristics and personal traits is false. Most such traits and characteristics are polygenic.

We also discovered chimeras, in which people occasionally inherit genes from different people in addition to their parents.

At one point I had my three billion base pairs of genes analyzed. Since "presumably" my own genes would not have changed since my birth, I wanted a geneticist to tell me what those genes would have predicted about me so I could compare how I actually turned out versus what the genes would have predicted. After months, a UCSF geneticist was not able to tell me much. Among the five characteristics the genes would have predicted, he said I would have blue eyes. That and the four other traits were very slim pickings and none were important.

Later, I read *Unique: The New Science of Human Individuality* by Dr. David J. Linden, a Johns Hopkins professor of neuroscience. I introduced myself and we had a Zoom call. He said simply that by and large most physical characteristics and traits are "polygenic" and also involve large numbers of environmental influences including culture. The numbers of genes involved in determining one's height, for example, is fifty or more, and diet and many other environmental factors play a part too. He says meaningful predictions can rarely be made from one or two genes (such as the well-known BRCA gene that may be used to help identify a risk for breast cancer). In short, a genetic predisposition is not predestination as some expected when the Human Genome Project was completed in 2003.

I chose to spend a good bit of my spare time over the next three or four years exploring all the new information and writing about why I thought Jews had become so uniquely moved to achieve. In addition, there were new books arriving with new data and new arguments responding to the question, "Why?" I wanted to think through the different theories more completely and further develop my own thoughts.

During that time, I was able to explore the top major arguments for disproportionate Jewish achievements. After carefully weighing these theories, I concluded that the driving force behind Jewish achievement has been Jewish culture—which was significantly influenced by a variety of historical circumstances. These are explored in detail in Appendix IV.

All of this new information and arguments about the different causes for disproportionate achievement form the core of my second (and last) book about the Jewish people and their astonishing accomplishments.

Chapter Fourteen

Threads, Inspirations, and Politics

There are no solutions. There are only trade-offs.
—*Thomas Sowell*

When asked to describe my political perspective, my initial response is that I am a Paul Gigot[45] conservative and have evolved over the years to be ever more confirmed in that view.

I am also more confirmed in the importance I place on my own independence in thought and action. I simply do not like to be pushed, hemmed in, or dependent on others. It is part of why I was reluctant to join a large company early in my career. This is one significant thread that has been important in shaping my views and values.

The nature of my conservative orientation has been inspired by many people. Important among them are Julius Rosenwald, Thomas Sowell, and Russell Kirk.

Julius Rosenwald

Julius Rosenwald, who was featured in my book *The Golden Age of Jewish Achievement*, continues to be a core inspiration to me. His values and the remarkable philanthropic donations he made, including some that are

---

[45] Paul Gigot is the longtime editorial page editor at the *Wall Street Journal*.

very germane to today's major issues of race, victimhood, and individual agency. He continues to significantly affect my thinking.

His is a stunning but little-known story about the one man responsible for the construction of 5,000 schools for Blacks built in the American South between 1916 and 1932. He was a second-generation German-Jewish immigrant born in 1862 at the family home about a block from Abraham Lincoln's Springfield, Illinois, residence.

He left high school after his sophomore year to work for his uncles in their New York store. At 23, with their support, he started his own successful clothing store which he later sold to invest in and run Sears & Roebuck. Richard Sears was a superb promoter and salesperson, and Alvah Roebuck was a self-made watchmaker, but it was Rosenwald, who bought 37.5 percent of the stock and later built Sears & Roebuck into the Walmart of its day. He was its CEO from 1908 until his death in 1932.

While serving on the board of Booker T. Washington's Tuskegee Institute, he learned that America's annual education spending was $21.14 per pupil, but only $4.92 for Whites in the South and $2.21 for Blacks. Rosenwald was compelled to act. He asked Tuskegee to draw up a set of plans for a generic one-room schoolhouse and then approached the parents of Black students in Southern towns with his unique offer. He would help them build schools and was willing to pay half the cost, but they had to match the value of his cash donations with their own contributions of time, money, and materials.

In making this offer, he said he wanted to avoid a dependence on welfare and, instead, create pride, self-respect, and commitment. Later, Rosenwald pointed out that their sacrifice was greater in proportion to their means than his was. Black in-kind contributions totaled $4.8 million. Rosenwald put in $4.4 million. Other Whites added $1.1 million and, thanks to Rosenwald's example, embarrassed local governments found a way to raise $18.1 million in taxes to cover the rest. None of that would have happened were it not for Rosenwald's philanthropic leadership.

Rosenwald also helped build twenty-five YMCAs, funded $2 million for university fellowships for Southerners, $2 million for the University of Chicago, and $3 million to help build Chicago's Museum of Science and Industry. In today's dollars, his total philanthropy over his lifetime approached $1 billion.

Thomas Sowell

Generally not well known, Thomas Sowell has been a vital force in the development of American conservative thinking, including that of Black conservatives. He also piqued my interest in the critical importance of culture long before I began to explore Jewish culture and its vital role in their remarkable achievements.

In the mid-1980s I began to read op-eds and books written by Sowell, and I found him and his writing extraordinary.

Born in North Carolina in 1930, he was orphaned at an early age. A great aunt took him in, and they moved to Harlem where he was admitted to the prestigious Stuyvesant High School for gifted students. He was ranked at the top of his class but dropped out in the tenth grade because of family and financial problems.

He left home a year later and moved into a shelter for homeless boys. He was destitute and kept a knife for his own protection. Over the next ten years, he says he was educated at "the school of hard knocks" doing menial labor while later completing high school by taking night classes. In 1951, he was drafted into the Marine Corps.

He counts the hard times he lived through as important and formative, and when he saw the fine homes and lifestyles of those better off through the windows of the subway cars, he began to believe in Marxism.

Using the GI Bill, Sowell entered Howard University and from there on it was straight up. After three semesters at Howard, his scores on the college boards and recommendations from two professors led to his transfer to Harvard from which he graduated magna cum laude in 1958 with a degree in economics. His senior thesis was on Karl Marx, and he counted himself a Marxist sympathizer. A year later, he earned a master's degree from Columbia and, in 1968, he earned his Ph.D. in economics from the University of Chicago where he studied under George Stigler and Milton Friedman.

Along the way, he had a summer intern job with the Federal Department of Labor dealing with hard research data. He watched fellow employees disregard objective economic evidence that countered Marxism because they believed their own careers might be at risk if they agreed with the research data. It caused him to lose faith in Marxism.

Next, he taught economics at Howard University, and then Rutgers, Cornell, Brandeis, Amherst, and UCLA. Since 1980, he has been a senior fellow at Stanford's Hoover Institution.

He has written at least forty-seven books and more than 1,000 columns for major newspapers and magazines including: *Forbes, The New York Times, Wall Street Journal, Washington Post, The Times of London, Los Angeles Times, Newsweek,* and others. Though not a user of social media, in June, 2020, he had nearly 550,000 followers on Twitter.

His trilogy: *Race and Culture, Migrations and Culture,* and *Conquest and Culture,* together with *Ethnic America,* look at cultures around the world in terms of their similarities and differences. These included differences among different groups (or tribes) of African Blacks, Asians, and others who immigrated to the same country or region. He could see significant differences in their respective successes and failures that were clearly not tied to their race, but to their cultural values. He noted how much more successful the offshore Chinese were in every country they moved to than the original residents[46] of the countries they

---

[46] Singapore was carved out of Malaysia because immigrant Chinese, driven by Confucian cultural values, were much more successful than the native Malays. The Malaysian government decided separating the

left. The same was true of different groups of Blacks. Caribbean Blacks, for example, are much more successful, both socially and financially, than their counterparts in America.[47]

Malcolm Gladwell, whose mother is Jamaican, has written at length about Jamaican culture and its successes. He believes British absentee landlords delegated sugar plantation management to Black slaves. It fostered their own sense of leadership and accountability and has made an enormous difference in their success versus other Blacks. The same is true for Winsome Sears, the recently elected lieutenant governor of Virginia, also born in Jamaica. She believes there are no limits to what Blacks can achieve. Moreover, Colin Powell also arose from Jamaican roots.

Ultimately, because of Sowell, Lawrence E. Harrison, David McClelland, David Landes, and a few others, I concluded that culture is one of the single most important phenomenon driving human behavior. Those values shape what we must and must not do and even what we would be prepared to die for. It also led me to conclude that all cultures are not equal. Some have been positive forces for good such as the cultures of the Marines and

---

two groups—thus allowing the creation of Singapore—was the wisest solution.

[47] Lawrence Harrison made a similar point when he looked at Haiti and the Dominican Republic. (Both occupy the island of Hispaniola, but have strikingly different cultures, literacy, and economic success.) He believed much of this arose from the fatalistic Haitian culture of voodooism. It meant they believed they had no control of their lives. Instead, fate controlled everything.

Navy Seals. Others, such as Hitler's Nazism and Pol Pot's Communism in Cambodia, have been forces for evil.

Sowell's Conflict of Visions

Sowell believes *A Conflict of Visions* is his most important book. I agree. In this era of fractured and embittered divisiveness, the book is even more important.

The book lays out two diametrically different visions of human nature. They date back to at least the time of Rousseau in the 1760s. Each vision provides its own implicit assumptions. Those assumptions have driven that group's philosophical and political thinking ever since.

The first is, the "unconstrained view." It sees a world where people can intervene directly to solve problems and achieve social and other goals. Results can be directly prescribed and accomplished. If you see an injustice, you can and should intervene to make things better. This view also generally sees humanity as perfectible. We begin as blank slates living in a world where there are no limits on what we can become and achieve. Through reason and willpower, humanity can move ever closer to perfection. Rousseau wrote man "is born free," but he "is everywhere in chains" and that "Men are not natural enemies." It is a utopian view and a social justice mentality.

In this view, our leaders, elites, and intelligentsia can solve our problems, and those who disagree are wrong, deplorable, and deserve to be shunned. There is a good bit of condescension in how all this is expressed. Their team is noble and pure, and if need be, some freedoms may have to suffer as the leaders impose their views of what is best on everyone.

The "constrained view" sees humans living in a nuanced world that is highly complex and beyond human comprehension. Those who hold this view generally understand and agree with the value in what is being sought but believe most direct interventions are overly simplistic and fatally flawed. They fail to take into account the interaction of the proposed solution with other phenomena in the real world. As a result, the "direct action" often results in unexpected adverse consequences that make things worse rather than better. School busing is but one small but very expensive example.

The constrained view believes man is not built perfect nor is he perfectible. Humans are flawed (think sin, Stalin, Hitler, Mao, and others). We all exist in a Darwinian world, where resources are limited, and trade-offs must be considered. Man does what he can and must do to survive and thrive. Progress can and must be made, but it must be provisional and tested. (This is reminiscent of the evolution of the Common Law over many centuries or Adam Smith's "invisible hand" that yields positive economic benefits without that having been its primary purpose.) Incremental steps are the best way to make life better over time. Sowell believes that "Interventions, if drawn upon at all, should attempt to complement the natural order rather than challenge it. You can never do just one thing and you must always consider the trade-offs."

A familiar biblical parable is a powerful example of how to "complement the natural order." Namely, we can best solve hunger by "teaching people to fish" (or farm), rather than giving them fish or food. A constrained leader augments the natural order with a practical long term solution. An unconstrained leader perceives and teaches that the hungry are victims and the direct way to solve the problem is to give them fish. Rosenwald pursued a parable-like solution. The story also illustrates my concerns about the dangers of conferring victimhood on a population rather than enhancing personal agency.

A Conflict of Vision's 1987 release predates by more than thirty years our current situation with supporters of both "visions" becoming ever more extreme and dug in.[48]

In the mid 1990s, I remember a conversation George Tedesco (my PLM colleague) had with an older Russian who told him how he and others had believed from their youth that Communism would inevitably triumph. It was scientific. It had a complete theory of history. They believed their victory in World War II (which they call "The Great Patriotic War"), would shortly usher in the great

---

[48] One interesting example of how deeply two visions can be embedded in one's psyche is demonstrated in Sir Eric Hobsbawm. Hobsbawm is a knighted British Jew, who, at Cambridge, joined the Communist Party and became the subject of an MI5 file from 1942 on. Even after the magnitude of Stalin's horrors became fully known, Hobsbawm remained loyal to the party. Kremlinologist Robert Conquest concluded that Hobsbawm suffered from a "massive reality denial." The commitment to one's paradigm can remain deep and long lasting.

economic and political success of Communism. Russia would become heaven on earth. He was disillusioned to the core by its failure.

Sowell's Early Positive Treatment Before Becoming a Pariah

I "went to school" on Sowell's books about culture, and he received impressive book reviews from major newspapers such as *The New York Times* for those efforts. Sowell was perceived as brilliant. As a University of Chicago economist, he had long been trained in the requirement for solid evidence in all economic research. But later, when he said he had "bootstrapped" himself to whatever prominence he earned, that he disagreed with conferred victimhood on Blacks, and his research proved that minimum wages cost jobs, he was derided.

When he opposed Affirmative Action, explaining, with hard evidence that Blacks had made much greater economic and academic strides before its enactment, the same thing happened. Later, he also challenged the ever more dominant orthodoxy of admissions policies favoring minority students at major universities. With all this, his views began to be shunned. The list of his critics became ever longer. It was politically incorrect for liberals to acknowledge the quality of his research and his writing.

In November 2000, *The New York Times* book reviewer Deborah E. McDowell went after him for saying he became a UCLA professor before Affirmative Action and later Black intellectuals may feel stigmatized by it. McDowell says, "Such shopworn sentiments are Sowell's stock and trade." She ends the review of his book, *A Personal Journey*, saying it "is a brittle, capacious book, despite its avuncular conclusion. There is no odyssey here, no journey. There is instead movement without growth in this largely unfaceted and self-regarding self-portrait."

There were Black conservatives before him, Booker T. Washington among them. In recent times Sowell's prominence has lent support to early Black conservatives and encouraged the recent emergence of many more.[49]

Roots of My Own Conservative Thinking

A decent touchstone for my conservative beliefs is offered in Russell Kirk's *Conservative Principles*. Kirk says: "Conservatives believe in thoughtful and incremental change rather than sudden and radically imposed changes. Continuity of long experience over time offers a far better

---

[49] Such as: Shelby Steele, Ben Carson, Walter Williams, Clarence Thomas, Robert Woodson, John McWhorter, Jason Riley, Senator Tim Scott, Fox TV's Harris Faulkner, Condoleezza Rice, Colin Powell, Allen West, Herman Cain, Lynn Swann, Michael Steele, Mia Love, Alveda King, Burgess Owens, Herschel Walker, Ward Connerly, Rosey Grier, Roy Innes, J. J. Watts, Judge Janice Rogers Brown, Alan Keyes, Candace Owens, Charles Payne, Larry Elder, Leo Terrell, Tyrus, Don King, Ernie Banks, Jackie Robinson, James Brown, Bo Jackson, Kayne West, Pearl Bailey, Ronnie Lott, Tony Dungee, Isaiah Washington, Chris Darden, Glenn Loury, Eldridge Cleaver, Bayard Rustin, Winsome Sears, and others.

guide to improved wisdom, policy, and actions than the abstract designs of coffee house philosophers."

Kirk's principles suggest that conservatives are guided by the beliefs enumerated below.

- There is an enduring moral order made for man, and that man is made for. Human nature is constant and moral truths are permanent. The twentieth century experienced the hideous consequences of a collapse in the belief of that enduring moral order.
- We should adhere to continuity, convention, and custom. The devil you know is better than the one you don't. The French Revolution, Nazism, and Russian and Chinese Communism have all shown the horrific results of radical change.
- Our rights and customs have arisen over a long history of incremental changes through which we've acquired a wisdom greater than any one person's utopian theory.[50] We should be guided by a principle of prudence. Sudden and slashing reforms are perilous.
- We should appreciate the importance of variety as distinguished from the narrowing uniformity and deadening egalitarianism of radical systems.

---

[50] This view was instrumental in the development of "the common law."

- We should be chastened by the fact that humans are not perfect and because of that, no perfect social order can be created. Every utopian attempt has failed.
- We should be guided by the knowledge that freedom and property are closely linked. Private property is a powerful instrument for teaching us about responsibility. "When everyone owns the cow, no one owns (or takes care of) the cow." The Soviet Union was a prime example. It failed miserably.
- We should uphold voluntary local communities and oppose involuntary collectivism. Centralized authority endangers cooperative volition.
- We should understand the need for prudent restraints upon power and human passions. Power corrupts and absolute power corrupts absolutely.
- It is also important to understand the necessity of both permanence and change and know that both must be recognized and reconciled in a vigorous society.

On Social Justice

There are a number of issues today that concern me. One of them is social justice.

I do not believe I ever heard the term "social justice" until recent decades. Certainly, it was not an expression used during my days in grade school, high school, college, or business school.

The Pachamama Alliance[51] says the concept "arose in the nineteenth century during the Industrial Revolution and subsequent civil revolutions throughout Europe that aimed to create more egalitarian societies and remedy capitalistic exploitations of human labor. Because of the stark stratifications between the wealthy and the poor during this time, early social justice advocates focused primarily on capital, property, and the distribution of wealth."

The article goes on to say that "by the mid-twentieth century, social justice had expanded from being primarily concerned with economics, to include other spheres of social life including the environment, race, gender, and other causes and manifestations of inequality." Later, it expanded still further to encompass . . . "slaves, exploited workers, oppressed woman and other 'victimized' human beings."

A March, 2012, article in *Nonprofit Management and Leadership/Volume 22, Issue 3*[52] begins saying, "In recent decades the phrase 'social justice philanthropy' has emerged to describe grant making for progressive social reform."

In no small measure, both articles represent the progression of liberal thought from Adam Smith's *Wealth of Nations* in 1776 through Marx's *Das Kapital* in 1867. Smith's conception of free markets, self-interest, the invisible hand, and economic prosperity brought immense

---

[51] https://www.pachamama.org/social-justice/what-is-social/justice
[52] https://onlinelibrary.wiley.com/doi/abs/10.1002/nml.20054

benefits, but they were not equally shared. That fact contributed to the emergence of Marxism, a utopian and messianic doctrine portrayed as history and science while arguing for the classless egalitarian society that Marx said was inevitable. The poor were victims. The system was rigged. The evolution of Communism would succeed and take over the world.

Unfortunately, the Marxist economic doctrine has never succeeded anywhere, but it still captures the hearts and minds of an immense following.[53]

I do not believe it is a coincidence that the Smith/Marx dichotomy echoes Sowell's *Conflict of Visions*. It appears to incorporate Smith's "constrained" vision that contrasts sharply with Marx's "unconstrained" vision.

The Pachamama and *Nonprofit Management* articles also seem to take us through the evolution of social justice and victimhood from the time of Marx to today.

Victimhood and Microaggressions

When I grew up, despite the Great Depression and WW II, my parents and grandparents did not want welfare. They considered themselves able and if they were not

---

[53] Interestingly, the common perception misses the fact that Adam Smith was an altruist who also wrote *The Theory of Moral Sentiments* in 1759, seventeen years before *Wealth of Nations,* and he was a popular professor of moral philosophy at the University of Glasgow. He was an altruist and not a ruthless capitalist. He did not create capitalism. *Wealth of Nations* simply described what he had found.

wealthy, they never saw themselves as victims, nor did they perceive any microaggressions against them.

My mother told me her cousin, Verne Harr, served in the Philippines and was captured when the Japanese took Corregidor, and the United States surrendered the Philippines. Verne survived the Bataan Death March, one of the most horrific travesties of WW II's Pacific theater. I knew him as a kid. Like so many WW II survivors, he said nothing about his war experiences and was never seen to be, nor did he act like, a victim.

For more than 2,000 years, the Jewish people were victims. Romans killed more than one million of them. The Diaspora was forced on them. They were discriminated against in the largely anti-Semitic world. Six million were slaughtered during WW II and though they may have known they truly were victims, that was not their mind set. They have made immense contributions to humanity. There never was a "social justice" program or reparations for Jewish people.

Victimhood, like social justice, has emerged to become a major contemporary issue. More recently, it has been joined by "microaggressions," "critical race theory," and "woke" as new members of the family and sources of anguish.

The term "microaggression" was coined by Harvard psychiatrist Chester M. Pierce in 1960. It did not catch fire until recently. As Dr. D. W. Sue, who popularized the term in 2008, has said: "I was concerned that people who use these examples would take them out of context and use them as punitive rather than in an exemplary way."[54]

The truth is, we currently live in a culture where many political and cultural groups and individuals emphasize their victimhood identity and compete in the "Victimhood Olympics."

Charles Sykes, author of *A Nation of Victims: The Decay of the American Character*, notes that this stems in part from the entitlement of groups and individuals for happiness and fulfillment. "When these feelings of entitlement are combined with a high individual-level tendency for interpersonal victimhood," he says, "social change struggles are more likely to take aggressive, disparaging, and condescending form."

In a way, all of this reminds me of grade inflation (the cheapening of something that should have retained its value and integrity). It also reminds me that when The Eagles came back together as a group in 1994 after a fourteen-year separation they decided they had to have at least one new song. Its title was "Get Over It."

A slight—intended or unintended—has become a major example of systemic racism, or some other form of discrimination. Social justice has gone from a peripheral notion to center stage. Where I had to lay out my college extracurricular activities on my business school application, today it feels like those who want to attend top universities

---

[54] https://en.wikipedia.org/wiki/Microaggression. Microaggression has a short pedigree. The first of 66 Wikipedia articles about "microaggression" came in 1970. Only twelve are cited from 1971 to 2010—but 54 are cited from 2010 to 2021.

need to have set up a social justice program for one or another kind of victims. Affluence and a liberal bent by most academics and admission committees may provide yet further impetus.

I worry it has become much too easy and common to confer victimhood on a group. They grow angry. They demand entitlement, they demand reparations. They do not take agency for their own behavior since they are "victims." On occasion they become violent.

For most conservative and successful Blacks, however, violence and victimhood has not been their "narrative." They knew life could be tough. They were often treated unfairly, but they took agency for themselves. Condoleezza Rice, Colin Powell, Shelby Steele, Ben Carson, Robert Woodson, John McWhorter, Jason Riley, Harris Faulkner, and many others do not play the role of victims. They achieve much. For me, one question is whether or not, and if so how, might we support them and other Black leaders in ways that might help nudge the larger culture in more positive directions.

Chapter Fifteen

Giving Back

"You Can't Take It With You"
Title of Kaufman and Hart's 1936 Broadway Play

Both of my parents grew up on small hardscrabble farms near Spokane, and my grandparent's history was much the same. None had significant savings or free time to donate. My parents lived through the Great Depression and World War II. For them, most animals were part of the farm. Some were there to help with the farm work; others for eggs, poultry, pork, or beef to sell or be eaten.

Joyce's parents and grandparents came from similar stock. They may not have been farmers, but they had the same Depression and WW II experience. Joyce's dad mostly served in the military, and her mom was a Pacific Telephone and Telegraph operator while raising nine kids. Like my parents, they had no significant money or free time. But they loved their families, most neighborhood kids, and animals of all sorts.

In later life, my dad belonged to service clubs (Shriners and Rotary), both of which supported major charities), and my mom supported her church and the Salvation Army. She was also generous with her time, serving underprivileged and shut-in women in hospitals, rest homes, and the like, with haircuts, shampoos and sets, and permanents.

Joyce and I grew up in an era of greater prosperity than our parents or grandparents ever experienced. We were far more fortunate. The United States economy had greatly expanded and yet, in our twenties and thirties, we had insufficient spare time and money to be generous in supporting causes we cared about.

That changed in the mid-1990s. The sale of Transcisco gave us our "go to hell money" as venture capitalist Don Valentine would describe it. It was not big money but unless I blew it, our financial independence was assured.

One early gesture was to help employees at Transcisco who I thought were not being treated fairly when the company was sold. Namely, a significant number of them had received recent awards of stock options from the company in the years before the sale. Most of the options were not yet fully vested. My view was that they should receive the benefit of that award so long as they were prepared to stay on and work for the new owner, Trinity Industries. Try as I might, I could not get the Transcisco board to agree. In the end, I set up a small side fund to accomplish the same thing. Namely, I set aside a percentage of my sale proceeds to be used by employees to exercise their options when they would have been vested. In the end, three quarters of the money went to the employees who requested it.

In my early fifties, I no longer needed to hold down a job unless there was one that really appealed to me. These were fortunate times representing a significant break from the very limited resources available to our parents. Joyce and I were able to devote more time to pro bono volunteering and donating some, but not large amounts, of money. A significant part of this was devoted to the notion of "Pay it forward," or, "Thank you!"

In an earlier chapter, I told of a cat killed when running under our car late one night while we were driving to Napa and how disconsolate Joyce became. Kids and animals have always been among her strongest passions, and she is devoted to both causes. She is also something of an agnostic or atheist. We tagged her as the "founder of the Church of Gonerism." Namely, "When you're gone, you're gone!" It was in that spirit that she expressed her fundamental belief that we should never intentionally harm another living thing (except perhaps a mosquito on a hot summer evening!). Her notion was (and is) how could you possibly harm or kill a critter or other living thing that has only one life to live for all of eternity.

Despite growing up hunting with my dad, and as a kid sometimes doing target practice on critters at my grandparent's Fish Lake Farm, Joyce converted me. I joined her in her "Jainist" philosophy.[55]

---

[55] One measure of her impact on me was an intervention while we were in Portugal. A man at an adjacent outside restaurant table was abusing his dog. I pushed him to stop and he did. Another, also while traveling, was a young man in Iceland beating up an old man across the street. I crossed the street and angrily confronted the younger man. He stopped and walked away. Both invoked a sense of duty that Joyce's values had instilled in me.

Early Efforts

Initially, one activity we shared was support to our George Ranch homeowners' association. Joyce served six years on the Architectural Control Committee while I served on the association's board and, as president, I headed up successful litigation settlement efforts and negotiations to recover damages for deficient roadway construction.

Joyce chose to join the Vintage House board that serves Sonoma's seniors with classes of all kinds, plus social events, and services such as ridesharing. She also served on the Mentoring Alliance board and for fifteen years was herself a mentor for two young girls in Sonoma's schools. This home-grown effort was created and led by a very talented neighbor, Kathy Witkowicki. Kathy built an organization that matches roughly 450 Sonoma Valley kids with mentors who work with parents, mentor counselors, and teachers to support the kids—including some for whom the relationship continues all the way through college.

Joyce fell in love with Best Friends Animal Society, and their wonderful pet rescue operation and sanctuary on 30,000 acres in Utah. For more than twenty years she has donated money and, on at least three occasions, she has gone to the sanctuary where she and other family members have donated time.

Meanwhile, Sonoma's historic and charming single-screen Sebastiani Theatre (built on the town plaza in 1933), was becoming endangered. It was vulnerable to plans being floated to convert the building to other uses by the managing partner of the partnership that owned the property. He was an unusual man who could be quite difficult. After some discussions with him and a bit of homework, I met with his limited partners. They then replaced the managing partner with a better and more agreeable leader.

Ed Stolman (my partner in some of this), and I then saw an opportunity to expand the theater's parking. With support from Sonoma's City Council, we purchased an adjacent parcel and arranged a swap of land with a neighboring parcel. That swap allowed an additional new parking lot to be built behind the theater for its use and for visitors to the stores and restaurants surrounding the plaza. The city bought the property from Ed and me at our cost.

Meanwhile, we continue to provide some limited annual financial support to the theater's foundation and the theater's wonderful longtime operator Roger Rhoten.

Grandkids' Education

In 1997 we set up a Grandkids Trust to support tuition when each grandchild was ready to go to college. We told our kids and stepkids at the time this was a "pay it forward" type of program. Joyce and I knew tuition could be a huge burden for the parents at that stage of their lives. Our hope would be they would consider doing something like it for their own kids and grandkids when the time came.

We began with Caitlin and paid for her four years of college. At that point her mom and stepfather began to accumulate assets. They were happy to take care of their other two kids, thus leaving more for their cousins. All three of the other grandchildren participated. Two graduated from college and the other took classes on and off but began working for Google and ended up with the salaried job he still holds.

In 2018, I asked for everyone's agreement to add Minh Tham to the beneficiaries. He is the son of Thanh Tham and Thao Nguyen. Thanh was a boat person who escaped Vietnam at the end of the war. When we met him, he was working for a state park in Sonoma. In 1989 we hired him to help us maintain our property while living in a studio apartment over our garage. He did a wonderful job and became a good friend.

When Thanh Tham could go back to Vietnam, he saw Thao Nguyen, who he babysat many years earlier. As chance would have it, he fell in love with her, married her and brought her to the United States. She became a schoolteacher, and Minh is their child. We love all three, and Minh is a very good student. He has always called us Grandma and Grandpa. College tuition would be a tall order for his parents which is why I asked to extend the list of beneficiaries, and everyone agreed. Minh graduated from UC Davis in June of 2021 with two degrees.

We were fortunate, in that my stepdaughter, Juliana, who had a fine arts degree from Boston University, had worked for a leading curator who managed art collections for wealthy people. When she was in her thirties, she said she felt more like a secretary, working at the curator's office in Jackson Hole, Wyoming. She decided she wanted to become a veterinarian.

She went back to college to take all the required undergraduate science courses to qualify for vet school at UC Davis. She was admitted and graduated. But, she had to finance both her second undergraduate degree and the UC Davis Veterinary school costs from loans. She now has her veterinary degree and works for Wildcare in Marin County treating wild animals and birds of all kinds.

She would never answer her mom when asked, "Do you still have debt left over from getting your second college and vet degrees?"

Juliana had helped me administer the grandkids' trust and, after the last bills were paid, I asked if she still had tuition loan debt. Her answer was "yes." As it turned out, there was still money left in the trust. With the agreement of the other beneficiaries, we wrote the check. Her debt is now paid off and she is debt free.

It all seems to us a wonderful outcome from the college tuition support program we had established in 1997.

Since 2000

Since 2001, I have devoted the bulk of my time to pro bono service with three entities in Russia: The U.S. Russia Investment Fund (TUSRIF), the U.S. Russia Foundation (USRF), and the Center for Entrepreneurship

(CFE). In that work, and as described in those chapters, we were pleased to be able to extricate the two Russian men who identified as gay, who worked for USRF in Moscow and were being targeted for abuse as we shut down our Moscow office. We brought them to the United States.

Joyce has continued to support and work for such programs as Meals on Wheels and book sales that support the local library.

Sonoma Valley Hospital

A second major pro bono involvement has taken much less time than my Russia involvement, but has been important for Joyce and me. It involves Sonoma Valley Hospital, and it first became important because of a fall Joyce had taken.

About 1 A.M. on a Saturday morning in December of 2001, I rushed Joyce to the Sonoma Valley Hospital emergency room. She had awakened me about twenty minutes earlier, leaning over the bed saying, "Steve, I hurt myself." I turned on the bedroom light to see blood all over one side of her face and clothing, and large gashes above and below her left eye.

I had gone to bed earlier. Still awake, Joyce heard coyotes howling next door in our neighbor's meadow. She was very worried about the neighbor's dog and our cats. She walked downstairs from our bedroom and outside to our deck and then decided to walk down the steps to our lower patio. On the way down, she missed a step and fell with her head smacking into the rock wall banister before landing face down on the slate patio. She knocked herself out and somehow later miraculously came to. Seeing the pool of blood where her head had been, she realized how serious it was and came upstairs to get me. (The following morning, I was shocked to see the size of the area of dried blood where she landed. She could have bled out.)

The emergency room doctor asked if there was a plastic surgeon either of us had used, and I gave him the name of one who removed a carcinoma below my eye. The ER doctor called him and was talked through the procedure by the plastic surgeon for a couple of hours. After 88 stitches, sedatives, and some Tylenol to take with us, we were on our way home.

Later, on Sunday morning, we drove down to the Marin County home of the plastic surgeon. We thanked him for everything he had done and asked for his thoughts about what the ER doctor had done. "Steve," he said, "I could not have done any better if I had treated her at the hospital near my office." We were very grateful. A fully functioning emergency room in our small town, a highly competent ER doctor, and a proven plastic surgeon had done superb work.

I felt we owed them something, and on Monday I wrote a commendatory letter to our small-town newspaper. Later that week, I met with Barbara Bamberg, the hospital's CEO and volunteered to be helpful in any way I could. Soon I was serving on a variety of committees, including one dealing with contingency planning.

As 2002 unfolded, two crises arose at Sonoma Valley Hospital. First, Medicare had always advanced sums over the year (roughly $1 million) that would be adjusted late in the year when final accruals and payables were settled up—which was also when the hospital would receive half of the annual parcel tax proceeds. In 2002, Medicare changed its policy, and the $1 million was recaptured in April and May. About the same time, Health Plan of the Redwoods, one of the hospital's largest customers, was going bankrupt. Another million dollars would dry up. Sonoma Valley Hospital was in great danger of becoming insolvent and unable to meet its payroll.

Having been involved in business turnarounds and bankruptcies, I grabbed a copy of the hospital's financial statements to see if there were costs to cut or assets to sell. I found a ten-year receivable and asked why they didn't negotiate a discount for an immediate cash payment. They said they couldn't. It was a "structured settlement" from litigation that arose from flawed construction a few years earlier. The insurance company that owed the money was unwilling to cash out a structured settlement.

A call to Harold Marsh, a neighbor who was then treasurer of Fireman's Fund Insurance Company, informed me that insurance companies were loath to pay off structured settlements fearing the recipient might later have further financial problems and, with that, have a valid claim against the insurer.

A little more digging revealed that the cover of CNA's (the insurer's) most recent annual report featured

Chris Benziger (a member of Sonoma Valley's Benziger Winery family). Inside, was a nice story about the family and its relationship with the CNA. A call to Chris led to a letter from him to CNA's chairman explaining how vital the hospital is to Sonoma. CNA relented and sent the hospital a large check which solved the liquidity problem. It put a smile on my face and the hospital's board sent a very gracious thank-you letter.

I continued to serve as an ad hoc volunteer on various committees and got to know many at the hospital, including its supporters and detractors.

A few years later, in 2006, some dissension within the board, local criticisms of the hospital, and a very controversial proposal to use eminent domain to purchase land for a new hospital site, led to the failed renewal of the parcel tax. That could have doomed the hospital. I returned from a Russia trip to find the hospital wanted me to co-chair a "coalition" that hopefully would turn around local attitudes so a new parcel tax effort might pass. Bob Edwards, my co-chair, was a leading critic. It quickly became clear that our most important problem was widely disseminated misinformation.

We hosted a series of monthly meetings at the Sonoma Community Center bringing in experts on topics such as hospital regulations, the state requirement for emergency departments and their economics, Medicare and Medi-Cal payments, and other topics. Over time it became clear the critics and the supporters were coming together. The next time, the parcel tax passed.

In the Fall of 2019, Bob Edwards called me to suggest I watch a video of a recent hospital board meeting. He wanted me to see the vitriolic criticisms being leveled at the board and CEO for their "incompetence." It was devastating and with a parcel tax renewal due to come up in little more than a year, such criticisms and disputes could be deadly.

The two of us and Gary Nelson, a former hospital board member—who knows the facts and numbers better than anyone in the community—decided to take a fresh look at Sonoma Valley Hospital. While we treated the critics with respect, we again found they were misinformed. The board was the best ever, the CEO had done a great job, money losing departments had been shut down, and an affiliation with UCSF, one of America's finest hospitals, was improving services and cutting costs. We also spotlighted the losses caused by under-reimbursement of costs by Medicare and Medi-Cal, and we complimented the hospital's plans for an expanded diagnostic center with a state-of-the-art MRI and CAT scanner and the use of UCSF neurologists to remotely diagnose and recommend immediate courses of treatment for stroke patients or make arrangements to transfer them to other facilities in the more complex cases.

We reported our findings to the board, the local newspaper, and the community. The two major critics moved out of Sonoma, and the parcel tax was passed.

Sonoma's Culture of Volunteerism and Philanthropy

We have not been singular in our support. Sonoma Valley is built on pro bono volunteerism. The elected hospital board members have superb backgrounds in medicine and leading hospitals, and they serve very long hours without pay. Wealthy donors helped establish the connection with UCSF, and others have become major donors to the Hospital Foundation. Steve Page, the recently retired well-known and well-liked head of Sonoma Raceway, led the parcel tax effort assisted by a large cadre of local experts, donors, and volunteers to get the parcel tax passed.

If you live in this small town, a huge proportion of the major events and social life center on support to worthwhile not-for-profit entities. One local leader, Les Vadasz, was found to have been the largest single donor supporting education in Sonoma County through his family foundation and his active hands-on approach to donating and overseeing education programs. A second Gary Nelson (there are two in this town) not only has been generous in support of the hospital, but has also led a very successful effort to raise money, build, and operate a superb charter school. Area winemakers organize many events that raise hundreds of thousands of dollars every year to go to not-for-profits in the Sonoma Valley. I could go on and on with many such stories.

I was recruited, and for a number of years, served on the board of the Sonoma Valley Fund. Its mission was and continues to be to encourage philanthropy. It assisted prospective donors in thinking through and establishing relations to administer distribution of donations in accordance with the wishes of the person or family. Joyce and I made a provision in our own wills for a donation to the Sonoma Community Foundation that would, in turn, be turned over to Sonoma Valley Hospital and Pets Lifeline.

Donations

When I look at our charitable donations of money over the last 20 or so years, I can see they tend to fall into two buckets. While I write the larger checks, Joyce writes many more of them to support animal welfare, kids, seniors, the homeless, and others.

I include the following list of her favorite animal not-for-profits with tongue in cheek thinking, *Geez, did she miss any*? Some of these are: Best Friends Animal Society, Pets Lifeline, Mutts with a Mission, Alley Cat Rescue, Wildcare, Fawn Rescue, San Francisco SPCA, Humane Society of Sonoma County, SF Zoo, Marin Mammal Center, Lyon Ranch Therapy Animals and Animal Sanctuary, Peaceful Valley Donkey Rescue, Tiger Haven, Ocean Conservancy, Pets in Need, Vested Interests in K9s, Catwatch, World Wildlife Fund, World Spay Day, and Dove Lewis Emergency Animal Hospital.

The list is not so long for kids, but the checks are bigger to Shriners Hospitals for Children and St. Jude Research Hospitals for children.

My own donations have often served as a "Thank-You!" for UCSF physicians who went far beyond what I would have expected. In one case, I developed retina problems in my right eye a week before a three-week trip to Italy. At UCSF, Dr. Alex Irvine used a laser to tack the retina back down, essentially "welding" it back in place. He cleared me for the trip and gave me contact information for a British doctor in London.

While in Florence one day, I noticed a prominent black spot in my right eye and called him. He had a resident from Verona in his office who suggested a retinal surgeon at a Catholic hospital in Rome. The next morning we drove to Rome and met Dr. Mario Stirpe, the surgeon who quickly determined I needed surgery. I had five hours of surgery and awoke to find three nuns patting the blankets to warm me up as I emerged from the anesthesia.

They had opened up the eye, removed the fluid, re-attached the retina, installed a permanent "buckle" around the eye, filled it with an oil and kept Joyce and me in the hospital for three days. When we got back home, Dr. Irvine removed the oil and filled the eye with water. He then did prophylactic laser procedures in the other eye to avert the risk of retinal tears. Twenty years earlier, it would have probably been impossible to save my vision in that eye. Twenty-seven years later, the retinas in both eyes are fine.

Because such surgeries often result in later cataracts, a colleague of his, Dr. David Hwang, did cataract surgeries in both eyes to get me to 20/20 vision. A few years ago, I awoke to find the vision in the left eye was distorted. The muscles holding the capsule that contained the interocular lens had failed. He immediately got me into surgery, moved the capsule and lens back where it belongs and secured it in place.

For many years, I had suffered with heartburn and used over-the-counter and prescription medications to keep it in check. But I discovered that over time, each drug became ineffective in less and less time. When I told Dr. Miranda Dunlop (our GP) about it, she called me back days later to tell me she went back to look at an esophageal exam done many years before. What she found was an undiagnosed hiatal hernia that that doctor had missed. She suggested a surgeon who did laparoscopic surgery through the groin to cut out the hernia and resew the esophagus to the stomach. The following morning I was discharged from the hospital, and I have never had heartburn since then. When I lost 10 pounds or so after the surgery, I laughed as I told the surgeon he never mentioned the procedure was also a form of bariatric surgery—a twofer for me!

Finally, for many years, my cholesterol was measured in the lowest decile suggesting I was in very good shape. That was good news for someone whose father had died at age 63 because of heart disease. Then in the space of less than a couple of years, I went from the bottom decile to the top. I asked my good friend and neighbor, Dr.

Danny Kaplan, a retired cardiologist, for his advice. He suggested I call Dr. Nelson Schiller, at UCSF, a classmate of his at Stanford. After a physical and lab tests, he prescribed significant doses of Atorvastatin, and various blood pressure drugs. He sees me annually and every other year, he does a stress echo test. My cholesterol has remained at very safe levels.

In all of these cases, I have made donations to UCSF and, in every case, it has been either to be used as directed by the physician or in a program he or she has suggested I consider. They are all both a "Thank-you" and support to vital medical research at a superb research hospital.

I expect that we will do more of these kinds of donations to and through specific UCSF physicians to support their work at UCSF or other programs they would like to have financial support.

Chapter Sixteen

Taking Stock

*The business of life is the acquisition of memories.
In the end, that's all there is.*
—*Mr. Carson* | Downton Abbey

In the preface, I expressed the notion that one of the purposes of this memoir is to revisit and think through the fortunate life I've lived. Had I written down my expectations as a child, or even after graduating from Harvard Business School, I could never have imagined how my life would unfold. The writing (and reflection) have given me an opportunity to "watch the movie all over again, and from the beginning."

With the passing of my sister, Glenna Rae, last August, and of my parents many years ago, I can now say, with tongue in cheek, that I am truly an orphan. A bit old, perhaps, but an orphan nonetheless. Some of what I think about Glenna's life and those of my dad and mom was covered earlier in this memoir. And yet, there is more to say.

Namely, when I think of my dad, I recall my mom saying that when he was very ill, he told her he believed he had never taken advantage of anyone. I believe that is true. He might have been demanding in his own way, but he was fair and he was honest. I know that when my sister was young, she could be highly critical of him, but when she and her first husband were having problems, it was Dad who stepped in, did some homework on the estranged husband, and told Glenna more than she knew before. It was very helpful. That was not the only time he helped her. Late in life she told family members that over the years she came to realize he was always there and if she needed help in any way, he would do whatever it took.

As a teen and young adult, I did not enjoy being his helpmate on the various projects he enlisted me to do, but boy did he teach me! He helped me a great deal by trusting me and putting me in a position to work for him and prove to myself I was up to the task, including the long drive to Minneapolis and back. I was fortunate to be able to help with his SBA loan and other business matters. He was a very honorable guy who lived through difficult times. He was always very responsible and never complained—even when pressures were great.

As I said earlier, my mom was the most important person in my life. She reminded me of Jenny Churchill, who was Winston's mother and an unfailing supporter for most of his early life. Mary Pinkney Hardy was the same for Douglas MacArthur. In fact, she moved near West Point when he was a student. He said of her: "Our teaching included not only the simple rudiments, but above all else a sense of obligation. We were to do what was right no matter what the personal sacrifice might be. Our country was always to come first." The key words "Duty, Honor, Country" were in MacArthur's most famous speech at West Point. He learned that first from his mom.

My mom was always there for me. If I stayed out late, she trusted me. If I said I was going to go to college and later to business school, she helped me pay for it. She encouraged me and she never demanded. She surprised and delighted me when she was named to the Washington Board of Cosmetology, not because of her academic history, but because of her reputation for the quality of her work and her integrity.

My mother had remarkable common sense. When I thought a bump on my head must be a tumor, she ran her hand over the spot and said, "Steve, it is a 'wen' not cancer. Have your dermatologist remove it."—and I did. When I told her my shoes really hurt, she said, "Your inexpensive shoes are the problem." I immediately bought Bally shoes and never had a problem after that.

She was always very clear. "If you love something, let it go." This was not a common expression in the 1960s, but I came to realize it was at her core—it applied to my departure to Seattle for college, to Boston for business school, and to San Francisco for a career. She was always at the other end of a phone call or ready to send me a plane ticket.

In her early eighties, she was diagnosed with Alzheimer's disease. Glenna and I had to tend to her and later found a superb 24/7 facility in Spokane for her to live out her days in complete safety. When she passed away, at age 90, it was a blessing, but I still miss her.

When my father passed away at 63, it seemed unfair. Had we known then what we have since learned about heart disease, he would likely have lived another ten years. In short, he was a very decent human being and I think he ended up pleased and proud of how I turned out. When he was gone, I had a mental image of him looking down at us with a smile on his face.

Travels

Earlier in my memoir I described my first trip to Europe in 1968 as the sole passenger on a flight to England's Lakenheath Air Force Base as part of a consulting assignment. It was topped off with a ride through beautiful English countryside en route to my hotel in London.

Joyce and I both loved traveling to new and interesting places. For a while, I thought it would be delightful to have an office in Mayfair and use London as a base for other travels. Then, Geneva was equally appealing—and the skiing would be much closer!

Later the serendipity of my career eclipsed both ideas with more travel opportunities than I could have imagined. We've been blessed with more than 100 overseas trips to every continent and to remarkable places that left us with many fond memories. You can view a few photographs of these on pages 202-209.

We still have a bucket list of destinations, particularly in Asia and South America. Given enough time, we may also throw in a few return trips to some of our favorite places.

Insights and Lessons

As noted earlier, one example of an insight learned along the way was discovering an ability in creativity that I doubted I had. I was at a stoplight in San Francisco when, in a flash, a left-field idea immediately came to mind. That flash resolved a large lawsuit at no cost to Transcisco.

Evidence of evolving entrepreneurial skill arose from the creation of Soviet-Finnish-America Transport (SFAT), the Russian tank car company that ultimately helped provide Joyce and me with financial independence.

Another lesson came when I was a fledgling management consultant. Beginning new engagements, I sometimes felt overwhelmed by the complexity of a problem, especially when I knew nothing about the industry, the company, or the people. I learned that if I simply put my head down and kept going, in a few more days or a week of interviews and digging, the fog would begin to clear. As I grew more comfortable, I found I actually knew a great deal about potential solutions and ultimately what to do.

This writing has also reminded me that I consistently found ways to cope with challenges. When I was consumed by a complex situation, a weekend of snow skiing was usually therapeutic. I could not get from the top of a difficult ski run to the bottom if a client's problem was front and center. Skiing forced me to let it go, focus only on the slope, and stay in the present moment.

When surprising and shockingly bad news came my way, I learned not to panic or immediately react unless it was critical to do so. Instead, at the end of a very long day, I could head home, have a drink or two, and hopefully get a decent night's sleep. By the next day, my mind would usually realize a sense of what to do, or at least, how to begin.

Serendipity

One other thing is very clear—there has been a stunning amount of serendipity in how my life unfolded.

In the love department, I met my first wife because I double-dated with a fraternity brother. I met Joyce, my second wife (and my last!) because she was at Wallbangers the day I walked through the door as its new president. I was only at Wallbangers in the first place because I had a racquetball court behind my office at Real Estate Data Inc. in Florida. I had moved there to take advantage of a great job opportunity to work with Dick First and learn from him. And at Wallbangers, there she was. Joyce and I have now been married 37 years. What are the chances of that?

The Jewish people became very significant in my life initially because of my experiences at REDI. Russia became equally significant because I had long hated Communism but saw a fascinating opportunity when Communism collapsed. The job at PLM (later Transcisco) arose because I knew Mark Hungerford and mutual acquaintances told him he should recruit me to turn the company around.

There I learned the railroad business, knew of our new railroad tank car technology, and realized Russia would be wise to use it. Again, pure happenstance.

My life and my experiences have been wonderfully diverse and interesting for me. They have afforded me great opportunities to thrive in many undeserved ways. I think that is probably true for nearly all of us, but perhaps chance does favor the prepared mind. Those experiences and values now provide Joyce and me with some useful guidance about what to do with our estate.

I have simply been blessed with a lifetime of good fortune by being born in America at a particular place and time of opportunity and I have a strong faith in the beliefs below.

I believe . . .

- Merit deserves to be celebrated and encouraged. It rewards and stimulates incredible achievements that benefit us all. Meritocracy will always trump mediocracy and uniformity.

- Hardship can be a blessing and stoicism is often appropriate.

- If one sees evil, they have a duty to do something about it.

- I strongly oppose elitism, feelings of superiority, and condescension that finds others who disagree with them to be "deplorable" or less valuable than themselves.

- We should try to keep an open mind and be able to debate both sides of most issues with empathy for those with whom we disagree.
- We should be humble, balanced, and open to compromise and never let the "perfect" become the enemy of the good. Such absolutes are counterproductive.

And last, but not least, both Joyce and I try to live by these simple tenets.

- Be loyal.
- Celebrate beauty, ethics, and family.
- Be responsible, smile, and don't complain.
- Try to make something of yourself. Make a mark.
- Be generous and responsible. Help others. Donate time if you can help.
- Work hard. Push yourself and take pride in what you are doing.
- Always try to be mindful of your duty.
- Also be mindful that life is rarely about absolutes and passionate adherence to a single objective.
- There are few, if any, "perfect" answers with no risk of adverse or unintended consequences.

- Most of life is about trade-offs, balance, and understanding. In a world of limited time and resources, it is the trade-offs we face and the choices we make that matter most.
- Try to avoid dogmatism.
- Never intentionally harm a child, an animal, or any other living thing.
- Don't steal and don't lie.
- Be generous in thanking those who help you.

ಬಿ ಬಿ ಬಿ

I remain a kid from Spokane, raised in one of the best communities in which any kid could grow up. I continue to think America is an exceptional country, never perfect but striving to improve. I have been very fortunate to travel widely, and yet I cannot name a country that has done so much or been such a positive force for good in my lifetime.

So Joyce and I will continue to stay engaged, smile, and feel blessed by our lifetime of good fortune, and hopefully make a positive difference where we can.

APPENDICES

Appendix I

A SUMMING UP - ACHIEVEMENTS OF JEWS

Distinction	Relevant Geography	Total Recipients	Projected Jewish Recipients	Actual Jewish Recipients	Jews as a Multiple of Projected	Jews as a Percent of all Recipients
The Greats of History						
Hart's Most Influential 100 in History	World[1]	100	0.2	8	35	8%
A&E's Millennium 100	World	100	0.2	8	35	8%
Time magazine's 100 of the 20th Century	U.S.[2]	67	1.4	13	9	19%
Intelliquest's World's Greatest 100	World	100	0.2	8	35	8%
Science						
Nobel Prize in Physics	World	181	0.4	48	116	27%
Nobel Prize in Physiology & Medicine	World	189	0.4	59	136	31%
Nobel Prize in Chemistry	World	151	0.3	30	87	20%
Total Nobels for Science	World	521	1.2	137	115	26%
Fields Medal (for mathematics)	World	48	0.1	12	109	25%
A. M. Turing Award (for computer science)	World	54	0.1	13	105	24%
Invention						
Encyclopedia Britannica's Great Inventors	World	267	0.6	13.7	22	5%
Education						
Enrollment in Ivy League Schools	U.S.	115,000	2,380	24,000	10	21%
Military and Aviation						
United States Astronauts	U.S.	268	5.5	9	2	3%
Economics						
Nobel Prize for Economics	World	61	0.1	22	157	36%
John Bates Clark Medal in Economics	U.S.	30	0.6	20	32	67%
Federal Reserve Chairmen	U.S.	14	0.3	4	14	29%
Politics and Law						
U.S. Senators (108th Congress)	U.S.	100	2.1	11	5	11%
U.S. Congressmen & Women (108th Congress)	U.S.	435	9.0	26	3	6%
Largest Political Donors (Mother Jones List)	U.S.	100	2.1	41	20	41%
United States Supreme Court Justices	U.S.	110	2.3	7	3	6%
Nobel Prize for Peace	World	95	0.2	9	41	9%
Sports and Games						
NFL Hall of Fame Inductees	U.S.	247	5.1	6	1	2%
NFL Team Owners (excludes "community owned" Green Bay)	U.S.	31	0.6	9	14	29%
MLB Prof. Baseball Team Owners (individually owned)	U.S.	26	0.5	5.5	10	21%
NBA Top 10 Coaches of All Time	U.S.	10	0.2	2	10	20%
NBA Basketball Team Owners	U.S.	30	0.6	10	16	33%
Naismith Basketball Hall of Fame Inductees	U.S.	285	5.9	20	3	7%
Olympics Medalists 1896 to date	see 5 below	16,167	66.9	231.74	3	1%
World Chess Champions - Years as Champion	see 5 below	122 yrs.	0.5	66 yrs.	131	54%
The Written Word						
Nobel Prize for Literature	World	104	0.2	13	55	13%
Pulitzer Prize for Fiction	U.S.	82	1.7	11	6	13%
Pulitzer Prize for Poetry	U.S.	89	1.8	17	9	19%
Pulitzer Prize for Non Fiction	U.S.	50	1.0	25.5	25	51%
Pulitzer Prize for Drama	U.S.	77	1.6	22	14	29%

This chart is reproduced from *The Golden Age of Jewish Achievement* and *The Debate over Jewish Achievement* written by Steven L. Pease

Appendix I (cont.)

A SUMMING UP - ACHIEVEMENTS OF JEWS

Distinction	Relevant Geography	Total Recipients	Projected Jewish Recipients	Actual Jewish Recipients	Jews as a Multiple of Projected	Jews as a Percent of all Recipients
Performing Arts and Comedy						
Kennedy Center Honorees	U.S.	157	3.2	41	13	26%
Conductors Major U.S. Symphony Orchestras	U.S.	202	4.2	66	16	33%
Composers "World's 50 Greatest" CD Collection	see 3 below	50	0.6	6	10	12%
Longest Running Broadway Musicals	U.S.	38	0.8	24	31	63%
Rock & Roll Hall of Fame Inductees	U.S.	238	4.9	29	6	12%
Jazz Grammy Awards	U.S.	216	4.5	22	5	10%
Grammy Lifetime Achievement Winners (Indiv.)	U.S.	125	2.6	18	7	14%
Rate It All Ranking of Stand Up Comedians	U.S.	82	1.7	25	15	30%
Visual Arts and Architecture						
Phaidon's 500 Artists	see 3 below	500	6.3	37	6	7%
Combined Lists (7) of Great Photographers	see 4 below	587	7.4	153	21	26%
Combined Lists (6) of Master Architects	World	309	0.7	32	45	10%
Hollywood						
Academy Award Winning Directors	U.S.	83	1.7	31	18	37%
Greatest Movie Directors - Reel.com	U.S.	55	1.1	15	13	27%
Greatest Movie Directors - Filmsite.org	U.S.	75	1.6	27	17	36%
Star Power 500 Top Actors & Actresses	U.S.	500	10.3	75	7	15%
American Film Institute Lifetime Achievement Awards	U.S.	35	0.7	8	11	23%
American Film Institute Greatest American Screen Legends	U.S.	50	1.0	6	6	12%
Radio and Television						
Radio Hall of Fame Inductees	U.S.	108	2.2	19	8	18%
Television Hall of Fame Inductees	U.S.	108	2.2	39	17	36%
High Tech Entrepreneurs and CEOs						
Entrepreneurs (Fortune's Richest 40 Under 40)	U.S	27	0.6	6	11	22%
Forbes' 400 (November 2007)	U.S	400	8.3	126	15	31%
Fortune 500 CEOs						
CEOs of Major 1917 U.S. Corporations5	U.S.	153	4.7	7	1	5%
CEOs of Major 1997 U.S. Corporations	U.S.	72	1.5	16	11	22%
Fortune 100 CEOs	U.S.	100	2.1	15	7	15%
Fortune's 25 Most Powerful People in Business	U.S	25	0.5	6	12	24%
Finance						
Private Equity Hall of Fame	U.S.	26	0.5	8	15	24%
Real Estate						
Forbes' "25 Real Estate Fortunes Among Forbes' 400"	U.S.	25	0.5	18	35	72%
Social Activists						
Ladies Home Journal's "100 Most Important Women"	U.S.	100	2.1	20	10	20%
Philanthropy						
Business Week's 50 Leading Philanthropists	U.S.	50	1.0	19	19	38%
All Nobels						
Total - All Nobel Prizes	World	781	1.8	181	101	23%

1) As of 2002, there were an estimated 14.3 million Jews in a world of 6.23 billion people. Jews were .00207 percent of the World's population.
2) As of 2002, the United States population was 280,562,489. Of that number an estimated 5,807,000 were Jews (2.07 percent).
3) U.S., Canada, Europe, Australia, New Zealand and Israel.
4) Western Hemisphere, Europe, Australia and New Zealand Jews were .0126% of population.
5) Jewish percent of the world population has changed over the 112 years of the Olympics. For this exhibit, the current percent (.00207) was doubled to approximate the average.

Appendix II
Thoughts on Jewish Culture

Jewish Culture

There is an immense difference between the various Jewish denominations in terms of what they believe, how they dress, and how they live. But when you read and listen to what Jews say about themselves and their values you find many common themes emerge to describe what they believe.

Here are the elements of Jewish culture that I feel most drove them to become disproportionately high achievers.

Ethical Monotheism

Jews were the first people to believe in a single God. That God is one and indivisible and is connected with a demand for ethical behavior. Unlike Greek and Roman gods, the Jewish God is not capricious or arbitrary. Humans are shaped by their own actions and, in Judaism, those actions have consequences.

Progress

"In the beginning" are the first three words in the Bible. It all began at a single point. Time is an arrow. It is not a circle. History has a purpose and it does not repeat. There is no reincarnation. The future will be better than the past and God has given them a role—and for many, a duty.

Free Will, Choice, Action, and Accountability

Perhaps no comment I made during *Golden Age* presentations was greeted with more heads consistently nodding in agreement than, "For Jews, it is what you do in this life that matters."

Faith and action count for Jews, but faith does not trump action. Unlike some religions, admission to heaven is not based on faith. As expressed by ancient rabbis, "Everything is foreseen, yet freedom of choice is given." There is free will. God creates options but does not direct responses.

Freedom comes with accountability, a linkage that ennobles and inspires. Almost no culture or race has more basis for feeling persecuted—and Jews do not forget their tortured history—but they rarely demonstrate the propensity of some cultures to see themselves as victims, deserving of an entitlement.

Rationality, Modernism, and Verges

Throughout the Diaspora, Jews lived on "verges"— places where different cultures came together. Individuals experienced interactions with other races and cultures that would have been impossible in their own insular worlds. Those interactions challenged their thinking and thus stimulated change and growth.

No culture has experienced more verges than Jews as they traversed the world. Jews processed new ideas by integrating dissimilar facts and cultures and developing new insights adding to their collective knowledge and capabilities. Few cultures are as open to new ideas, and as pragmatic about change, and so inclined to adopt solutions that work.

Tolerance for Competing Views

As the title of a collection of Jewish quotations says, *Two Jews, Three Opinions*. In his book *What Is a Jew*, Rabbi Morris N. Kertzer notes, "The most distinctive feature of the Jewish religion has been its hospitality to differences."

Consider the frequent role of Jews as leaders on different, and often opposing, sides of major issues. Nobel laureate Paul Samuelson was a leading Keynesian when he wrote his classic college textbook *Economics*. Fellow Jew Milton Friedman, also a Nobel laureate, became the foremost economist to discredit much of the Keynesian dogma. Noam Chomsky is a critic of nearly everything done by the Israeli government and the United States. Two of his constant adversaries are Alan Dershowitz and David Horowitz, who are strong supporters of Israel.

In the end, such contrasts demolish simple-minded anti-Semitic stereotypes of Jews as monolithic, single-issue advocates of one dogma or another. On the contrary, what seems to engage the Jewish mind is energetic involvement on all sides of an issue.

Assertiveness and Verbal Skills

For most Jewish people, standing up and speaking out is valued—to see a wrong and not work to change it is irresponsible. One must be capable of thinking and reaching conclusions, and that skill must be coupled with a willingness to air those views, have them challenged, and challenge others in return.

Speaking out and speaking well is important in Jewish culture. In both bar mitzvah and bat mitzvah ceremonies, the 13-year-old must stand before family and friends to publicly assert, "Today, I am a man" or "woman."

In the significant numbers of Jewish people who practice in major law firms, hold political office, work in journalism, literature, the media, and entertainment, one sees these skills manifested every day. In fact, there is a cultural expectation of verbal skill.

Education

Throughout history, the need to write things down, and the ability to read and understand this trove became fundamental to keeping the religion, the tribe, and Jewish culture alive across the years and miles of the Diaspora.

Jews were the first to demand that parents educate their children. Mandated when most Jews were still farmers, and well before the invention of the printing press, this was an expensive, time-consuming proposition for an end result—literacy—of little benefit to farmers. But over the centuries that followed, as Jews became urban, and as their brethren moved to distant locales, literacy took on increasing importance.

From the twelfth century on, the duty to educate and be educated was absolute. This value was reinforced with the smartest and best-educated Jews frequently serving as rabbis. For much of 2,000 years, rabbis were more than simply religious leaders; in most communities they were also the local civil authority and revered head of the community. Intellectual skill, more than physical skill, conferred prominence.[56]

---

[56] Though circumstances in the 1700s and 1800s made education difficult in the Pale of Russia (a region of the western Russian empire where Jewish people were permitted to live), a generally illiterate

Though destitute and testing poorly on IQ tests when they first arrived in the United States from the Pale of Russia, "Jews rose to have not only higher incomes than other Americans, but also more education and higher IQs. Jews not only pursued more education, but better education—from higher quality colleges and careers in more demanding and remunerative fields such as law, medicine, and science."[57]

The same thing happened elsewhere around the world where Jews had the opportunity. These high levels of education, including advanced degrees from the best schools, allowed Jews to practice demanding scientific, literary, education, artistic, professional, and entrepreneurial careers. It facilitated their high achievement.

Family

Family support was critical in an environment where discrimination reinforced the need to take care of one's own. Marriage and family have long been indispensable in Jewish life. Jews are more inclined to marry and less likely to divorce, and Jewish fathers are less likely to desert their families.

Jewish population still craved learning. Thomas Sowell's book, *Ethnic America*, notes that roughly half the Eastern European Jews were illiterate when they arrived in the United States.

[57] From *The Golden Age of Jewish Achievement*. By the 1950s, more than one-fourth of Jewish males had four or more years of college, while less than 10 percent of the U.S. population had that much education. As of 1990, more than half of all Jews over age 25 were college graduates with 30 percent also completing postgraduate study. By contrast, 21 percent of the corresponding (U.S.) White population had completed college with 9 percent completing postgraduate studies.

Jewish fathers have a duty to support their children, educate them and teach them a trade, and children have a duty to honor their parents. In many Jewish families, the day-to-day job of raising kids, instilling values, and encouraging academic performance has been the job of a loving—even demanding—Jewish mother.

Scores of Jewish family rites strengthen home and religion. Traditions, such as Shabbat (the Friday night and Saturday celebration of the Sabbath) keep the family close. While I may have been out partying with friends on a Friday night in Spokane, my Jewish friends were home with their families engaged in a spirited conversation over dinner.

Healthy Diet and Moderation in Drink

Traditional Jewish culture follows kosher dietary practices arising from Biblical injunctions about what Jews should eat and drink, and how these things should be prepared and served.[58] Kosher "disciplines Jews toward holiness" in satisfying the basic need for food. It cultivates respect for the distinctive requirements of being Jewish.

For non-Jews, some kosher practices seem strange. Although safety concerns about eating pork and shellfish 2,000 years ago are perhaps no longer warranted, Orthodox Jews would respond that safer food is irrelevant. The Torah calls for kosher.

Many Jews enjoy alcohol, but most avoid excess. Recent research suggests there may be a genetic basis for such restraint. Drinking in moderation is both healthy and a survival skill. Among all immigrant groups, rates of

---

[58] All vegetables are kosher. Pork is prohibited, as are certain kinds of seafood. Blood must be removed, and dairy products must not be served with meats. Because they are creatures of God, animals must be killed in a humane fashion. Their death should not be taken lightly.

violent crime and alcoholism are lowest among Jewish people.

Skills, Autonomy, and Independence

Diaspora Jews were rarely farmers or landlords, and they were unwelcome in many established trades and industries controlled by locals. Still, they had to survive. If they were to provide for their families in a hostile world, skills were vital. Even those who dislike you will pay for your services if what you do is valuable and you do it better than other available sources.

Historically, Jewish people shied away from large organizations. Anti-Semitism made it unwise to trust the goodwill of others or serve an institution where a change in sentiment could put you at risk. Better to control your own destiny and succeed or fail based on your own performance.[59]

Jewish people created new industries where there were no established barriers, such as the ready-to-wear clothing industry, the feature film and television business, and high-tech companies. When banks and law firms were already staffed by old-line, white-shoe Gentiles, Jewish people started their own banks and law firms—and later

---

[59] The major paths open to Jews were the professions (such as doctor, lawyer, scientist, or entertainer) and working as merchants, financiers, and entrepreneurs. In each such field, skills are distinguishable, and excellence is valued. Professions typically allow one to function outside large organizations and relocate if threats arise. Merchant and middleman skills were viewed as "beneath" most locals, while finance and lending were needed but prohibited by some religions. Jewelry and precious metals had the further advantage of being compact relative to their value. They could be moved quickly and quietly if circumstances warranted.

their own country clubs as well—when they found those doors closed to them.

Even Jewish beliefs support autonomy. There is no pope, Christ, or priest serving as a religious intervener between the individual Jew and God, and each synagogue selects its own rabbi.

Hard Work, Tenacity, and Excellence

Jewish people rarely had family wealth to fall back on. Parents had to instill awareness that life was serious, play was not a priority, and determination mattered. Tenacity and superior talent made you valuable and discrimination costly.

As a child, I was told a good definition of maturity was accepting (or believing in) the importance of deferred gratification. Clearly, Jews have believed in this. Determination and hard work were complemented with superior skills, and that excellence provided a sense of achievement. Financially rewarding, achievement was also a ticket to respect; but more, it was psychological compensation for the world's false view that you might be unworthy. In any meritocracy, Jews excelled.

A Willingness To Be Different

The Biblical story of the Jews began with Abraham's willingness to be different. Abraham packed up and left virtually everything he knew. He had confidence in his God and in himself, enough to leave his home and go where God directed him. It was an astonishing thing for a person to do 4,000 years ago.

Jews often dressed and ate differently, spoke their own languages, kept to themselves, performed work no one else was willing to do, and generally refused to assimilate. This was not so much an accident of taste as a code of religious mandates keeping the tribe together. It lessened the likelihood of assimilation for a dispersed people.[60]

Being different allowed Jews to stand apart and to live by their principles and their wits and thereby overcome negative stereotypes through superior performance. Indeed, virtually every Nobel Prize is an award for being different, for having thought through a problem in a new way that yields dazzling new insights.

Money

Jewish culture comes in for a good deal of both respect and derision when the subject is money. While a Scot may be kidded about being frugal in a charming sort of way, Jewishness can elicit a rather more broad-brush, often pejorative, treatment. To some, Jews are miserly or hoarding. Others see them as ostentatious. Still others see them using money as an instrument of control. Envy and anti-Semitic stereotypes come into play.

In a meritocracy, however, money is a reward for success, a scorecard of achievement, a proxy for status, and an insurance policy for survival. It goes to those with talent who work hard to earn it. It also provides the means to survive if, as in the 1930s, there is risk to you and your family. One reason for Jewish involvement in diamonds

---

[60] While there was a price to be paid, the code survived for thousands of years. It only began to slacken with the growth of the Reform movement in Europe and the United States, and the subsequent shift to secularism. Among some of the ultra-Orthodox Jews, separateness, if anything, has grown.

and jewelry is the transportability of that concentrated form of wealth to augment security.

Threatened for as long as Jews have been imperiled, wealth may be seen as insurance and a way to help compensate for discrimination. Jews are remarkably generous. Often missed is the disproportionate philanthropy of Jews to secular causes. (See Appendix II for more on this subject.) Many Jews feel a special duty to help those in need. Wealth provides the means to fulfill this responsibility.[61]

I cannot end this discussion about money without also acknowledging the many Jews for which money has not been nearly so important. A good friend recently reminded me of the large number of Jewish professionals, such as physicians, teachers, and scientists—including most Nobel Prize winners—who have been remarkable achievers and never sought great riches. They have accomplished much, benefited many, and never become wealthy.

Justice

Perhaps arising from the long history of anti-Semitism, Jewish culture strongly identifies with the underdog. Many of them believe they have a duty to care for, and demand justice for, others, as much as for themselves. And in the concept of *tikkun olam* (which means "Repair the world"), they were "chosen" to take

---

[61] Since temple times, the *kuppah*, or collection box, has been the community welfare box to which Jews were obligated to donate. Many of them think of charity as an item to budget for, just as they would the mortgage payment. It is an obligation (*tzedakah*), not an afterthought. One reason for accumulating great wealth is to help those in need.

action. The world and injustice will not heal themselves. "If not me, who? If not now, when?"

One sees in the activist liberal orientation of many Jewish people the consequence of long-standing cultural values akin to Sowell's "unconstrained" view. By intervening, they helped establish trade unions, helped get Blacks the right to vote, cured polio, developed birth control pills, split the atom, pioneered psychotherapy, and effected thousands of other interventions that benefit us.

Appendix III

Statistics and Stories of Jewish Accomplishments

Charles Murray's book *Human Accomplishment* looks at those who achieved excellence in the arts and sciences from 800 BC to 1950. He devoted part of that book to what he calls the "astounding" disproportionate representation of Jewish people among history's great figures. Following "the Jewish Emancipation" (which he dates from 1790 to 1870), he measures the representation of Jewish people among the 1,277 great historical figures between 1870 and 1950. Based on their percentage of the population, he says 28 should have been Jewish people. "The actual number was at least 158." His observation is corroborated in other listings of "history's greats."

Michael Hart's book, *The 100—A Ranking of the Most Influential Persons in History*, counts eight Jews among the 100 (Jesus, St. Paul, Einstein, Marx, Moses, Freud, Pincus, and Bohr). This is 35 times what one would expect by chance.

In the sciences, Jews have won 26 percent of all the Nobel Prizes ever awarded—29 percent of the prizes since 1950, after the Holocaust destroyed a third of their numbers. Given their small population, Jews should have earned only one of the 502 Nobel Prizes awarded for physics, chemistry, medicine, and physiology. They have won 123.

The Fields Medal, awarded to the world's brightest mathematicians under the age of 40, is the honor that John Nash, of the book and movie *A Beautiful Mind*, had hoped to win. Instead, he took a Nobel in economics as a consolation prize. One-fourth of the Fields Medal winners are Jews.

Encyclopedia Britannica provides a list of "Great Inventions." Of the 267 individual inventors, more than thirteen were Jewish people, including Zoll (the defibrillator and the pacemaker), Land (instant photography), Gabor (holography), and Ginsburg (videotape). Jewish people are represented on the list 22 times more than one would expect based on their population.

Jewish people are disproportionately counted in most of the arts. Since their respective dates of inception, America's leading symphony orchestras have been led by Jewish conductors one-third of the time. They have created nearly two-thirds of Broadway's longest running musicals. Probably one-fourth of the greatest photographers of all time have been Jewish people, as have 10 percent of the world's great master architects. Of movie directors who earned Oscars, 38 percent were Jewish. In broad artistic recognition, nearly 30 percent of the Kennedy Center Honors and 13 percent of the Grammy Lifetime Achievement Awards have gone to them.

As "People of the Book," the sobriquet Mohammed used to describe them, it is perhaps not surprising that Jewish people have earned 13 percent of the Nobel Prizes for literature and 51 percent of the Pulitzer Prizes for nonfiction. Their outpouring of books, screenplays, newspaper, and magazine articles is prodigious.

Certainly Jewish people have been seminal thinkers in philosophy (Spinoza, Maimonides, Marx), deconstruction (Derrida), economics (Marx, Ricardo, Friedman, Samuelson, Becker, Kuznets), physics (Einstein, Bohr, Gell-Mann, Feynman, Szilard), mathematics (Von Neumann, Mandelbrot, Fefferman, Zelmanov, Erdos), chemistry (Heeger, Kohn, Kroto, Olah), linguistics (Chomsky), paleontology (Gould), medicine (Flexner, Chain, Goldstein and Brown, Salk, Sabin, Prusiner), law (Brandeis, Cardozo, Frankfurter, Tribe, Dershowitz), anthropology (Boas), psychiatry and psychology (Freud, Adler, Erikson, Fromm, Rapaport, Maslow), sociology (McClelland, Riesman, Glazer, Lipset), and many other fields.

In education, it is difficult to name an academic discipline in which they have not played a leading role. Their research and teaching helped shape entire disciplines. They now head five of the eight Ivy League schools, and Jews are 21 percent of all Ivy League students. Any review of the lists of faculties of most schools will evidence a disproportionate number of Jewish teachers. They are, for example, roughly 30 percent of the faculty of the Harvard, Stanford, and Yale law schools.

In politics, they were 11 percent of the United States Senate and 6 percent of the House of Representatives in 2009. They were 42 percent of the 100 largest political donors to the 2000 election cycle, and since 1917, when Judge Louis Brandeis was appointed, 17 percent of Supreme Court justices have been Jews. Before Justice Ruth Bader Ginsburg passed away, Jews were three of the nine Supreme Court Justices. Now they are two: (Kagen and Breyer), and soon, only one, as "diversity" now calls for a Black woman.

As economists they are gifted. They have earned 38 percent of all Nobel Prizes for economics and 67 percent of the John Clarke Bates Medals for promising economists under age 40. They were instrumental in the creation of the Federal Reserve System and have headed it for 25 of the last 35 years.

In philanthropy, a December 2004 *Business Week* listing of America's fifty most generous benefactors included at least nineteen Jewish families and individuals. Their charitable donations totaled nearly $10 billion over less than five years. More than 90 percent of their donations went to secular causes in support of education, health care and medicine, arts, culture, and the humanities. It is remarkable that 38 percent of America's most philanthropic people come from a group representing only two percent of its population.

Much of the wealth behind that philanthropy came from success as entrepreneurs. In that role, Jews created whole new industries. Increasingly, they also occupy the corner office as CEOs of some of America's largest and most important companies. Of the 2003 CEOs of *Fortune*'s 100 largest companies, 10 to 15 percent were Jews. Of *Fortune*'s 2003 list of the 25 most powerful people in business, six (24 percent) were Jews. Of the thirty entrepreneurs included in the 2004 *Fortune* "America's 40 Richest Under 40," at least five of the top ten were Jewish as were 23 percent of the *Forbes* 400. I have not gone back to update all these categories, but when I browse more recent versions of such lists, they generally seem to continue to be much the same despite the passage of the years.

Here are a few more stories of Jewish pioneering in major industries and in those activities touching our lives in so many important ways.

In specialty retailing, major chains such as Gap Stores, Limited, Mervyn's, Barneys, Men's Warehouse, Home Depot, Ritz Camera, Bed Bath & Beyond are just a few of the Jewish creations. In television retailing, both QVC and Home Shopping were largely shaped by Jews.

The world's foremost demonstration salesperson, Ron Popeil, used television to sell products that he invented.

In diamonds, De Beers and the Lev Leviev Group are the dominant forces in the worldwide diamond trade, while Zales, Helzbergs, Whitehall, and Friedman's are among the leading diamond and jewelry retailers.

We drink our Starbucks coffee and have sipped Seagrams wines and distilled spirits. The Dove Bar, Häagen-Daz, Ben & Jerry's, and Baskin-Robbins ice cream lead to our later signing up for Weight Watchers, Jenny Craig, and Nutri-System programs or buying Slim-Fast in the supermarket. All these companies were founded by Jewish entrepreneurs.

We may lounge in our Fairmont, Loews, Hyatt, Helmsley, or Wynn hotel, or cruise on any of the seventy-three ships of Carnival or twenty-eight of Royal Caribbean. These companies were founded or largely shaped by Jews.

In publishing, America's newspaper of record is *The New York Times*, and in the nation's capital, Katherine Meyer Graham and her son, Donald, ran *The Washington Post* before it was sold to Jeff Bezos. The Pulitzer Prize is the legacy of the family that still runs the *St. Louis Post Dispatch* and *Arizona Daily Star*. Reuters, Newhouse, Triangle, and Ziff Davis are just a few of our leading magazine publishers. Random House, Alfred A. Knopf, Simon & Schuster, and Farrar, Straus and Giroux are but four of the major book publishers created and run by Jews.

In finance, the story is much the same. Premier names like Goldman Sachs, Lehman Brothers, Bear Stearns, Salomon Brothers, Lazard Freres, and Wasserstein Perella are just a few of the contemporary names of a legacy dating back to the Rothschilds, Warburgs, Kuhn-Loebs, and Seligmans. In private equity, names like Kohlberg Kravis Roberts, Thomas H. Lee Partners, Blackstone

Group, Hellman & Friedman, Quantum Fund, Steinhardt Partners, Claxton, Arthur Rock, Alan Patricof, Gene Kleiner, and Ben Rosen are today's legends taking the place of Bernard Baruch and Henry Morgenthau Jr. Of the twenty-six individuals named to the Private Equity Hall of Fame, at least eight (31 percent), and perhaps as many as eleven, are Jewish.

Jews were generally not allowed to own real estate outside the ghetto for the better part of 1,800 years. They have compensated by becoming a major force in development and management of property all over the world. Today, of the five largest real estate investment trusts listed by *Forbes* magazine in May, 2002, four were headed by Jews.

Michael Bloomberg, New York's former mayor, created Bloomberg LP, the enterprise that gave him the wherewithal to take on a second career. It is the largest financial information company in the world.

Few people know that the shell of Shell Oil traces back to a London curio shop where the Samuels family featured seashells before two sons started trading kerosene. Nor would they know that the Amoco part of BP Amoco was the creation of the father and son team of Louis and Jacob Blaustein, who also invented the railroad tank car. Amerada Hess, Aurora Oil, Marvin Davis, Occidental Petroleum, and Kaiser-Francis are just a few more of the petroleum businesses started or principally shaped by Jews.

America's great legacy of the Guggenheim Museums and Smithsonian's Hirschhorn Museum and Sculpture Garden have their origins in the success of two great mining operations established by Jewish families.

In business services, Manpower is the world's largest temporary staffing company, just as ADP is the largest payroll processing company and H&R Block is the largest preparer of tax returns. All were started by Jews.

And lest anyone think Jews are not on the leading end of new technology, consider that Jews:

- Created the world's largest and for years most valuable computer company (Dell, Michael Dell).

- Co-founded the world's most successful search engine (Google, Sergey Brin).

- Headed for a time, the world's largest software company (Microsoft, Steve Ballmer).

- Co-founded and head the world's second largest software company (Oracle, Lawrence Ellison).

- Co-founded, led, and served as chairman of the then world's dominant microprocessor and memory chip company (Intel, Andrew Grove). Served as CEO or COO at three of the world's four most valuable internet companies at the time (Yahoo, Terry Semel; eBay, Jeff Skoll; and IAC, Barry Diller).

- Co-founded and headed the communications protocol/chip company whose chips were in most United States cellphones and were slated to be utilized in the next generation of cellphones to be used worldwide (Qualcomm, Irwin Jacobs).

And this does not consider the vital role of Jewish people as labor leaders and advocates for the poor and the oppressed. While Jews were busy creating the garment industry, their fellow Jews, Bessie Abramowitz, Sidney Hillman, David Dubinsky, and others, were organizing that industry's labor force. In that same era, Samuel Gompers headed organized labor for much of the early twentieth century. Later, Saul Alinsky, Abbie Hoffman, Jerry Rubin, Betty Friedan, and Gloria Steinem were just a few of the Jews devoted to social change.

While there are not many prominent Jewish athletes in today's professional sports, most would be surprised to know that in 2009 they were two of the ten top NBA coaches of all time. Five of the 216 members in the NFL Hall of Fame are Jewish, and Jews owned 25 percent of the NFL football teams and 28 percent of the NBA teams. Meanwhile, Jews served as commissioners of all five major professional sports: baseball, football, basketball, hockey, and soccer. And, where the games have more to do with brains than brawn, Jews held the world chess championship title for roughly two-thirds of the time since it began in 1834. In bridge, the legend of the game, Charles Goren, was Jewish.

Appendix IV

Historical Events That Influenced the Jewish Culture of High Achievement

Listed below are major historical events that significantly contributed to Jewish culture of high achievement are:

- The Roman conquest and destruction of the Second Temple in 70 CE gave rise to Rabbinic Judaism and mandatory education for Jewish people. It also helped the Oral Law to evolve and later become the written Talmud. Both remain important influences to this day.

- The Roman-imposed Diaspora, which meant Jewish people would be stateless for 2,000 years without kings, popes, or armies. They had no temple, but they had synagogues, which sometimes functioned as community centers and schools. Their rabbis often served as local leaders.

- Jewish people became "international," living in minority enclaves among dominant cultures. They learned from many of those cultures, and they communicated with family, friends, colleagues, and religious leaders (the Responsa) across the world for 2,000 years.

- They became an urban people (rather than rural farmers), and they evolved to become traders, merchants, lawyers, doctors, lenders, and other skilled professionals and businessmen where their individual talents truly mattered. In most such careers, autonomy and self-reliance mattered greatly. A few also became court Jews or tax collectors, for which they were often reviled.

- They often lived at verges, where multiple cultures interacted, such as in Spain, with its Muslim and Catholic cultures. Jewish people learned from both, sometimes serving as intermediaries between them. Traders and international financiers, such as the Rothschilds, were very skilled in serving multiple cultures.

- They became multilingual in order to live and work among other countries and cultures.

- Circumstances helped nudge Jewish people away from strict religious prohibitions such as "usury" (interest earned from lending). They had to be pragmatic, and the Talmud was altered to accommodate such needs.

- They had to operate pragmatically to survive. They respected other cultures, avoided disputes, and controlled their own behavior and anger. Diplomacy and logic trumped parochial traditions, customs, and dogmatism.

- Literacy allowed Jewish people to excel, but those unable or unwilling to become literate often dropped out, no longer thinking of themselves as Jewish, and in Darwinian fashion, the best and brightest survived and did well.

- The Enlightenment expanded opportunities for Jews. For roughly 120 years, after Martin Luther unleashed the Reformation, religious warfare killed millions of Europeans. When the slaughters ended, Catholics and Protestants could be at peace with one another. They could meet, talk, and reason together, and they could and did bring Jewish people into those conversations. The -

Enlightenment curtailed dogmatism, while reason and science emerged and prevailed all over Europe. Jewish people had their own Enlightenment in the years that followed and began to reform their own religion, adopting a more secular lifestyle.

- Napoleon unleashed the Jewish Emancipation first for French Jews and later for all Jews in the French-controlled empire. Jews could own land, they could vote, and they could serve in the military. They were full citizens.

- Anti-Semitism has existed for more than 2,000 years and was often terrifying, humiliating, and brutal. The Holocaust killed six million. In 2005, noted Jewish British historian Sir Eric Hobsbawm wrote that, coupled with the Emancipation and Enlightenment, anti-Semitism resulted in a tension that, together with Jewish culture, stirred Jews to become disproportionate high achievers.

- Immigration to America gave Jews hope and a home. Jews first arrived in America in 1654 from South America fleeing the Inquisition. They have been here ever since. In 1880, pogroms in the Pale of Russia drove two million more Jews to move to America. This migration was not without some levels of hostility and occasional anti-Semitism; but apart from Israel, America has proven to be the most hospitable country in the world for Jews. Said simply, they have thrived. In a 2008 interview, Edgar M. Bronfman said, in response to a question about anti-Semitism, "When Al Gore lost the election in 2000, and nobody blamed it on Joe Lieberman because he was a Jew, I knew anti-Semitism in America was essentially over."

Appendix V
Theories of Jewish Achievement

I was able to explore and analyze the other major theories for disproportionate Jewish achievements. They are described below, together with my thoughts on where they do and do not make well-reasoned arguments.

1. Chance

If you consider the breadth of domains Jews lead and the numbers of prominent Jews in most of these domains, luck simply cannot explain the phenomenon.

2. God's Chosen People

Consider the hardships Jews faced over the 2,534 years before Israel was created—having to live as dispersed minorities, often persecuted, and then slaughtered in the Roman Rebellion and Holocaust. The same God who allowed these tragedies conferred the Nobel Prizes, Oscars, and many other honors on Jews? Today, the concept of "chosen" is more associated with *Tikkun Olam*—that Jews have a special duty to help repair the "broken world," and they are "chosen" to "re-unite the sparks of divine light" shattered when God created the world.

3. Cheating, or the deck is stacked in their favor

You do not cheat to become one of the Forbes 400. Nor do you cheat to win a Pulitzer Prize, an Oscar, or become an Ivy League president. This idea really represents anti-Semitism at its most illogical.

4. A Second-Generation Jewish immigrant phenomenon

Many Nobel Prizes were won by children of the roughly two million Jews who immigrated from the Pale of Russia between 1880 and 1924. Their parents were illiterate, spoke Yiddish, and were broke. Among these Nobel Prize winners were Milton Friedman, Saul Bellow, Richard Feynman, Edwin Land, and many others. They were pushed to get education and strived to achieve and compensate for their parent's difficult conditions and behavior. The problem with the second-generation theory is that third-, fourth- and fifth-generation Jewish people continue to win disproportionate numbers of Nobels and other distinctions, and they are not handicapped by poverty or embarrassment over their illiterate parents. The theory does not hold up.

5. Brains, drive, and circumstances: Malcolm Gladwell's *Outliers*

Gladwell's 2008 book *Outliers* posited that you needed brains, drive, and the luck to be in the right place at the right time to succeed. He used Bill Gates as an example. Gates was certainly smart and driven, and he happened to attend one of the few schools that had access to a time-sharing computer terminal. Gladwell had other examples. The problem is that it does not explain the breadth of Jewish success. One cannot review the lives of all those high-achieving Jewish people and conclude they were all at the right place at the right time.

6. Genes: Rabbinic Judaism versus Catholic celibacy

This theory observed that the Catholic meritocracy put its best and brightest in service to the Church—

becoming celibate priests, bishops, cardinals, etc. Rabbis were encouraged to marry and have children; thus, the numbers of bright Jewish people grew while the numbers of bright Catholics declined.

There are several problems here: first, Eastern Orthodox Catholic priests were always allowed to enter the priesthood as married men with families. Second, priesthood celibacy generally only existed from roughly 1123 to 1517. When the Reformation commenced in 1517, Lutherans and all Protestants could marry and have families—and they did.

7. Genes: Survival skills learned over two millennia of persecution

Jewish people have been persecuted for more than two thousand years. Perhaps, through genetic selection, the best and brightest do survive and thrive. That may well have contributed to the cultural capital so vital for Jewish people, but it is hard to parse the genetics from the cultural influences. The Roma have been oppressed for as long as Jewish people, but they are not counted among the high achievers.

8. Genes: Nature/DNA and IQ heritability

This one makes some valid points but misses contradictory data. It says, Ashkenazi Jews have a long history of higher IQs (106-112) than American and European Whites (+/- 100). In 2002, Dr. Robert Pollack wrote that the total world Ashkenazi population shrank to about 3,000 families in the early seventeenth century. The survivors may have shared high IQs, which would have resulted in higher IQ populations in succeeding generations.

The higher IQs led to many distinctions (Nobels) in domains where intelligence matters. But there are problems. Many domains of disproportionate achievement do not involve IQ, and Jews still outperform other groups. Moreover, Haredim (Ultra-Orthodox) Jews are Ashkenazi, but show no propensity for high achievement in secular activities.

Finally, Ashkenazi Nobel laureates win Nobels at rates all out of proportion to their higher IQs. That is, they substantially beat Whites with equivalent IQs. The theory is interesting but inadequate.

9. Genes: Nature/DNA—the Cochran, Hardy, and Harpending theory

This is another interesting but inadequate theory. In 2005, three University of Utah professors issued a paper that received wide coverage. It argued that certain well-known genetic ailments shared many by Ashkenazi Jews (such as Gaucher's disease, idiopathic torsion dystonia, and others) were correlated with high IQs.

It also said that in medieval times and in most countries, Jewish people had limited career options such as financiers, traders, merchants, etc. In most such careers, high IQs were essential for success. Wealth and success in those careers encouraged large families in succeeding generations to be genetically endowed. Leading geneticists took issue with the theory and the three professors never backed it up with easily performed experiments to prove or disprove the theory's validity. As a result, the theory remains interesting, controversial, and unproven.

10. Nature/Nurture—Botticini/Eckstein, Murray Genes and IQ

In 2012, Botticini and Eckstein published *The Chosen Few* making the point that it was only when Rabbinic Judaism became dominant, after the Jewish revolt against the Romans, that education was made mandatory for all Jews (not just the immediate family members and priests as practiced by Sadducees). The Romans destroyed the Sadducees as traitors, and Rabbinic Judaism became dominant.

With the Roman imposed Diaspora exiling Jewish people to small enclaves around the world, Jewish people had to be able to communicate across thousands of miles and years in order to survive. That would only be possible if they were literate. Jewish people incapable or unwilling to become literate dropped out and stopped being Jewish. Many became Muslims. With that, Jewish people self-selected for intelligence and motivation. By the time of the Muslim ascendancy, basic literacy among Jewish people was nearly universal. Jewish people were thus much better educated than the peoples among which they lived. They could do those valuable jobs others could not do.

Charles Murray, author of *The Bell Curve,* who had read and differed with Cochran, Hardy & Harpending, felt the higher IQs and disproportionate achievements of Jews were largely genetic. The best and brightest Jews had survived and thrived. My response was that the high IQs were the result of culture that mandated education. In essence, Jews believe in free will, share a family of important cultural values—of which education is one of the most important. Even with my Presbyterian legacy. I do not believe Jews were "predestined" by genetics. Instead, I think that because of their culture they may have developed a genetic predisposition for enhanced IQs, but that is not the same thing as predestination.

Where I came out

In the end, I concluded the driving force has been Jewish culture, and that culture was significantly influenced by historical circumstances.

INDEX

A

AAEF (*See:* Albanian-American Enterprise Fund)
ABC (*See:* American Broadcasting Company)
ACI (*See:* Arcata Communications Information)
AFL-CIO, 139
AMTORG (*See:* Amerikanskaya Torgovlya)
AOL (*See:* America Online)
APAX, 145-46
ARDC (*See:* American Research and Development Company)
ASI (*See:* Agency for Strategic Initiative)
AT&T, 41
Abraham, 291
Abramowitz, Bessie, 302
Academy Awards, 220
Academy of Sciences, 166
Adams, Tom, 161-62
Addis Ababa, 230-232
Adventure Capitalism (*Economist* article), 135
Affirmative action, 246-47
Afrikaner, 36
Agency for Strategic Initiative (ASI), 157
Airbus, 133
Aish Ha Torah, 214
Alaska, 31-32
    Anchorage, 33, 54
Albanian-American Enterprise Fund (AAEF), 140
Alcaldessa, 80
Alighieri, Dante, 161
Alinsky, Saul, 302

Allen, Paul, 133
Alliance, Nebraska, 93, 95
Alvin Ailey Dance Company, 42
Amazon/Amazon.com, 226, 229
America Online, 25, 30
American(s): 7, 85, 108, 144, 148-49, 151, 154, 171, 193, 219, 221, 230, 239, 253, 288, 308; conservative thinking, 239, 247; gays, successful, 180; initiative, successful, 138; South, 238
American Ballet Theater, 42
American Broadcasting Company (ABC), 222
American Research and Development Company (ARDC), 126-27
Americans, 7, 85, 108, 144, 148-49, 151, 154, 171, 193, 219, 221, 288
American Stock Exchange, 99
Amerikanskaya Torgovlya (AMTORG), 85, 102, 105, 113, 139, 141-42, 202
Ames, Aldrich, CIA, 107
Amsterdam, 84, 87
Anderson, Arthur, 21
anti-Semitic, anti-Semitism, 216, 225, 252, 286, 290, 292-93, 305-06
Antibes, 87
anticipate, 8, 63, 65
apartheid, 36
apparatchiks, 108
Apple, 69, 129
Applied Imaging, 122
Arab Oil Embargo, 91
Arabs, 62

Arbitrazh court system, 165, 170
Arcata Communications Information (ACI), 25, 38–39
Arcata National Corporation, 30, 38, 39-40, 43, 45-47, 50, 68, 96, 109
Architectural Control Committee, 258
Armstrong, Gene, 93, 100, 124
Ashkenazi Jews, 308-09
asylum, 182, 198
Athens, 82
Atlantic Richfield, 30, 37
Atorvastatin, 271
Auerbach, David, 213
Austria/Austrian 84, 87, 113
Azalea Art Press, 342

B
BRCA gene, 236
Bacow, Lawrence, 220
back of the envelope deals, 40
Bahrain, 175
Baker Scholar, 29, 149
Bamberg, Barbara, 263
Bancels, Stephane, 135
bankruptcies/bankruptcy, 71-73, 100, 108-09, 151, 264; bankruptcy law, 151, 170, 174
Banks, Ernie, 247
Barsimson, Jacob, 221
Baruch, Bernard, 300
Basel, 79
Basin Street West, 41
Bataan Death March, 252
Bates, John Clarke Medal, 40, 297
Bauman University, 156
Bay Area (San Francisco), 65, 69, 101

Bayh-Dole Act (patent and trademark law amendments act), 130, 166
Beat the Dealer, 29
Beaux Arts Ball/group, 53, 64
behavioral training, 71
Bellow, Saul, 307
Belova, Anna, 156-57
Benziger, Chris, 265
Berger Hewitt, Danny, 230-31, 339
Berger Hewitt, Marilyn, 230-231, 339
Berliner, David, 119–20
Bernstein, Leonard, 217
Berry, Clarence, 31
Berry Holding Company, 31
Beyrle, John, 163, 171, 177, 182, 185
Bezos, Jeff, 133, 299
bipolar, 97
Biegun, Steve, 162, 182, 191
Bill, Wyoming, 97
BioSource Technologies (aka Large Scale Biology), 119
biotech, 119
Birkelund, John P., 139
Biscayne Bay, 64
Black Thunder coal mine, 97-98
Blacklin, Scott, 169
Black(s), 238, 241-42, 246, 254, 294, Jamaican, 242
Black Conservatives: 239, 247
　Brown, James, 247
　Grier, Rosey, 247
　King, Alveda, 247
　Love, Mia, 247
　McWhorter, John, 247, 254
　Rustin, Bayard, 247
　Jackson, Bo, 247
　Owens, Burgess, 247
　Robinson, Jackie, 247

313

Black Conservatives (cont.)
    Rogers Brown, Janice (Justice), 247
    Sears, Winsome, 242, 247
    Steele, Michael, 247
    Steele, Shelby, 247, 254
    Washington, Booker T., 238, 247
Bloomberg, Michael, 300
Blumenthal, Michael, 141-42
Board for International Broadcasting, 164
Boeing, 34, 133
Boise, Idaho, 93
Bolshoi Ballet, 200
Bonner, Yelena, 192
Borisov, Sergey, 148, 157
Boston, 10, 17, 19, 23, 46, 227, 274
Boston University, 260
Botticini, 310
Botticini/Eckstein, 310
Bourla, Albert, 135
Bower, Marvin, 26
Boys State Program, 90
brake, 56, 99
Brand Rating Research, 38-39
Brandeis, Louis (Judge), 297
break-even, 94, 110
breast cancer screening, 74
Brin, Sergey, 301
Brilling, Steve, 15
Britain, 36, 105
Britell, Jenne, 162, 178
Broder, David, 42
Bronfman, Edgar M., 305
Brooks, David, 229
Brooks, Sid (bankruptcy judge), 165, 174
Browder, Bill, 150-51, 193
Brown, Janice Rogers (Judge), 247
Brownstein, Neil, 120

Bryant, Bill, 109
Brzezinski, Zbigniew, 139
Burlington Northern, 93, 109
Burns, George, 217
Burns, William, (Ambassador), 189
Bush, George H. W. (President), 139, 144
Bush, George W. (President), 161-62, 177, 204
business turnarounds, 264, 341
Butko, Valerie, 105
Butters, Tami, 4, 338

C

CBS (*See:* Columbia Broadcasting System Inc.)
CEELI (*See:* Central and Eastern Europe Law Initiative)
CFE (*See:* Center for Entrepreneurship)
CMP, 25, 27-31, 33, 37
CNA, 264-65
CTC Media, 145-46
Cain, Herman, 247
California, 31, 38, 41, 65, 67-9 81, 101, 115, 123, 129, 225, 230, 341
Cal Tech, 127, 215
Calhoun family: Andrew, Bernadette, John, Kevin, (Caitlin Jolicoeur), 213
Calvey, Michael, 148-49
Cambridge, Massachusetts, 17
Cami, Dick, 47-48
Canadian Teamsters, 48
Capetown, 35
capital, cultural, 227, 308
Carlson, Edward (former CEO/Western International Hotels), 33
Carmel, 42, 82

carried interest, 30, 115, 129-30, 151, 185
Carson, Ben, 247, 254
Carter, Jimmy (President), 130
Cascades, 64
case, case method, 19-22, 106, 111, 170
Cathedral of Christ the Savior (Moscow), 155-56
Caufield, Frank, 30, 42-43, 68, 73, 75-6, 116, 119, 129, 142, 162, 178, 182, 203
Center for Entrepreneurship (CFE): 127, 137, 145, 148, 154-56, 158-60, 165-66, 174-75, 177-79, 182-84, 189, 192, 200, 262, 338; board, 155, 175 182, 200; events, 179; founded, 148; fund, 179; mission, 154; supporters, 179; USRF, 160, 261
Central and Eastern Europe Initiative (CEELI), 165, 170, 173
Chamfleury, Pierre de, 121
Channel Islands, 61
Chateau de la Chevre de la 'Or, 87
Chicago, 18, 37, 75-77, 239-40, 246
"Chief," 5-55, 338
chimeras, 235
China/Chinese, 7, 133, 241, 248
Chomsky, Noam, 286, 297
Chubais, Anatoly, 106
Church of Gonerism, 257
Churchill, Winston, 228, 273
  Jenny, 273
CIA, 107, 108, 189
Cipriani Hotel, 82
Cirillo, Joe, 52
Clancy, Jack, 55

Clarke, John, 40, 297
Cleaver, Eldridge, 247
Clement, Norm, 35-36
Clinton, Hillary, 168
Cloherty, Pat, 142, 145, 154, 184
coal-fired power plants, 91
Cochran, Hardy, and Harpending theory, 309-10
Coeur d'Alene Lake, 11
Cohen, Ronald, 145
Cold War, 6, 156, 177
Collins, James (Ambassador), 161-62, 177, 203, 338
Collins, Karen (Saldin), 16-17, 27-28, 40-42, 44-45, 53-55, 58, 63-65, 79-80, 90, 341, 337-39, 337-39
Collins, Mark, 123
Collins, Naomi, 162, 203
Columbia Broadcasting System (CBS), 222
Columbia School of Journalism, 230
Comcast, Comcast Cable, 163, 222
command economies, 103, 136, 138, 144
Commie Modern, 85
Committee of 20, 167
Communism/ist(s): 7, 136, 243, 245-46, 248, 251, 277, Party, 243
Community Action Agency, 25, 34
Commonwealth Club, San Francisco, 229
companies, startup (*See:* startup companies)
Comstock Park, 234
Conflict of Visions, 243-46, 251
Congregation Shearith Israel, 229

315

Congress, 23, 51, 130, 196
Connerly, Ward, 247
Conquest, Robert
 (Kremlinologist), 245
Conservative, 1, 16, 80, 93, 96,
 215, 237, 239, 247-48, 254
consists (mile long), 91
constrained view, 243-44
Container Corporation of
 America, 79
convection, 102, 112, 117,
 convection oven, 118
Cook, Paul, 30, 119
Cooper Companies, 83
Coral Gables, 44, 53-55, 61, 63,
 79, 339
Corfu, 79
Corregidor, 252
corrupt, corruptions, 135-36,
 143, 147, 151-53, 193, 249
Costco, 118
Côte d'Azure, 84, 87
Cowles, David, 184
Credit-Anstaldt Bank, 103
Cresap, McCormick & Paget
 (CMP), 25, 27-28, 30-31,
 33, 37
Crocker, Charles (Charlie),
 75-76, 116
Cubans, 59
Cut Bank, Montana, 10
Cyprus, 104–5

D

DARPA (*See:* Defense
 Advanced Research
 Projects Agency)
DEC (*See:* Digital Equipment
 Corporation)
DPEP (*See:* Delta Private Equity
 Partners)
DVP (*See:* Deucalion Venture
 Partners)

D'Alemberte, Lyn, 66
Daly, Deborah, 228
Daly, Ed, 33-4
Damar (for David, Martin
 Nitka), 50
Danny (Berger Hewitt), 232-33,
 339
Darden, Chris, 247
Das Kapital, 250
Datis, 123
Davis, Fred, 73
Davis, Gil, 48
Davis, Thomas J., 129
Dawe, James, 111
deal flow, 117
*Debate Over Jewish Achievement
 (The)*, 214, 218, 233, 337,
 341
Defense Advanced Research
 Projects Agency
 (DARPA), 127-28
Dehlendorf, Bob, 40, 96
Del Monte, 79
Delovaya, Rossiya, 157
Delta Leasing, 147
Delta Private Equity Partners
 (DPEP), 145-46, 152,
 185-86
Deng Xiaoping, 133
Denneny, Michael, 228
department store chain(s), 35,
 220
Deucalion:
 Deucalion Securities Inc,
 73; Deucalion Publishing,
 73, 226-227; Deucalion
 Venture Partners (DVP),
 73, 100, 102, 114, 116,
 119, 121, 124–25, 127,
 226-27
Diaspora, 62, 252, 285, 287, 290,
 303, 310

Digital Equipment Corporation (DEC), 126-27
DiJulio, Jim, 28
Dmitriev, Kirill, 149
Dnieper River, 86
donations, 24, 233, 237-38, 268-69, 271, 298
Doomsday Nuclear Time Clock, 7
Doriot, Georges (General), 22, 126
Douglas, Bill, 21
Draper and Johnson, 129
dual mandate, 138, 148, 154, 189
Dulbecco, Lloyd, 68
Dungee, Tony, 247
Dunlop, Miranda, M.D., 270
Durban, 35
Dutch East India Company, 221
Duval, Glenna Rae (Keller, Pease, Ragland), 3, 272-74

E
ENIAC, 127–28
E-Z-EM, 75
EBRD (*See:* European Bank for Reconstruction and Development)
ERISA (*See:* Employee Retirement Income Security Act)
EURECA (*See:* Enhancing University Research and Entrepreneurial Capacity)
Eastham, Steve, 184
Economist Magazine, Nov. 27, 2021, "Adventure Capital," 135
Edwards, Bill, 67
Edwards, Bob, 265-66
Ehrlichman, Peter and Debbie, 42

Einstein, Albert, 217, 224, 295-96
Eisenhower, Susan, 163
Elder, Larry, 247
elements of Jewish culture, 284
elevator speech, 223
elitism, 22, 278
Ellington, Duke, 42
Employee Retirement Income Security Act (ERISA), 127, 129
employee suggestion program, 48
employee survey(s), 47-48
English Channel, 82, 101
Enhancing University Research and Entrepreneurial Capacity (EURECA), 165-69, 171, 174
Enlightenment, 304-05
Enterprise funds, 103, 136-41, 144, 154, 163, 177, 186, 189, 195-96, 200
Entrepreneur(s): 39, 46, 49-50, 63, 74-76, 97, 99, 108, 112-13, 126, 129, 130-34, 142, 146-50, 154-59, 160, 165, 193, 214, 222, 288, 290, 298-99; Entrepreneur of the Year, 148, 155; in Russia, 156; innovation, 132, 154, 156; local, 158; mentoring younger, 155; prospective, 148; serial, 341, talented, 133
Entrepreneurial, 39, 44, 91, 112-13, 131, 144, 148, 150, 157, 166, 174, 217, 276; capacity, 165-66
Entrepreneurship, 127, 130-32, 137-38, 145, 148, 154, 158-59, 165 174-75, 217; private enterprise, 132;

Entrepreneurship (cont.)
    Student Entrepreneurship Award, 156
Ephrati, Eric, 74, 77
epigenetics, 234-35
Ernst & Young, 52, 148, 155, 158
Erox, 120-21
Estonia, Tallin, 85, 103, 112
ethical monotheism, 284
Ethiopian Jews, 231
Europe, 34, 61, 64, 87, 166, 169, 171, 178, 183, 250, 275, 292, 305-06
European, 74, 77, 100, 103, 167, 173, 176, 178, 181, 288, 304, 308
European Bank for Reconstruction and Development (EBRD), 100, 103, 140, 142, 172
Europe Law Initiative, 165, 170
Evil Empire, 195
Ewing, Marion Kauffman Foundation, 130, 132, 141, 148, 154, 159, 174-75

F
FBI (*See:* Federal Bureau of Investigation)
FDA (*See:* Food and Drug Administration)
FLEER (*See:* Fund for Large Enterprises)
FSB (*See:* Federal Security Services)
Facebook, 171-72
Fairchild Air Force Base, 6, 13
Fairchild Camera and Instrument, 128
Fairchild Semiconductor, 115, 128
Fairchild, Sherman, 128

Faulkner, Harris, 247, 254
Federal Aviation Agency, 23
Federal Bureau of Investigation, (FBI), 107-08
Federal Reserve Bank, 162, 178
Federal Reserve System, 297
Federal Security Service (FSB), Russia, 143
Federal Trade Commission, 23
Feynman, Richard, 224, 296, 307
Fields Medal, 295-96
financial independence, 144, 256, 276
find a need and fill it, 112
Finland, 86, 104, 195
Finsterwalder, Karl, 103
Fireman's Fund Insurance Company, 264
Firestone, Tom, 163
Firestone, Duncan, 151
First, Dick, 39, 43, 45, 48-50, 55, 64-65, 216, 277, 339;
    First family, 339
Foley, Tom (Congressman), 23-24
Food and Drug Administration (FDA), 77
Food Saver, 118
Forbes, 46, 134, 218, 221, 241, 298, 300, 306
Ford, Tom, 68, 116, Ford Land Company, 68
Ford Motor Credit, 95
forehead thermometer, 74
foreign agent, 170
forensic audit, 183
Fort Ross Annual Conference, 171
Fortune magazine, 119
Fortune 500, 38, 45, 178
founder(s), 30-31, 45, 57, 66-67, 69, 72, 76, 100, 115, 122, 128-29, 150, 174,

216, 224, 257
France, 74, 79, 101, 134
Freeman, Ron, 103
Freund, Jim, 49, 217
Friedan, Betty, 302
Friedman, Milton, 217, 240,
    286, 296, 299, 300, 307
Friedrich, Roland, 88
Frist, Bill, 162
Fund for Large Enterprises
    (FLEER), 139, 141-42, 186
Fursenko, Andrei, 168

G
GE Capital, 147, 163, 178
GEG (Spokane airport code),
    25-6
GEN (*See:* Global
    Entrepreneurship
    Network)
GEW (*See:* Global
    Entrepreneurship Week)
GSEA (See: Student Entrepre-
    neurship Award)
Gables High, 53
Garceau, Ken, 9
Gaskins twins, 10
Gates, Bill, 133, 307
gay(s), 173, 180-81, 262
Gemmell, Clark, 15
Genentech, 116, 129
genes, genetics, 119, 122, 228,
    234-36, 289, 307-10, 311
genetic predisposition, 234
Gennady, 172-73, 181, 338
Genovese, Vito, 40
Gentile(s), 214, 226-27, 290
George Ranch Homeowners
    Association, 258
Georges V Hotel, 87
German Marshall Fund, 163,
    185
Gessen, Masha, 180

Gettysburg Address (Lincoln's),
    109
Gibbons, George, 101
Gibbons, Lou, 101
Gigot, Paul, 237
Gilbert, Sir Martin, 228
Ginsburg, Ruth Bader, 297
Gladwell, Malcolm, 242, 307
Global Entrepreneurship
    Network (GEN), 159,
    165, 174
Global Entrepreneurship Week
    (GEW), 159-60
Global Van Lines, 13-14
go to hell money, 125, 256
Goldberg, J. J., 224
Golden Age of Jewish Achievement,
    214, 218-19, 288, 337, 341
Goldenson, Leonard, 222
Goldman Sachs, 149, 299
Goldwater Girl, 16
Gompers, Samuel, 302
Gonzaga (University), 9
Google, 260, 301
Gorbachev, Mikhail, 106, 143
Gorky Park, 85
Graham, Donald, 299
Graham, Katherine Meyer, 299
Graham, Loren, 166
Grammy Lifetime Achievement
    Awards, 296
grandkids' trust, 261
Great Depression, 2, 251, 255
Great Falls, 14
Great Patriotic War, 86, 246
Greater Detroit Jewish
    Community Center, 233
Greatermans, 35-37
green card, 173, 182, 198-99
Gref, Herman, 157
Grinstein, Gerald, 23
Grove, Andrew (Andy), 129,
    224, 301

319

Guff, Drew, 148
Gulag Archipelago (The), 191
Guriev, Sergey, 172
Gudonov, Boris, 42

H

HAKKA, 100, 102, 105, 136
HBS (*See* Harvard Business School)
Haas, Peter, 26
Haganah, 62
Haggard, Merle, 83
Haiti, 242
Hammer, Armand, 85
Happonnen, Pertti, 105
hard currency, 103, 105, 112-13
Harr, Verne, 252
Harrison, Lawrence E. (Larry), 227, 229, 242
Harvard, 19, 22–29, 40, 162, 215, 220-21, 240, 252, 297
Harvard Business School (HBS), 10-11, 15, 18-30, 44, 106, 126, 142, 149, 212, 215, 272, 341
Harvard Law School, 18, 212
hat-in-hand, 93
Hatch, Lee, 9
Heidrick & Struggles, 164
Hellman & Friedman, 300
Helsinki, 86
Hempel, Gardiner, 38, 45
Herber, Norman, 35-37, 216
Herber, Toni, 37
Hermitage Fund, 150, 193
Hewitt, Don, 231
Hewitt, Marilyn (Berger), 230-33, 339
high achievers, 49, 135, 217-18, 224, 234, 284, 305, 308
high fixed cost, low variable cost business, 70
history's highest achievers, 217

Hitler, 6-7, 243-44
Hobsbawm, Sir Eric, 245, 305
Hodes, Rick, 230-32, 339
Hoffman, Abbie, 302
Hoerni, Jean, 128
Holocaust, 6, 215, 295, 305-06
Horn, Karen, 162, 178, 338
Hotel du cap Antibes, 87
Howard University, 240-41
Human Genome Project, 236
Hungerford, Katy, 42, 97, 101, 337
Hungerford, Mark Calvin, 42, 90-103, 109, 153, 277, 337
Huntington, Samuel P., 227
Hwang, David, M.D., 270

I

ITMO (*See:* Institute of Technology, Mechanics and Optics)
INTH (Russian investment), 145-46
Indiana University's Russian and East European Institute, 162
injustice, 243, 294
Innes, Roy, 247
Institute of Law and Public Policy, 167
Institute of Technology, Mechanics and Optics ITMO), 165, 167, 174
Intel Corporation, 129, 224
Intel Higher School of Economics, 167
Intourist Hotel and Tour T51, 84
Irvine, Alex, M.D., 269
Israel/Israeli: 7, 49, 62, 74, 215-16, 226, 229, 231, 305-06; Israel Day Celebration, 224;

economic miracle, 227; government, 286; victory, 7, 62
Ivy League, 220, 297, 306

J
J. H. Whitney & Company, 126
Jacobsen, Finn, 21
Jackson Hole, 261
Jainist philosophy, 257
Jamaican culture, 242
Japanese American, 10, 29
Jesus, 295
Jewish/Jews:
    Appendices I-V, 282-311; Chapter Thirteen, 214-236; accomplishments, statistics and stories, 295-302; achievement theories, 306-11; Book Council event, 229, 233; community centers, 230, 233; cultural values, 241, 294, 310; culture, 236, 239, 284-294, 303, 305, 311; disproportionate achievement, 49, 125, 217-18, 234, 236, 284, 293, 295-97, 305-310; entrepreneurs, 222, 299; families, 222, 289, 298, 300; fathers, 288-89; friends, 15, 49, 215-17, 223, 289; history, 49, 62, 214-17, 221, 226, 284-85, 287, 293, 295, 303-305, 308; Jewish Life Television, 229; mother, 233, 289; people, 36, 49, 98, 214-15, 218-19, 236, 252, 277, 286-87, 290-91, 294; success, 224, 307; victims, 6, 252
Jobs, Steve 133
Johannesburg, 35–37
Johnson, Lyndon (President), 34
Johnson, Richard, 184
Jolicoeur, Caitlin, 108, 203, 213, 260
Judaic, 225
Judaism, 284
    Rabbinic 303, 307, 310
Juneau, 33
Junior Achievement, 167

K
KGB, 140, 143
KPIs (*See:* Key performance indicators)
Kalinin, Alexander, 157
Kalinka, 200
Kaplan, Danny, 225, 271
Kauffman, Ewing Marion, 131-32
Kauffman Foundation, 130-32, 141, 148, 154, 159, 174
Keller, Glenna Rae (Duval, Pease, Ragland), 3, 272-74, Ed, 4
Kemp-Roth tax, 130
Kennedy, Craig, 163
Kennedy Center Honors, 220, 296
key performance indicators (KPIs), 176, 179
Keyes, Alan, 247
Keynesian dogma, 286
Khodorkovsy, Mikhail, 144, 150, 172
Kibbutz, kibbutzim, 7
Kiev (now Kyiv), 84, 86
Kimsey, Jim, 30
King, Don, 247
King County, 58-59
Kirk, Russell, 237, 247

Kirkland, Lane, 139
Kirkus Discoveries, 229
Kislyak, Sergey (Russian ambassador), 169
Kleiner, Eugene, 128-29, 300
Kleiner, Perkins, Caufield, & Beyers (aka Kleiner Perkins), 30, 75, 116, 128-29, 132, 300
Kohlberg Kravis Roberts, 299
Korkunov, Andrey, 156
Koufax, Sandy, 217
Kozloff, Ted, 49-50, 216-17
Kozminski, Jerzy (Polish ambassador), 140
Kremer, Charles, 98-99, 217, 339, Naomi, 98
Kremlin, 107, 150, 164, 168, 171, 193-94, 196; Kremlinologist, 245
Kroon, Rick, 21
Kreuger National Park, 35
Kushner, Harold, Rabbi, 223, 226-27, 234
Kuzin, Vladimir, 105, 107

L

LCT (*See:* Liquid Crystal Technologies
LGBTQ, 172-73, 176, 180-81, 185-86, 198
Lake Baikal, 200
Lakenheath Air Force Base, 34, 275
Lake Tahoe, 29, 82, 96
Lake Washington, 13
Landes, David, 242
Lang, Lang, 80
Large Scale Biology, 120
Larsen, Michael, 223-24
Lauren, Ralph, 222
Lease Partners, 120
Lee Partners, Thomas H., 299

Leningrad (St. Petersburg), 84, 86, 143, 147, 195, 200
Lenin's tomb, 85, 339
Levada, 194
level the playing field grants, 184
Levi Strauss, 26
Levy, Larry, 15, 215
Lewis & Clark High School, 8, 10-11
Lewisburg, West Virginia, 41
Library of Congress, 51
Liechtenstein, 87
Lincoln Center, 42
Lincoln Park Synagogue, 229
Linden, David J., 235
Liquid Crystal Technologies LCT), 65, 73-77, 79
Lockheed Martin, 133
Loevinger, Richard, 112
Lombard Street, 82
London, 34, 81, 100-01, 171, 222, 275, 300
Lonely Ideas: Can Russia Compete, 166
Lord Acton, 135
Los Angeles, 27, 29, 35, 50, 61-62, 169, 219, 229
Los Angeles Times, 181, 241
Lott, Ronnie, 247
Loury, Glenn, 247
Lugar, Richard (Senator), 187
Lusk, Rufus, 60
Luther, Martin, 304
Lutherans, 308
Luzhkov (Moscow mayor) 106-07
Lynch, Bill, 337
Lynn, Bob, 61

M

MI5 file, 245
MPS (*See:* Ministry of Rails, also Russian Ministry of Rails)

MacArthur, Douglas, 273
MacArthur, Mary Pickney Hardy, 273
Machu Picchu, 209
Mad Shitter (the), 60
Mafia, 40, 76
magna cum laude, 16, 240
Magnitsky, Sergei, 151
Magnitsky Act, 151
Magnuson, Paul (Judge), 163, 165, 338
Magnuson, Warren G. (Senator), 15, 23
Maimonides, 296
Mala Mala, 35
Malaysia, 241
Malek, Fred, 40
management consultant/consulting, 18, 26, 76, 341
Mandela, Nelson, 37
Mandelbrot, 296
Manhattan, 18-19, 42, 229, 232
Manpower, 300
Mao, 6, 244
Mariinsky, 200
Marin County, 223, 261, 263
Marine Corps, 240
Marion Labs, 131
Marion Kauffman Foundation, (*See* Kauffman Foundation)
Marion Merrell Dow Pharmaceuticals, 131
Marriott Corporation, 40
hotel, 194
Marsh, Harold, 264
Marshall Fund, German, 163, 185
Marshall Plan, 139
Marx, Karl/Marxism, 240-41, 250-51, 295-96
May Day, 86

McCain, John (Senator), 162
McClelland, David, 242, 297
McDowell, Deborah E., 247
McGovern, Katy (Hungerford), 42, 337
McKenna, Regis, 69
McKinsey, 26-27, 40, 149
McWhorter, Charlie, 41-43
    Christmas list, 43
    White Ghost, 41
Medi-Cal, 265-66
Medicare, 264-66
Medvedev, Dmitry (former President of Russia), 168
Memorial, 191-92
Mendocino, 82
Menlo Park, 38, 40
mensch, 43
Mentoring Alliance, 258
merit, 278
meritocracy, 278, 291-92, 307
Merrell Dow Pharmaceuticals, 131
Merello, Lucy (Peterson), 214, 337
Mexico, 28, 30, 119
Meyers, Philip, M.D., 75
Miami, 39, 44, 46, 48, 53-55, 58-59, 61, 63, 64-65, 339
microaggression, 251-53
Microsoft, 301
Middle East, 62
Midwest, 92
Mihm, Michael (Mike), (federal judge), 162, 164, 338
Miles City, 14, 95
Minister of Education and Science, 168
Minister of Economic Development (Russian), 157
Ministry of Economic Development (Russian), 158

Ministry of Education (Russian), 167
Ministry, Interior (Russian), 150-51
Ministry of Petrochemicals, (Russian), 105-06
Ministry of Rails (MPS), Russian), 102-3 105-06, 161
Minneapolis, Minnesota, 14, 273
Minnikhanov, Rustam, 157
Mireau, Karen (Rimmer), 336
mirror image identical twins, 81
Mob, mobsters, 40, 48, 76
Mohammed sobriquet (People of the Book), 296
Moderna, 134
Monster (the), 94
Mont Blanc, 77
Montana, 10, 14, 54, 90-92, 95
Monterey Jazz Festival, 42
Montgomery, Herb, 111
mood rings, 74
Mooney, Bill, 65
Moore, Gordon, 128-9
Morgenthau, Jr., Henry, 300
Morehouse, Diane (née Ragland, 4, 338; and Dan, 4
Morrison, Knudsen, 93
Morrisroe, David, 215
Moscow: 55, 84-86, 105-06, 108, 113, 143, 146, 148, 150-51, 155-60, 162, 168, 170-72, 175, 177, 185-86, 193-94, 198, 200, 202-03, 262; American Chamber of Commerce in Moscow, 150, 169, 185; Embassy, 162, 177; National Research University, 156;

Moscow State University, 155, 162; Ritz-Carlton, 84
Mother Teresa, 81, 228-29
Mother Teresa Clinic, 230-31
Mother Teresa-Tirana International Airport, 140
Mount Parnassus, 73
Mount Rainier, 13
Murray, Charles, 229, 295, 310
Murray, Joel, 75
Musk, Elon, 133
Muslim(s), 304, 310

N

NATO (*See:* North Atlantic Treaty Organization
NBA (*See:* National Basketball Association)
NBC (*See:* National Broad-Casting Company
NPR (*See:* National Public Radio)

NYSE (*See:* New York Stock Exchange)
NASDAQ (*See:* National Association of Securities Dealers Automated Quotations)
NGO, 8, 11, 136-37, 139, 148, 157, 170, 176, 179, 182, 187-89, 192-93, 198
Napa, 81, 257
nation of victims, 253
National Association of Securities Dealers Automated Quotations (NASDAQ), 25, 32
National Basketball Association (NBA), teams, 302
National Broadcasting Company (NBC), 222, 230

National Court Clubs Association, 67
National Public Radio (NPR), 225
National Venture Capital Association, 148
National Security Council, 162, 175, 187, 191
Nationwide Marketing, 118
natural order, 244-45
nature/DNA, 308-09
Navy Seals, 243
Nazi/Nazism, 10, 86, 243, 248
Nelson, Gary, 266-67
Nelson, Willie, 79, 83
Never Again (statue), 86
Nevsky Prospect, Russia, 147
New Jersey Turnpike, 18
New Republic, 181
New Science of Human Individuality (The), 235
New York Stock Exchange (NYSE), 110
New York, 26, 34, 37-38, 41, 51-52, 62, 75, 145, 153, 222-24, 228, 230, 232-33, 238, 300
New York Review of Books, 180-81
New York Times, 180, 229-30, 241, 246-47, 299
Nitka, David, 49-50, 61, 64, 125, 216
Nitka, Laurette, 62
Nitka, Martin, 61-62
Nixon, Richard (Vice President/President), 40-41, 129, 231
No Party Preference, 80
Nobel Prizes/Nobels/laureates, 128, 194, 215, 217, 284, 290-91, 293-95, 304-05, 307

Nonprofit Management, 250-51
normal country, 144
North Atlantic Treaty Organization (NATO), 195
Norway, 21
Nizhny Novgorod (University), 166, 169
Noyce, Robert, 128-29

O

OMB (*See:* Office of Management and Budget)
OPORA, 145, 148, 157-58, 165, 167
Office of Management and Budget (OMB), 187
Oklahoma Gas and Electric, 101
Old Russia Hand, 163-64
oligarch(s), 137, 147, 150
Order of Friendship, 151
Ortmans, Jonathan, 174, 338
Oscars, 296, 306
Osso, Kenny, 14
Ostromoff, Paul, 61
outdoor recreation plan, 32
outliers, 307
Owens, Candace, 247

P

PAEF (See: Polish American Enterprise Fund)
PAFF (*See:* Polish American Freedom Foundation)
PLM (*See:* Professional Lease Management)
PLM Railcar Maintenance Company (*See:* Professional Lease Management)
Pachamama Alliance, 250-51
Pacific Coast Stock Exchange, 29
Pacific Telephone, 255

325

PAFF (Polish American Freedom Foundation), 139-40
Pale of Russia, 221, 287-88, 305, 307
Palestine, Palestinians, 62, 216
Palo Alto, 66-67, 119
Paris, 30, 61, 82, 84, 87, 121
Pasteur, Louis, 138
Patricof, Alan, 145, 300
Payne, Charles, 247
Peale, Norman Vincent (Reverend), 112
Peale, Ruth Stafford, 112
Perm 36, 191–92
Pease family: Glen, 2; Glendon Leroy, 2, 210; Glenna Rae, 3, 272-74; Joyce (Sorem), *Preface*, 42, 73, 79-89, 100-01, 145, 203-04, 206-08, 213, 255-59, 262, 268-69, 275-80, 339, 341; Lillian, 2; Ruth Shepard, 2, 210-11; Steve (Steven L.), 2-3, 43, 54, 63, 76, 202-13, 223-24, 227, 262-63, 274, 341-42
Pelham, 41, 51–52
Pelosi, Nancy, 146
People of the book, Mohammed Sobriquet, 296
perpetual foundation, 176
Peterson, Lucy Merello, 214, 337
Pherin, 120-21
pheromones, 120-21
Phi Beta Kappa, 16, 341
philanthropic/philanthropy, 131, 218, 237, 239, 250, 265-66, 291, 293 298
Philippines, 62, 252
Pierce, Chester M. (Harvard psychiatrist), 252
Piketty, Thomas, 134
Pillsbury Company, 111

Pine, Richard, 224
Piraeus, 82
play the field, 13, 80
Poland/Polish, 139-40 ,163, 186-87, 216; shtetel, 62
Polish American Enterprise Fund (PAEF), 139-40
Polish American Freedom Foundation (PAFF), 139-40
Pollack, Robert, 308
Pol Pot's Communism, 243
polio, 217, 234, 294
polygenic, 235
Pomar, Mark, 164, 171, 185-86
Pomerance, Brad, 229
Popeil, Ron, 299
Porsche(s) 82
Portuguese Jews, 221
Powell, Colin, 242, 247, 254
Power of Positive Thinking (The), 112
Prague, 170
predisposition, 236, 311
Presbyterian, 215, 310
Prim, Craig, 109
Prim, Wayne, 68
privatization, 106, 136, 143-44, 156
pro bono, 40, 88, 98, 136, 144, 182, 257, 261-62, 267 341
Professional Lease Management: Chapter Six, 90-113; (PLM), 38, 48, 77-78, 90-100, 102, 109-112, 116, 120, 124-25, 141, 153, 245, 277, 337, 339; experience, 120; name, 78; PLM International, 90, 99; PLM Railcar Maintenance Company, 78, 90, 99;

senior management team, 95; stock, 94; Transcisco, 90, 99, 141-42
Pulitzer Prizes, 220, 296, 299, 306
Pullman Standard Railcar Company, 97
Purdue University, 166
Putin, Vladimir, 136-37, 143, 148-51, 157-58, 168, 175, 191, 194-95
Pyrrha, 73

R
RAEF (*See:* Russian American Enterprise Fund)

REDI (*See:* Real Estate Data Inc.)

RERC (*See:* Real Estate Research Company)
R. J. Reynolds, 119
racism, 10, 253
racquetball: 47, 70 clubs, 63, 65; court, 63, 65-67, 277; match, 66; regulation, 47; skills, 66
Radical Chic and Mau Mauing the Flack Catchers, 25
Radio Free Europe/Radio Liberty, 164
Radisson Royal, 147
Ragland family: Diane (Morehouse), 4, 338; Glenna Rae (Duval, Keller, Pease) 3, 272-74; Steve, 4; Tami (Butters), 4, 338
Railcar Maintenance Company: 48, 78; railcars, 90-1; 93, 97-99, 109, 112, 136; railroads, 91-92, 102, 112; retrofitted, 103, 141,

tank cars, 85, 113, 141-42, 278, 300, 341
Reagan, Ronald, 41, 80, 90, 130, 184
Real Estate Data Inc. (REDI): Chapter Three, 45-64; 25, 38-39, 65, 143, 216, 277, 339; competitor, 49; employees, 47-48; employee survey, 47-48; founder, 57; Jewish founder and CEO, 216; market, 50; sales force and salespeople, 49, 56-58, 61-62, 216
Real Estate Research Company (RERC), 122, 140
Reasoner, Harry, 29
Red Army Choir, 200
Red Notice, 151, 193
Red Square, 84-85, 339
reflows, 147, 188
Reformation, 304, 308
refuseniks, 191
Regis McKenna, 69
Reno, Janet, 65
research universities, 127, 166
Responsa, 303
Reshetnikov, Maksim, 157
Revlon, 222
revolution, 105, 147, 250
revolutionary, 218, 221
Revolutionary War, 221
Rice, Condoleezza, 162, 247, 254
Rigdon, Greg, 163
Riley, Jason, 247, 254
Ritz Carlton (Moscow), 84
Rock, Arthur, 128-29, 300
Rockefellers, 126, 162
Rockwell, George Lincoln, 10
Roebuck, Alvah, 238
Rogstad, Ken, 16, 58

Rojansky, Matthew, 183
Roman(s), Catholic, 35,
    conquest, 303; cultures,
    304, gods, 72, 284;
    rebellion, 306
Rosen, Ben 300
Rosenwald, Julius, 237-39 245
Ross family: 81, Joyce (*See:*
    Sorem), Pease, 81; Heiler,
    Janice, 81
Rossiya, Delovaya, 157
Rotary, 255
Rothschilds, 299, 304
Rousseau, 243
Rule of Law: 127, 137, 145, 161,
    165, 170, 173, 177, 180;
    Committee 165, 170;
    efforts, 165; programming, 173; programs, 173,
    338
Russell, Bill, 46
Russia/Russian(s):
    Chapters Eight, Nine,
    Ten, Eleven, Twelve,
    136-200; 6-8, 32, 84-86,
    88, 100, 102-08, 113, 125,
    127, 132,136-200, 214,
    221, 245-46, 248, 261-62,
    265, 276-78, 287-88, 305,
    307, 338, 341; ambassador, 169; (former) 161,
    189; attorney/lawyers,
    151, 173, 180, 193;
    business angels, 158;
    companies, 136, 151,
    large, 147); economy, 103,
    108, 143, 161; Enterprise
    Fund, 103; enterprise
    funds, 103, 136, 138,
    140-41, 144, 154, 177,
    182, 189, 195-96, 200;
    entrepreneurs, 137-38,
    145, 148-49, 154-61, 165,
    193; entrepreneurship,
    127, 130-32, 137-38, 145,
    148, 154-56, 158-59, 165,
    169, 174-75, 178-79, 189,
    261; government, 8, 105,
    148, 151, 174, 192, 195;
    Old Russia Hand, 163-64;
    Russian railroad tank cars,
    85, 102-03, 112,-13,
    141-42; 341; roulette, 32;
    studies, 163-64, 175;
    television, 145, 155; trips
    to, 104, 107, 142; universities, 166-67
Russia Direct Investment Fund,
    149
Russia Venture Company, 156
Russian Agency on Youth
    Affairs, 158
Russian American Chamber of
    Commerce, 150
Russian American Enterprise
    Fund (RAEF), 140-42
Russian Association of Business
    Education, 158
Russian Interior Ministry,
    150-51
Russian Microfinance Center,
    158, 167
Russian Minister of Economic
    Development, 157
Russian Ministry of Economic
    Development, 158
Russian Ministry of Education,
    167
Russian Ministry of Petrochemicals, 102, 105
Russian Ministry of Rails, 102,
    107
Russian Union of Entrepreneurs, 158

Russian Union of the Organ-
    ization of Business
    Angels, 158
Ryan, Charles (Charlie), 148,
    152, 178, 338

S
SAE (*See:* Sigma Alpha Epsilon)
SBA (*See:* Small Business
    Administration)
SBICs (*See:* Small Business
    Investment Companies)
SFAT (*See:* Soviet-Finnish-
    America Transport
Sabin, Albert, 217, 234, 297
sabra, 7
St. Jude Research Hospitals, 269
St. Petersburg (Leningrad), 84,
    86 195, 200
St. Petersburg Institute of
    Technology, Mechanics
    and Optics (ITMO),
    165-67, 174
Saldin family:
    James (Jim), 54, 338;
    Karen, 16-17, 27-28,
    41-42, 44-45, 53-54, 58,
    63-65, 79, 80, 90, 341,
    343, (*See: Collins, Karen*);
    Kerry, Kim, Kurt,
    Montana, 54
Salestar, 217
Salk, Jonas, 217, 234, 297
Salvation Army, 255
Samuelson, Paul, 217, 286, 296
San Francisco, 26-28, 30, 40-41,
    44, 63, 65, 68, 76-7, 79,
    82, 87-88, 95, 106, 108,
    111, 205, 223, 226, 229,
    268, 274, 276
Sanborn Map Company, 41,
    50-52, 63, 205
Sanders, Melba, 42, Stan 42

Sand Hill Road, 68
Sappienza, Rocco, 75
Sarro, Ilja, 339
Sasha, 107–8, 203
Saunders, Greg, 53
Sberbank, 157
ScaleUp, 159
Scandinavia, 21
Schiller, Nelson, M.D., 271
Schramm, Carl, 141, 148
Scott, Tim, 247
Sea Ranch, 88
Sears, 222, 238
Sears, Richard, 236
Sears, Winsome, 242, 247
Sears & Roebuck, 222, 238
Seattle, 1, 11-13, 19, 26-28, 55,
    58, 274
Sedov, Victor, 154
Senor, Dan, 229
self-publishing, 226
Semel, Terry, 299
Senate: Commerce Committee,
    15; Foreign Relations
    Committee, 187
senator(s); 15, 23, 152-53, 162,
    162, 187, 247
Sequoia, 129
serendipity, 275, 277-78
Shakharov, Andrei, 192
Sharansky, Natan, 191
sharks, 72, 108
Shearith Israel (Congregation),
    229
Shepard, Happy, 2, 210
Shepard, Raymond, 2, 210
Sheremetyevo Airport, 84
Sherwood, James, 100
shtetel, 62
Shockley, William, 128
Shriners, 255, hospital for
    children, 269
Shuvalov, Igor, 157

Siberia, 85, 103, 150
Siberian oil wells, 112
Sigma Alpha Epsilon, 9, 11-13
Silberstein, Charles, 50-52
Silbiger, Steven, 225
Silicon Valley, 68, 128
Simonet, Richard, 52
Simpson Timber, 26
Singapore, 241-42
Singer, Saul, 229
Sioux City, 95
Siva, 120
Sixty (60 Minutes), 29, 231
Skadden, Arps, Slate, Meagher & Flom, 49, 216
Skolkovo Innovation Center (Moscow), 158
Skoll, Jeff, 301
Slakey Brothers Inc., 37
Slate, 49
Small Business Administration (SBA), 11, 15, 129, 146, 273
Small Business Investment Companies (SBICs), 127, 129, 140
Small Grants program, 167
Smith, Adam, 244, 250-51
Smith Jr., John F. (GM chairman), 139
Sobyanin, Sergey, 157
Sochi Olympics, 108
social justice, 243, 249-54; mentality, 243; program, 254
Société Générale, 147
Solomon, Haym, 221
Solzhenitsyn, Aleksandr, 164, 191
Sonnenfeldt, Michael, 224
Sonoma City and County: 80, 83, 87-89, 107-08, 226, 258-60, 262, 264-68, 341;
Alcaldessa, 80; Benziger, 265; City Council, 259; culture, 267, 341, Pets Lifeline, 268; Raceway, 267; schools, 258; seniors, 258; Sonoma Community Center, 265; Sonoma Community Foundation, 268; Sonoma County, 267-68; Sonoma Index Tribune; 337; Sonoma State University, 80; Sonoma Valley Fund, 267; Sonoma Valley Hospital, 262-66, 268; wine country, 341
Sorem family: 72, 83, 207, 213 Bernadette (Calhoun), 81, 213; CJ, 213; David, 81, 213; Joel, 82; Jonathan, 213; Joyce (Pease), *Preface*, 42, 73, 79-89, 100-01, 145, 203-04, 206-08, 213, 255-59, 262, 268-69, 275-80, 341; Juliana, 81, 213; Lisa, 213; Maggie, 213
Soul (This is a): The Mission of Rick Hodes, 230, 233
South Africa(n), 35-36, 216
South America, 64, 275, 305
South Florida, 63-4
Soviet(s) 6-7, 85-86, 112, 127,
Soviet-Finnish-America Transport (SFAT): 85, 90, 100, 102-9, 113, 136, 140-42, 178, 200, 276; CEO, 90, 104-5; board meetings, 104, 142; Chair Valery Butko, 105, earnings, 108-09 fleet, 103, 105; in Russia, 102, 105; Moscow bank accounts,

105; shares, 106-07; story, 103
Soviet(s)/Soviet Union, 7, 22, 86, 105, 112, 127, 138, 164, 249
Sowell, Thomas, 237, 239-40, 242-47, 251, 288, 294; book, 246, 288
Soweto, 37
Space Race, 127
Space Station, 133
Spanish Inquisition, 221
Sparrow, 193
speaker of the House, 24
Spencer, Roberts, Woodward, and McDowell, 65
Spinoza, 296
Splitgerber, Jeff, *Preface*, 336
Spokane, 1-3, 6, 10-15, 19, 24-26, 28, 42, 87, 215, 234-35, 255, 274, 280, 289, 341
Sputnik, 7, 127, Sputnik V, 149
Stadnik, Alexander, 171
stage fright, 71
Stalin, 6-7, 192, 244-45
Stallcop family, David (Dave), 9-10, Glenda, 9-10, 12-13, Linda, 10, 12
Stanford, 68, 130, 149, 155, 241, 271, 297
Stanford Memorial Church, 68
Stanford's Hoover Institution, 241
Stansbury, Michael, 18, 23, 212
Start Up Nation: The Story of Israel's Economic Miracle, 227
startup companies, 31, 50, 92, 114-16, 126, 128, 136, 158, 179
Startup Huddle, 158
State Department, 144, 152, 161, 163, 168
Stern, Howard, 75
Stigler, George, 240
Stirpe, Mario, M.D., 269
stoic(ism), 43, 278
Stolman, Ed, 223, 226, 259
Story First Communications, 145
Strauss, Levi, 26, 222
street-smart, 46
Streisand, Barbara, 217
structured settlements, 30, 262
Student Entrepreneurship Award (GSEA), 155
study groups, 20-21
stutter, 57
Stuyvesant High School, 240
Summer Palace (St. Petersburg), 86
Supreme Court Justices, 297
Sutter Hill Ventures, 129
Suzzallo Library, 13
Swann, Lynn, 247
Sweeney, Jerry, 72
Switzerland, 74, 77, 79, 84, 87; Alps, 64, 77, 82, 101
Sykes, Charles, 253
synagogues, 215-16, 229-30, 291, 303
Syntex, 119

T

TUSRIF (*See:* The U.S. Russia Investment Fund)
TWA (*See:* Trans World Airlines)
Taft, California, 31
take or pay contracts, 92
Tallin, Estonia, 85, 103, 112
Talmud, 303-04
Taming the Wild East: New Russian Entrepreneurs Tell Their Stories (Pat Cloherty), 149, 155

Tandem Computers, 116, 129
Tarre, Michael, 215
Tatarstan, 157
Teamsters (Canadian), 48
Teapot Dome oil fields, 31
technologies, 39, 128, 130, 132
technology, 7, 39, 74, 102-03, 113, 115, 119, 122, 127-28, 133, 166, 278, 301
Tedesco, George, 97, 101, 245; Dorothy, 101
Telushkin, Joseph (Rabbi), 224-225
Tefft, Nancy, 9
Terrell, Leo, 247
Tham, Minh, 213, 262, 339
Tham, Thanh, 213, 260
Thao Nguyen, 213, 260
The U.S. Russia Investment Fund (TUSRIF): Chapter Eight, 138-153; 100, 103, 125, 136-38, 140-42, 144-47, 150-54, 157, 161-63, 174, 177-78, 183-90, 192, 195-97, 214, 261; 2014 final report to USAID, 190, 337; and USAID, 137, 184, 190; and USRF, 157, 195-96; board, 103, 142, 146, 151, 162, 188, 197; and USRF for Ukraine, 196, board dinners in Washington, 146; 189; chair and CEO, 267; DPEP, 145-46, 152, 85-86; directors, 145-46, 154, directorship, 125, 144; escrow, 174, 188, 190, 194, 196; grant, 86, 188; history, 190; investment portfolio, 152, 161; portfolio liquidation, 184;
structure, 146
This is a Soul: The Mission of Rick Hodes, 230, 233, 343
Thiel, Peter, 180
Thomas, Clarence, 247
Thompson, Don, 39
Thorpe, Edward, 29
Tikkun olam, 293, 306
Titov, Boris, 158
tobacco, 119
Top of the Home, 47
Torah, 289
trade-offs, 237, 244-45, 280
traitorous eight founders, 128
Transcisco/Transcisco Industries, 78, 84, 87, 90, 99-103, 108-10, 113, 136, 141-42, 153, 256, 276-77
Trans World Airlines (TWA), 25-26
Trans-Siberian Express, 200
travels, 87, 275
Trinity Industries, 90, 110, 256
tuberculosis of the spine, 231-32
turnaround(s), 52, 63, 72-73, 226, 264, 341
Turnbull, Bill, 87
Tyrus, 247
Tzedakah, 293

U

UC Berkeley, 81, 127
UCLA, 127, 167, 174, 241, 247
UCSF, 235, 266-67, physicians, 263, 266, 269, 271
USAID (*See:* United States Agency for International Development)
USRF (*See:* U.S. Russia Foundation for Economic Expansion and the Rule of Law)

U.S. Foreign Corrupt Practices Act, 147
U.S. Russia Business Council, 150, 153
U.S. Russia Foundation for Economic Expansion and the Rule of Law (USRF): 8, 100, 106, 108, 127, 137, 145, 153, 157, 160-61, 163, 165-67, 169-179, 181-83, 185, 189-98, 261-62; 338 board dinner, 166, 189; board meeting, 169; board members, 178, 191; boards, 143, 157, 166, 190-91, 193-94, 196; business, 194; CEO, 171; 175-76, 178; co-chair, 162-63, 181-82, 200; directors, 178, 182, 185, 193; in Moscow, 262; inception, 165, 183; motivations, 108; obligation, 181; programs in Russia, 171; staff in Washington, D.C., 179, website, 195; U.S.S.R., 108, 142-43
Ukraine: 86, 108, 137, 175, 194-98; democratic, 196; invasion, 194-97; proposal, 195-98; proposed TUSRIF grants, 186, 188; southeastern, 108; Ukrainian people, 149, 196; victims, 196
unconstrained view, 243, 245, 251, 294
undesirable, 8, 170, 172, 174, 176
union(s), unionize, 47-48, 92, 223, 294

Union of Entrepreneurs of Novgorod Region, 158
Union of the Organization of Business Angels, 158
unit trains, 93
United Artists, 222
United States Agency for International Development (USAID): 127, 132, 136-37, 140-41, 152-54, 161, 163-64, 174, 177-79, 184-87; 188-90, 194-97; activity in Russia, 153, 164; and State, 153, 161, 163, 187; Certificate of Appreciation, 189; escrow and grant, 194-197; evaluation, 189; grant agreement and priorities set, 177; grant dollars, 188; inquiries, 152; report on the outside evaluation audit of the Enterprise Funds, 189; support, 195-99; technical assistance 152, 184-85, 190
unhappiness, 185
United States Institute of Peace, 188
University of Maryland, College Park, 166
University of Washington, 9, 11, 28, 341
Uston, Kenny, 29, 30
Utah, 119, 258, 309

V

VEB.RF bank, 157
VSOE (*See:* Venice Simplon Orient Express)
Vadasz, Les, 129, 224, 267
Valentine, Don, 66, 256

333

Valium, 4
values, 1, 56, 99, 135, 214, 227, 237, 241-42, 257, 278, 284, 289, 294, 310
Venice, 79, 81-82, 100-01
Venice Simplon Orient Express (VSOE) passengers, 81, 100-01
venture(s), 68, 76, 88, 102, 107, 115, 120, 129, 136, 138
venture capital: 22, 25, 30, 63, 66-68, 77, 88, 114-16, 120, 125, 130, 142, 145, 178; boutique,100, 116; capitalist, 25, 116, 120, 126, 145, 148, 178, 226, 256, 341; early pioneer, 22, 66, 116; experience, 63, 125, 142, 183; financing, 63, 114; firms, 68, 77; 115-16, 126, 129, 132, 145; fund, 136, 148; industry, 22, 67, 114, 123, 125, 135; investment, 30, 102; investors/partnership(s), 30, 100, 110, 114-15, 123, 128-29, 138, 182, 341; new, 115, 129, 138, 341; prominent, 120; successful, 126-27, 178
verges, 285, 304
victimhood, 238, 245-46, 251-54
Victoria, British Columbia, 28
Vietnam, 34, 129, 260
Vimpelcom, 156
Vinik, Jack, 50
vintage cars, 100-1
Virginia, 41, 92, 242
Vladivostok, 200
vodka, 104
Voice of America, 164
Volga River, 104
Volkman, Janet, copyeditor, 337

vomeronasal organ, 120
Voodoo, 242
Vykhodtsev, Sergey, 155

W

WNET, 230
WW II (*See:* World War II)
Walker, Herschel, 247
Wallander, Celeste, 175-76
Wallbangers, 63, 65-67, 69-71, 80, 277
Wall Street, 26, 122
Wall Street Journal, 134, 198, 237, 241
Walmart, 238
Walsh, Bill, 40
Warsaw Pact, countries, former, 138
Washington, D.C., 17, 23-24, 27, 39-40, 51, 60, 68-69, 141, 146, 153, 163, 166, 171, 173-76, 179-80, 187-90, 197-98, 203-204
Washington Post, 42, 181, 230, 241, 299
Washington State, 6, 15, 19
Washington's Tuskegee Institute, 238
Watts, Ronnie, 46
Wealth of Nations, 240-51
Webster, Gary, 16
Weill Symphony Hall, 80
Western NIS Enterprise Fund, 195-96
West, Kayne, 247
West Point, 30, 40, 142, 273
White, Kendrick, 169
White Ghost, 41
White House, 40-41, 161, 187
Whitney & Company, 126
Whitney, Cornelius Vanderbilt, 126
Whitney, David, 12

Whitney, J.H., 126
Whitworth College, 16
whiz kids, 46
Wildcare (Marin County), 259, 269
Wilde, Oscar, 161
Wilder, Billy, 161
Williams, Walter, 247
Wilson, Flip, 114
Witkowicki, Kathy, 258
woke, 252
Wolf, Tom, 35
Wolff, Ellen, 15
Woodson, Robert, 247, 254
World Airways, 33-34
World War II/WW II, 2, 4, 6, 22, 41, 126-27, 176, 215, 246, 251-52, 255
written cases, 19
Wyoming, 92, 97, 261

X
Xiaoping, Deng, 133

Y
YMCA(s), 239
Yakima Valley Community Action Agency (YVCAA), 25, 34
Yegor, 172-73, 180-82, 198-99, 338
Yegor Gaidar Fellowship Program in Economics and Public Policy, 167
Yeltsin, Boris, 136, 143
Yergin, Daniel, 169
Yiddish, 307
Young Turks, 40
Yves-Saint-Laurent Parfums, 121
Yvgeny, 203

Z
Zablotsky, Alexander, 105
Zephyr, 117-118
Zeus, 73
Zoom, 235
Zuckerman, Marty, 49, 216
Zvedre, Yevgeny, 166

Acknowledgments

When I think of the word "memoir" it conjures up the notion of one person writing about his life, or selected parts of it. It is all his work and it is a singular effort for which, if it is interesting and well written, he deserves the credit.

That is not so, at least not in this case. I had lots of help from many people. So, any blame is still mine, but if you should find it of interest, it is in no small measure because it has been a shared effort.

I must begin with my neighbor, Jeff Splitgerber, who first approached me with the suggestion to write my life story. When I expressed skepticism with the idea, he followed through by setting up a meeting with Karen Mireau.

Karen is a "Literary Midwife" who assists authors in turning their manuscripts into publishable works. Her diplomacy is stunning and she draws out the best from clients with her charm and grace. What a pleasure!

Also invaluable was copyeditor Janet Volkman, first introduced to me by Bill Lynch, then the publisher of the Sonoma Index Tribune. She did an excellent job in copyediting my first book *The Golden Age of Jewish Achievement*. I again had the pleasure of calling on her fresh eyes (and red pencil) to discover typos, awkward grammar, misspellings, and all the rest in this memoir.

Lucy Merello Peterson worked with me to produce the *TUSRIF Final Report* and she edited *The Debate Over Jewish Achievement*. She also reviewed a draft of this memoir and provided a wonderful blurb.

Katy Hungerford McGovern was very helpful in reading everything I wrote about her husband, Mark, and the experiences we shared in the various incarnations of Professional Lease Management (PLM) over many years. She offered unique insights and it was fun to share our reactions and thoughts.

Karen Collins was helpful in going over the parts of the manuscript that mention her and the times we spent together. I am very glad she did. She reviewed the text and made suggestions about a few things I had not mentioned. She also suggested two amusing anecdotes, one of which allowed me to profile her wonderful dad, who I nicknamed "the Chief."

My nieces, Tami and Diane, encouraged me to write the book, read an early version, and sent me a copy of the picture that appears on the front cover of this book.

Jim Collins was invaluable in his review of the Russia chapters and in his suggestions to add an overview introduction and to re-order the chapters.

Karen Horn was terrific in reading and commenting on the writing, as well as pointing out what else I might want to cover in the Russia chapters.

My sincere thanks also goes to Jonathan Ortmans, who has long been part of CFE and USRF, to judges Michael Mihm and Paul Magnuson for their review and suggestions for the Rule of Law material, and to Yegor and Gennady for their permission to use their first names in the text.

Charlie Ryan was helpful in reviewing the writing on Russia. He has been a great colleague to work with ever since we sat next to each other in a banquet hall on the upper floor of GUM, directly across Red Square from Lenin's tomb.

Charles Kremer helped with the PLM chapter and, like me, he found those years and experiences very important in our respective careers.

The First family (namely Dick First's seven kids), were pleased to hear about the chapter devoted to their dad and my years at REDI. They said Dick had told them I was a graduate of "Dick First University." They also fondly recalled experiences with Karen and me during the years we lived in Coral Gables and worked in Miami.

Many thanks as well to Marilyn Berger Hewitt who helped with my rendition of her wonderful story about Danny, Rick Hodes, and herself, plus reading and suggesting other worthwhile changes.

Also many thanks to Ilja Sarro (our videographer, Minh Tham and Karen Rimmer for creating a wonderful website for this memoir.

Last, but not least, I must thank my beautiful wife, Joyce, for her endless patience, help, and love . . .

About the Author

Steven L. Pease has had a varied career as a management consultant, venture capitalist, pro bono director of not-for-profit organizations, and as a CEO who headed up and in some cases led the turnarounds of several public and private companies.

As a serial entrepreneur, he conceived and later served as deputy-chair of a Russian railroad tank car company, and a general partner of a venture capital partnership. Over a period of more than 20 years, he served as a pro bono chair, co-chair, CEO, and director of three Russian nonprofit organizations—all sponsored by the United States government. In those roles, he travelled much of the world.

Born and raised in Spokane, Washington, Steve is a Phi Beta Kappa graduate of the University of Washington with a master's degree from Harvard Business School. He also has written two books: *The Golden Age of Jewish Achievement* and *The Debate Over Jewish Achievement*.

He is active in community affairs in the small wine country town of Sonoma, California, where he lives with his wife Joyce (and their two cats!)

To Contact the Author:
please email
spease@vom.com
or call (415) 264-9597

৯ ৯ ৯

For Direct Book Orders:
please visit Lulu.com,
Amazon.com,
and other online venues

Learn more about Steve Pease at:
https://www.nothingventuredstevepease.com
and on YouTube

৯ ৯ ৯

To Contact the Publisher:
please email
Azalea.Art.Press@gmail.com
or call (510) 919-6117

www.ingramcontent.com/pod-product-compliance
Lightning Source LLC
Chambersburg PA
CBHW020348170426
43200CB00005B/93